NETL
A System for Representing and Using
Real-World Knowledge

The MIT Press series in Artificial Intelligence

Artificial Intelligence: An MIT Perspective, Volume I: Expert Problem Solving, Natural Language Understanding, Intelligent Computer Coaches, Representation and Learning by Patrick Henry Winston and Richard Henry Brown, 1979

Artificial Intelligence: An MIT perspective, Volume II: Understanding Vision, Manipulation, Computer Design, Symbol Manipulation by Patrick Henry Winston and Richard Henry Brown, 1979

NETL: A System for Representing and Using Real-World Knowledge by Scott E. Fahlman, 1979

The Interpretation of Visual Motion by Shimon Ullman, 1979

NETL
A SYSTEM FOR REPRESENTING AND USING
REAL-WORLD KNOWLEDGE

SCOTT E. FAHLMAN

The MIT Press
Cambridge, Massachusetts, and London, England

PUBLISHER'S NOTE

This format is intended to reduce the cost of publishing certain works in book form and to shorten the gap between editorial preparation and final publication. The time and expense of detailed editing and composition in print have been avoided by photographing the text of this book directly from the author's typescript.

Third printing, 1985
Copyright © 1979 by
The Massachusetts Institute of Technology

Printed in the United States of America.

Library of Congress Cataloging in Publication Data

Fahlman, Scott E.
    NETL, a system for representing and using real-world
knowledge.

    Slightly edited version of the author's thesis,
M.I.T., 1977.
    Bibliography: p.
    Includes index.
    1. Artificial intelligence--Data processing.
2. NETL (Computer system) I. Title.
Q336.F33   001.53'5   78-10483
ISBN 0-262-0609-8

Table of Contents

SERIES FOREWORD

Artificial intelligence is the study of intelligence using the ideas and methods of computation. Unfortunately, a definition of intelligence seems impossible at the moment because intelligence appears to be an amalgam of so many information-processing and information-representation abilities.

Of course psychology, philosophy, linguistics, and related disciplines offer various perspectives and methodologies for studying intelligence. For the most part, however, the theories proposed in these fields are too incomplete and too vaguely stated to be realized in computational terms. Something more is needed, even though valuable ideas, relationships, and constraints can be gleaned from traditional studies of what are, after all, impressive existence proofs that intelligence is in fact possible.

Artificial intelligence offers a new perspective and a new methodology. Its central goal is to make computers intelligent, both to make them more useful and to understand the principles that make intelligence possible. That intelligent computers will be extremely useful is obvious. The more profound point is that artificial intelligence aims to understand intelligence using the ideas and methods of computation, thus offering a radically new and different basis for theory formation. Most of the people doing artificial intelligence believe that these theories will apply to any intelligent information processor, whether biological or solid state.

There are side effects that deserve attention, too. Any program that will successfully model even a small part of intelligence will be inherently massive and complex. Consequently, artificial intelligence continually confronts the limits of computer science technology. The problems encountered have been hard enough and interesting enough to seduce artificial intelligence people into working on them with enthusiasm. It is natural, then, that there has been a steady flow of ideas from artificial intelligence to computer science, and the flow shows no sign of abating.

The purpose of this MIT Press Series in Artificial Intelligence is to provide people in many areas, both professionals and students, with timely, detailed information about what is happening on the frontiers in research centers all over the world.

Patrick Henry Winston
Mike Brady

PREFACE

The goal of the M.I.T. Press Series in Artificial Intelligence is to make available to a wide and interdisciplinary audience some of the work that is occuring at the frontiers of artificial intelligence research. In many cases, this means that the books in the series will be snapshots of work in progress, rather than the rounded, well-polished presentations that characterize older, more stable fields.

This book is such a snapshot. It is a slightly edited version of my Ph.D. thesis, completed in September of 1977 at the M.I.T. Artificial Intelligence Laboratory. It assumes that the reader is familiar in general with the principles of digital computers and has some appreciation for the difficulties involved in making these devices behave intelligently. It does not assume a knowledge of particular details or languages, except in the section on software simulation of the knowledge network and the appendices on hardware implementations. It is my hope that this book will be of interest to psychologists, linguists, and others not directly connected to the fields of computer science or artificial intelligence.

I would like to express my gratitude to the following people, who made essential contributions to this project:

To my thesis supervisor, Gerald Sussman, and my readers, Patrick Winston and Marvin Minsky, for their advice, support, and patience. I would also like to thank each for the special gifts that he brought to the task: Sussman, his contagious energy and enthusiasm; Winston, his broad perspective and good sense; and Minsky, his sense of direction.

To Drew McDermott, Bob Moore, Michael Genesereth, Mitch Marcus, and Jon Doyle for the many stimulating arguments and discussions that we have had about knowledge-representation and related topics.

To McDermott, Genesereth, Doyle, Candy Bullwinkle, Bill Martin, Guy Steele, Steve Rosenberg, Jim Stansfield, and

Johan de Kleer for reading drafts of the thesis and for making many useful comments and criticisms.

To Tom Knight, Jack Holloway, Kurt VanLehn, Ben Kuipers, David Marr, Carl Hewitt, Bob Woodham, Richard Stallman, Richard Greenblatt, Brian Smith, Chuck Rich, and Howie Shrobe for contributing good ideas, for pointing out things that I ought to read, for providing tools that were a pleasure to work with, for general moral support, and for combinations of the above.

To Bob Sjoberg and Brian Reid for their help in the area of digital calligraphy.

Finally, and most of all, I would like to thank my wife, Penny, for her support and understanding. This book is dedicated to her.

For two of the four years covered by this research, I was supported by an I.B.M. Graduate Fellowship. The laboratory was funded in large part by the Defense Advanced Research Projects Agency, as noted below.

Scott Fahlman

This report describes research done at the Artificial Intelligence Laboratory of the Massachusetts Institute of Technology. Support for the Laboratory's artificial intelligence research is provided in partby the Advanced Research Projects Agency of the Department of Defense under Office of Naval Research contract N00014-75-C-0643.

If a cat can kill a rat in a minute, how long would it be killing 60,000 rats? Ah, how long indeed! My private opinion is that the rats would kill the cat.

> *--- Lewis Carroll, on the advantages of parallelism*

1. Introduction

1.1 Preview

The human mind can do many remarkable things. Of these, perhaps the most remarkable is the mind's ability to store a huge quantity and variety of knowledge about its world, and to locate and retrieve whatever it needs from this storehouse at the proper time. This retrieval is very quick, very flexible, and in most cases seems almost effortless. If we are ever to create an artificial intelligence with human-like abilities, we will have to endow it with a comparable knowledge-handling facility; current knowledge-base systems fall far short of this goal. This report describes an approach to the problem of representing and using real-world knowledge in a computer.

The system presented here consists of two more-or-less independent parts. First, there is the system's parallel network memory scheme. Knowledge is stored as a pattern of interconnections of very simple parallel processing elements: node units which can store a dozen or so distinct marker-bits, and link units which can propagate these markers from node to node, in parallel through the network. Using these marker-bit movements, the parallel network system can perform searches and many common deductions very quickly: the time required is essentially constant, regardless of the size of the knowledge-base. The network is similar to the parallel marker-propagating network proposed by Quillian [1968, 1969], but is much more tightly controlled. This system is presented as a faster, more effective, and much simpler alternative to the currently popular approach of using domain-specific meta-knowledge, in the form of local procedures, to guide and limit serial searches in a large knowledge-base.

The second, more traditional part of the knowledge-base system is a vocabulary of conventions and processing algorithms -- in some sense, a language -- for representing various kinds of knowledge as nodes and links in the network. This set of conventions is called NETL. In many ways, NETL is similar to existing systems for representing real-world knowledge, such as the partitioned semantic networks of Hendrix [1975a, 1975b, 1976] and the frame-based KRL system [Borow & Winograd, 1976], but it differs from existing systems in three respects:

First, NETL incorporates a number of representational techniques -- new ideas and new combinations of old ideas -- which allow it to represent certain real-world concepts more precisely and more efficiently than earlier systems.

Second, NETL is built around a single, clear, explicit organizing concept: an effective knowledge-base system, in addition to storing and retrieving isolated facts, must provide the user with the ability to create and use *virtual copies* of descriptions stored in the memory. By "virtual copy", I mean that the knowledge-base system *behaves* as though a portion of the semantic network has been copied (with some specific alterations), but it does not actually create the redundant structure in memory. The descriptions that are copied in this way may be arbitrarily large and complex, with parts, sub-parts, and internal relationships. This entire structure is inherited by the copy, not just a few global properties. NETL is not unique in *providing* such a virtual copy facility, but it is unique in *stating* this goal explicitly, in clear and simple terms, and in relating all of its representational machinery to this goal. This adds considerably to the conceptual clarity and unity of the resulting system, and it provides us with a way of determining whether the system's accessing mechanisms do what they are supposed to do.

Finally, NETL has been designed to operate efficiently on the parallel network machine described above, and to exploit this machine's special abilities. Most of the ideas in NETL are applicable to knowledge-base systems on serial machines as well.

A simulator for the parallel network system has been implemented in MACLISP, and an experimental version of NETL is running on this simulator. A number of test-case results and simulated timings will be presented.

1.2 The Knowledge-Base Problem

Suppose I tell you that a certain animal -- let's call him Clyde -- is an elephant. You accept this simple assertion and file it away with no apparent display of mental effort. And yet, as a result of this transaction, you suddenly appear to know a great deal about Clyde. You can tell me, with a fair degree of certainty, how many legs he has, what color he is, and whether he would be a good pet in a small third-floor apartment. You know not only that he has eyes, but what they are used for, and what it implies if they are closed. If I try to tell you that Clyde builds his nest in a tree or that he is a virtuoso on the piano or that he amuses himself by hiding in a teacup, you will immediately begin to doubt my credibility. And you can do this very quickly and easily, with none of the sort of apparent mental effort that would accompany, say, adding two four-digit numbers. This effortlessness may be an illusion, but it is a compelling one.

"Elephant", of course, is not the only concept that behaves in this way. The average person knows a huge number of concepts of comparable or greater complexity -- the number is probably in the millions. Consider for a moment the layers of structure and meaning that are attached to concepts like lawsuit, birthday party, fire, mother, walrus, cabbage, or king. These are words we use casually in our daily lives, and yet each of them represents a very substantial package of information. In technical fields (except, perhaps, for the more austere parts of mathematics) the situation is the same. Consider how much you would have to tell someone in order to fully convey the meaning of concepts like meson, local oscillator, hash-table, valence, ribosome, or leukemia. And yet, once these concepts are built up, they can be tossed around with abandon and can be used as the building blocks for concepts of even greater complexity.

The point is not just that we can handle large chunks of knowledge as though they were atoms; the important thing is that we can find our way through these complex, nested structures to whatever individual fact or relationship we might need at any given time, that we can do this in a very flexible and efficient way, and that we can somehow avoid having to look individually at each of the vast number of facts that could be -- but are not -- relevant to the problem at hand. If I tell you that a house burned down, and that the fire started at a child's birthday party, you will think immediately of the candles on the cake and perhaps of the many paper decorations. You will not, in all probability, find yourself thinking about playing pin-the-tail-on-the-donkey or about the color of the cake's icing or about the fact that birthdays come once a year. These concepts are there when you need them, but they do not seem to slow down the search for a link between fires and birthday parties. If, hidden away somewhere, there is a sequential search for this connection, that search is remarkably quick and efficient, and it does not become noticeably slower as the knowledge base expands to its adult proportions.

This impressive ability to store and access a large and diverse body of knowledge is a central feature of human intelligence. The knowledge-base system provides essential support for the other components of intelligence: the peripheral processes that handle such things as vision and speech understanding, and the linear, sequential, conscious kinds of thinking that characterize our problem-solving behavior. The knowledge base is the common ground for these diverse elements, the glue that holds everything else together.

It follows, then, that any *artificial* intelligence, if it is to be even remotely human-like in its capabilities, must include a knowledge-base system with abilities comparable to those possessed by humans. To date, in the field of AI research, we have been unable to achieve or even approach this goal. We can make -- and have made -- a certain amount of progress toward understanding the sensory and problem-solving areas of thought by confining our investigations to relatively knowledge-free problem domains -- tasks like cryptarithmetic puzzles and the symbolic integration of mathematical expressions. We can make still more progress by patching together tiny knowledge bases, just sufficient to serve as scaffolding for whatever test cases we are working on at the moment. But until we can find an adequate solution to the knowledge-base problem, all of our work will be fragmented and somewhat distorted. Sooner or later, we will have to confront that elephant.

The problem is not that we are unable to store and retrieve enough *explicit* knowledge -- that problem was solved long ago. In the property lists of LISP, in the hash-tables of LEAP and SAIL [Feldman & Rovner, 1969], and in the indexing structures of the PLANNER-related languages [Hewitt, 1972; Sussman, Charniak, Winograd, 1971; McDermott & Sussman, 1972], we can store away an arbitrarily large body of assertions and can easily retrieve any one of these later with a matching query. But the key word here is "matching": the datum to be found must be explicitly present, and it must be in the proper format for the match to succeed. These systems (ignoring, for a moment, their procedural components) give us no direct access to the much larger body of information that is *implicit* in the set of facts at hand. If we know things about "every elephant" or "every animal" or "every object bigger than a breadbox" and the questions are about Clyde, we need some way to connect the question to the answer. That means deduction, and deduction means search. To be sure that it has found all of the information relevant to Clyde, a knowledge-base system would have to examine a potentially very large set of related concepts.

The problem, then, is to find a way to perform this search in a reasonable time, even when the data base is huge. We can perform the deductions in antecedent fashion as new facts are added; we can perform them in consequent fashion in response to specific queries; or we can use some combination of these approaches, but the problem remains basically the same: our current search techniques are much too slow to handle a knowledge-base of sufficient size to produce a human-like intelligence, even in a restricted problem-domain.

Note that I am not referring here to the difficult deductions that people perform consciously: solving puzzles, formulating hypotheses, deducing the voltage at some point in an electronic circuit, deciding whether some complex block-structure is stable, and so on. These, it seems to me, are legitimately the responsibility of the problem-solving parts of intelligence, and it is not too disturbing if they run rather slowly. It is the deductions that people find to be trivial and automatic, if indeed we notice them at all, that will concern us here. These are so tightly bound up with the operation and the contents of the knowledge-base that we must attack them as one problem. One of the major contributions of Charniak's thesis [1972] was to demonstrate just how much pre-existing knowledge comes into play in the understanding of a seemingly simple story intended for young children. It is significant that something like this had to be pointed out at all -- *this* is the kind of effortlessness that we must try to achieve in our machines.

The most general and mathematically elegant of the deductive systems, those based on some form of the predicate calculus, are ridiculously slow. The best of these, on the fastest computers, adopt a downright glacial pace when faced with more than a few dozen facts at a time. The **PLANNER**-style languages are somewhat better, since they give the user the ability to hand-craft, in the form of data-base demon programs, the exact deduction strategy to be used in dealing with each possible type of input or query. An optimal mix of antecendent and consequent reasoning can thus, in principle, be employed, and the searches can be guided to consider first those paths that are most likely to be productive. In actual practice, however, the principal advantage of such systems over the unguided deductions of the theorem provers is that the procedural systems do not have to be able to deduce every consequence of the knowledge at hand, but only those consequences that the system designer knows his programs are going to need. This makes the **PLANNER**-style knowledge-base an adequate tool for constructing the kind of limited test-system scaffolding that I mentioned earlier -- my own BUILD program [Fahlman, 1974a] is an example of such an application -- but it is still inadequate for implementing the sort of knowledge-base that we will ultimately need.

The problem is that systems produced in this way tend to be very brittle. Only a carefully selected set of deductive paths has been implemented, so it is very easy for unanticipated queries or situations to cause the system to wander from these paths. At best, this lands the query back in the quagmire of undirected search; at worst, it causes outright failure. A solution to this is to build more and wider paths in an attempt to completely pave the area of interest, but this is paid for in vastly increased search-times. Even an optimized search, if it is to be reasonably complete, must sooner or later examine all of those concepts which might have something to say about the question at hand. If we are ever to endow our programs with something resembling common sense, we must somehow give them access not only to the most prominent and useful of an object's properties -- those that an optimized search would find first -- but also to those "fringe" properties that are usually insignificant but that may be of pivotal importance in a particular situation. An elephant's wrinkles are certainly well down in its list of prominent features, but to a tick they are home, and to a tick-remover they are the major obstacle to be overcome. Any single property of this sort may be used only infrequently, but the collection of them is so large that at any given time we are likely to be using some such property. The point is that we can rearrange the order of the paths to be searched to gain efficiency, but it is dangerous to leave anything out. We are left with a certain irreducible kernel of search to be performed, even if our strategies are very clever.

And who is going to write all of these search-optimizing programs? If these are to exploit the local regularities of the currently-existing knowledge and the local meta-knowledge about the likely patterns of knowledge-use, then the body of search-programs must be augmented and altered as the system learns new things. Unless there is to be constant human intervention in the system's inner workings, the computer itself is going to have to write these programs. Unfortunately, it is hard even for humans to write effective search-optimizing programs in such a non-uniform environment. It requires not just technical skill but a good understanding of exactly how the knowledge-base is going to function. It seems unlikely that an automatic programming system will be able to exhibit such understanding any time in the near future -- in fact, it seems probable that to achieve such an understanding, the system would already have to contain the type of broad, flexible knowledge base that we are trying to develop here.

Despite these problems, the procedural approach to representing knowledge is still the dominant paradigm in the field of artificial intelligence (or at least that part of the field that has resisted the siren song of predicate calculus). Minsky, in his paper on frame-systems [1975], advocated the use of a combination of declarative information and local procedures to represent structured knowledge, and most of the workers that have followed Minsky's lead, notably Winograd [1974, 1975], Kuipers [1975], the FRL group at MIT [Goldstein & Roberts, 1977; Roberts & Goldstein, 1977], and the KRL group at Xerox-PARC and Stanford [Bobrow & Winograd, 1976], have continued in this vein. These researchers have been primarily concerned with the problems of flexibly representing relatively small bodies of knowledge, and of integrating the declarative components of their systems with the procedures. To the extent that they have addressed the problem of efficient search in a very large knowledge base, however, they have generally subscribed to the view that meta-knowledge, embedded in local search-guiding procedures, can eventually carve the searches down to a manageable size without destroying the generality of the system. This optimism may be justified, but to succeed by this route -- if indeed it is possible at all -- will require a tremendous investment of time and effort. In this report we will explore an approach that is much simpler and more direct.

1.3 The Parallel Network Approach

In my proposed knowledge-base system, we forget about trying to avoid or minimize the deductive search, and simply *do* it, employing a rather extreme form of parallelism to get the job done quickly. By "quickly" I mean that the search for most implicit properties and facts in this system will take only a few machine-cycles, and that the time required is essentially constant, regardless of how large the knowledge base might become. The representation of knowledge in this system is entirely declarative: the system's search procedures are very simple and they do not change as new knowledge is added. Of course, the knowledge base must contain descriptions of procedures for use by other parts of the system, including those parts that perform the more complex deductions, but this knowledge is not used by the knowledge base itself as it hunts for information and performs the simple deductions for which it is responsible.

The parallelism is to be achieved by storing the knowledge in a semantic network built from very simple hardware devices: *node units*, representing the concepts and entities in the knowledge-base, and *link units*, representing statements of the relationships between various nodes. (Actually, the more complex statements are represented by structures built from several nodes and links, but that need not concern us here.) These devices are able to propagate a variety of marker bits -- somewhere between 8 and 16 distinct markers seems to be the right number for human-like performance -- from node to node, in parallel through the network. This propagation is under the strict control of an external serial computer that is called the *network controller*. It is the propagation and interaction of the various marker-bits that actually constitute the deductive search.

The result is a network memory very similar to the one proposed by Quillian a decade ago [Quillian 1968, 1969], but with a very important difference: the network system I am proposing is much more tightly disciplined. The controller is not only able to specify, at every step of the propagation, exactly which types of links are to pass which markers in which directions; it is also able to use the presence of one type of marker at a link to enable or inhibit the passage of other markers. It is the precision of such a system that gives it its power, but only if we can learn to use it properly.

Note that this is a very different kind of parallelism from that displayed by a relatively small set of serial machines working together. Ten CPUs, at best, speed up the processing by a factor of ten. Usually the improvement is much smaller because the CPUs begin to squabble over shared resources or because most problems cannot be broken up into ten independent, equal-sized parts. The proposed network, on the other hand, can perform many deductions in time proportional to the length of the longest branch of the search-tree, regardless of how many nodes the tree may contain overall. For short, bushy trees (knowledge bases consist mostly of short, bushy trees), the speed-up could be huge: a tree that is five or ten links deep might contain millions of nodes in its branches, so a million-fold speed increase is possible. Of course, this would mean that the parallel network must contain millions of hardware processing elements, but each element is very simple -- a few decoding gates, an internal state flip-flop, and enough other flip-flops to store the marker bits that may be present on that element. The knowledge itself is stored not inside the elements, but in the pattern of interconnections among them. (We will see later how this interconnection might be accomplished.) With current technology such a network would be very expensive, perhaps prohibitively so, but there is nothing mysterious or undefined about it.

The network scheme is not without its own problems, and we will examine these in detail, but the speed advantage in certain important areas is great enough to *qualitatively* alter our ideas about what is easy and what is hard. The network-based system easily performs many of the mental operations which seem effortless to people, but which have proven to be very costly (or very complicated) for serial computers: finding the implicit properties of an item in a large hierarchy of types and sub-types (an "IS-A" hierarchy); dealing with multiple, overlapping contexts or world views; locating the known entity in the knowledge-base that best matches a list of distinguishing features; detecting any glaring inconsistencies between new knowledge and old; and so on. This rough correspondence of abilities does not necessarily imply that the human knowledge base uses a parallel network (though that is an interesting conjecture), but it does suggest that such networks might be *one* way to produce a system with human-like capabilities.

All of this talk about human abilities may cause some confusion as to my goals in this research. Let me state very clearly that this is meant to be artificial intelligence research, not psychology. People are able to do certain things with stored knowledge, and we want to find *some* way to make a machine do these things. The resulting theories may or may not prove to have some relevance to the human knowledge-handling system; it will take much careful experimentation to determine what the similarities and differences might be. It does seem to me that this general type of parallelism is *a priori* more plausible as a model for human knowledge-handling than systems which depend for success on the brute speed of current serial computers, since it is hard to see how the neurons of the brain could achieve such speed. Because of the speed advantage deriving from its parallelism, a network of the type I have been describing can achieve reasonably fast results even if the propagation time of its elements is in the millisecond range, instead of the microseconds or nanoseconds that we are accustomed to in our computers.

If my principal concern is not the modeling of human knowledge handling, why is there so much concern about what is hard and what is easy for people? Quite simply, I am using my own rather haphazard introspection in this area as a sort of heuristic guidance mechanism to tell me where to look and what to look for. If people seem to perform some task effortlessly, that is a pretty good indication that some efficient solution exists, though not necessarily on the kind of computer hardware that we are using at present; it is therefore worthwhile to expend a certain amount of effort trying to find the processing strategy that makes the task so easy for the brain. If, on the other hand, both people and conventional computers have trouble with some task, it is possible that no good solution exists, and it is unlikely that the operation in question is an essential part of human-like intelligence; much less effort is indicated in such cases. Such intuitions, unreliable as they may be, are still a lot better than nothing. In the end, a theory in AI must stand or fall on its performance, the breadth and variety of the intelligent responses that it can produce or explain, and the extent to which it inspires better theories as its shortcomings become apparent -- not on the correctness of the psychological speculations that led to the theory.

One question should perhaps be dealt with before we go on: What is the value of a solution to the knowledge-base problem that is based on imaginary or impossibly-expensive hardware? I believe that there are four answers to this question. First, the expensive hardware of today may well be very inexpensive in the future. If we can clearly specify what we want and why we want it, the necessary technology is much more likely to come about. Second, there is the argument of pure science: the creation of useful systems is only a part of the goal of AI; equally important is the goal of understanding, in precise mechanistic terms, how the activities that make up intelligence can be accomplished, and how the time required by each method is related to the size of the knowledge-base. For this purpose, the expense or practicality of the hardware is irrelevant, as long as the system is well-defined. Third, there is the possible usefulness of this theory as a source of models and ideas for psychologists, linguists, and others concerned with the question of how the human mind functions. Finally, and in my view the most important consideration, there is the usefulness of the parallel network theory as a *metaphor*: an intellectual tool that will help us to factor out the constantly-distracting technical problem of search-efficiency from the more complex issues of how to represent and use the knowledge, given that the search is accomplished somehow. Regardless of whether the deductive searches are ultimately performed by parallel hardware or by serial software, this separation of the problem will, I believe, help us to see more clearly the purely representational issues that we must deal with.

As I mentioned at the start of this report, the general idea of the parallel network system and the specific conventions and procedures of the NETL system are to a large degree independent. NETL has been specifically designed to run efficiently on the parallel network hardware, real or simulated, but it contains a number of ideas for improving the precision and representational power of knowledge-base systems in general, whether serial or parallel. Section 2 of this report will describe the parallel network system, along with its uses and general principles of operation; section 3 will cover the representational conventions and processing algorithms of NETL. A simulator for NETL is currently running in MACLISP on the PDP-10, and several test problems of assorted sizes have been run. These tests will be described in section 4, followed by overall conclusions in section 5. Appendix A will consider the possible hardware technologies for implementing the parallel network. Appendix B will summarize the node and link-types currently defined in NETL.

2. Overview of Knowledge-Base Operations

2.1 Type Hierarchies and Inheritance

Before we look at the details of the parallel network system and its operation, it would be useful to have a clearer picture of what we want it to do. As we have seen, it is not enough for the knowledge base just to store and retrieve isolated facts with no deduction; on the other hand, we cannot expect it to deduce quickly *everything* that could be deduced from the available body of knowledge. We would certainly accept such a capability if it were available in some practical form, but there is no real prospect of this, and such a capability is far in excess of what we need to produce a human-like level of intelligence. What we want from the knowledge base, then, is some intermediate level of deductive ability: we want it to perform those deductions that, to people, seem trivial and obvious (if indeed we notice them at all).

How can this set of obvious deductions be characterized? One possibility is to describe them in terms of type hierarchies and property inheritance. As we will see later, this characterization is not entirely adequate: it does not provide us with any clear idea of how to handle the inheritance of the internal structure of a description. Still, the type hierarchy is the starting point for the characterizations we will eventually want to use, so it is important to understand its importance in a knowledge-retrieval system.

There are two types of nodes that represent concepts in the network: individual-nodes and type-nodes. The individual-nodes, as the name implies, represent individual entities that may or may not exist in any particular context. Type-nodes represent not individual entities but template descriptions from which any number of individual copies may be created. Each type-node is associated with a particular set (represented by an individual-node) for which it serves as the exemplar -- the description of the typical member of that set. Every set-node has a type-node, and every type-node has a set-node. CLYDE is an individual-node. (Here and in the future, words written completely in capitals will refer specifically to some node, link, or other computer-thing; the concepts themselves will be written in the normal English style. Thus, CLYDE is the node that represents the elephant named Clyde.) TYPICAL-ELEPHANT (or just ELEPHANT) is a type-node attached to another node, named ELEPHANT-SET, that represents the set of all elephants. (The word "elephant" is represented by yet another node, distinct from TYPICAL-ELEPHANT but connected to it. Unless otherwise specified, the nodes we will be talking about represent real-world concepts rather than words or other linguistic entities.) It is important to keep the set-node and the type-node distinct, because their properties are different: the set of elephants has a certain size, expressed as the number of elephants in the world; the typical elephant has a certain size expressed in meters or kilograms.

Anything that we have to say about "the typical elephant" or about "every elephant" is thus attached, in the form of a property or a statement-structure, to the TYPICAL-ELEPHANT node. I am using a weak sense of the word "every" here: I mean that the property is true of every elephant for which it is not explicitly cancelled. We will see later how to declare that some fact is sacred (uncancellable) and therefore true of all elephants without exception.

Now, when we say that Clyde is an elephant, what should happen? First, we must establish a set-member relationship from Clyde to the set of elephants. Far more important, however, is the establishment of a *virtual-copy* (abbreviated VC) relationship between CLYDE and TYPICAL-ELEPHANT. We will explore the full implications of the virtual-copy concept shortly; for now, it is enough to say that this VC relationship causes Clyde to inherit all of the properties that are attached to the TYPICAL-ELEPHANT node. We accomplish both of these effects by the creation of a single link, called the VC link, from

CLYDE to TYPICAL-ELEPHANT. (There is an implicit MEMBER-OF statement linking a set-node to its type-node and this membership is inherited by all the virtual copies of the type-node, just like any other property.)

To create a subset or type-of relationship between elephant and mammal, we do essentially the same thing. By creating a VC link between TYPICAL-ELEPHANT and TYPICAL-MAMMAL, we set up the desired inheritance of properties: if every mammal is warm-blooded, then every elephant should be as well. Every elephant also inherits membership in the set of mammals, and an implicit part-of or subset relationship is established between ELEPHANT-SET and MAMMAL-SET. Some semantic network systems use distict link types to distinguish "is a type of" from "is an instance of"; because, in this system, the nodes themselves distinguish types and individuals, we can get away with using the single VC link, which treats individual-nodes and type-nodes alike.

Like all links in this system, the VC links can be crossed by markers in either direction, as ordered by the external control computer, but this does not mean that the VC links are symmetrical. While marker sweeps may be run in in either direction, the intent of the links is to establish the inheritance of properties in one direction only, from the more general class to the more specific one or from the type to the instance. We do not want the typical elephant to inherit Clyde's particular properties, nor do we want the typical mammal to inherit the properties attached to the typical elephant.

The virtual-copy links are transitive, directional, and they do not form loops. Furthermore, every concept-node in the system (with one or two exceptions) has at least one VC link to some more-general category, and a path of VC links upward to the most general type-node in the system. This node is named THING, and it encompasses everything (every THING) else. The network of VC links, then, welds the nodes of the network into a single tangled hierarchy (or, if you prefer, a partial ordering) of types, subtypes, and individuals. This hierarchy forms the backbone of the knowledge-net -- the rigid organizational structure that keeps everything else from collapsing into a heap.

In order to talk about this hierarchy more coherently, I will adopt some directional metaphors. The VC links will always be spoken of (and will appear in diagrams) as pointing *upward*: MAMMAL is *above* ELEPHANT and *below* VERTEBRATE. The THING node is at the *top* of the hierarchy, and the various individual entities are at the *bottom*. (One never makes a copy or instance of an *individual-node* in normal kinds of description, though such operations may play a role in metaphorical description.) Other relations will be spoken of and drawn as running sideways, more or less. I will also sometimes speak of the *parent* or *parents* of a node, meaning those nodes immediately above the given node in the hierarchy, and the *ancestors* of a node, meaning those nodes somewhere above the given node. Obviously, *offspring* and *descendent* are analogous, but downward in the hierarchy. Such conventions will save a lot of words in the long run.

Because of the transitivity of the VC links, properties may be inherited through many levels of the type hierarchy. Consider a node like COW. (We will let the elephants rest for a while.) Properties attached to the COW node itself, or to any node above COW in the hierarchy, are meant to apply to *every* cow. Explicit exceptions may be made, but in the absence of these, the inheritance is to hold. Properties hung from nodes below COW are meant to apply to only *some* cows. In figure 1, for instance, we see that all cows (unless there are specific exceptions) are warm blooded and have udders, but that only some cows are black-and-white while others are brown. There are not, to the system's knowledge, any purple cows, but this is not ruled out. If asked what color cows are, the system would look at the COW node and at all the nodes above COW in the hierarchy, but would find no COLOR property on any of these nodes. It would then have to answer that cows are no particular color. It might go on to look down the hierarchy, and report that some cows are brown, while others are black-and-white.

It is important in constructing any search or marker-propagation strategy always to respect this transitive property of the VC links. If every cow is a mammal and every mammal is an animal, then every cow is an animal, whether or not there is a VC link *explicitly* saying so. It follows from this that it should always be possible to split a VC link, for instance to add UNGULATE between COW and MAMMAL. Once we have created VC links from COW to UNGULATE and from UNGULATE to MAMMAL, the original VC link from COW to MAMMAL becomes redundant. The system can garbage-collect this link or leave it in place, whichever is more convenient. As you can see, a node may be above or below another, or may be between two other nodes on the hierarchy, but it makes very little sense to talk about distances from one node to another, since this is so fluid and may be different by different paths.

As I mentioned earlier, the VC hierarchy is a tangled one. That means simply that a node may have more than one immediate parent, as well as an arbirarily large number of offspring. To put it another way, the tree branches upwards as well as downwards. In addition to being an elephant-mammal-animal-physob-thing, Clyde may be a male, a vegetarian, a circus performer, and a veteran of the Punic Wars, and each of these identities may add a few properties and other statements to Clyde's overall description. Figure 2 shows the form of the resulting hierarchy, with a non-tangled hierarchy for comparison. The importance of this two-way branching to the property-finding procedures is illustrated in figure 3 which shows that part of the hierarchy which can be seen from a typical mid-level node X. In the familiar non-tangled hierarchy or tree structure, a node may have many descendents, but only a single strand of ancestors. Therefore, to find some property of X it is only necessary to trace up this single strand. In the tangled hierarchy, the descendents still fan out, but now the ancestors do as well. The hierarchy containing the ancestors of X can spread out to very considerable dimensions before it again converges

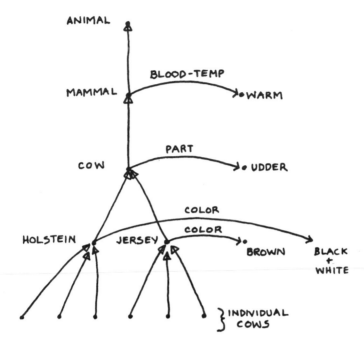

Figure 1: A portion of the COW type-hierarchy.

toward the top-level THING node. Because of this, X is in a position to inherit a very large and diverse set of properties. In a serial system this could be an embarrassment of riches, but with the parallel network system it is possible to investigate such a lattice in no more time than it would take to scan a single strand of the same height.

It might seem that in propagating markers through these tangled hierarchies, there is some chance of markers sneaking through unintended paths and marking everything. With a little care, we can avoid this. First, we must never let the VC links form a loop. (This is a stronger requirement than is absolutely necessary, but we have no real need for such loops anyway. In NETL, there is a separate link-type for representing the *equivalence* of two or more concepts. Note that in many relationships other than VC -- "hates", for example -- we do allow directed loops.) Second, we must always mark either upward or downward from a node or set of nodes, never both at once. If we observe these rules (and they are very easy to observe) there is no way to end up above a node while trying to mark down from it, or below it while trying to mark upward.

The kind of property inheritance that I have been describing is nothing new, of course. It appears in Quillian [1968, 1969] and, in one form or another, in every semantic network that has been designed since then. And, without the diagrams, it is just a form of logical syllogism with roots going back through Raphael's SIR system [1968] to Aristotle. The use of *tangled* hierarchies has been possible in most such systems, but people have only recently begun to concentrate on this aspect of inheritance and on its implications for efficiency in retrieving desired properties. Some comments by Terry Winograd, in a lecture describing Halliday's systemic grammar, triggered my first real appreciation of the need to allow tangles (multiple upward links) in a type-hierarchy, and only later did I realize what this implied in terms of deductive search for a system with a very large knowledge network. This, in turn, renewed my interest in Quillian-style parallelism to handle the search problem.

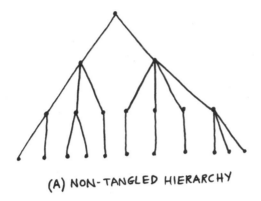

(A) NON-TANGLED HIERARCHY

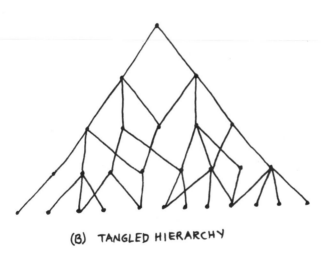

(B) TANGLED HIERARCHY

Figure 2: Tangled and non-tangled hierarchies, viewed externally.

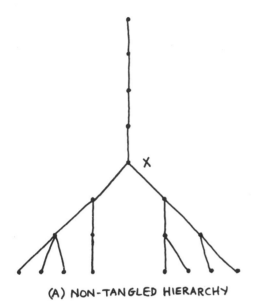

(A) NON-TANGLED HIERARCHY

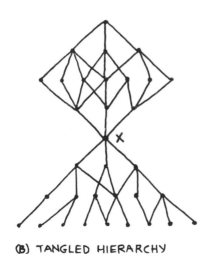

(B) TANGLED HIERARCHY

Figure 3: Tangled and non-tangled hierarchies, viewed from interior node X.

Though it seems a minor point, I think that this business of drawing the type hierarchy in a standard direction is important: it has no effect on the representational system itself, of course, but it makes it much easier for the designer of the system (and anyone else trying to decipher the diagrams) to visualize what is going on. If, as I believe, the type hierarchy is the most important single organizational structure in the knowledge network, it should be given prominence comparable to its importance. If a system is drawn (on paper or mentally) as a chaotic tangle of links of all kinds, it is much harder to visualize its behavior as an orderly, structured flow of events.

2.2 The Virtual Copy Concept

Property inheritance is a part of what we need from a knowledge base but, as I mentioned earlier, it is not the whole story. Somehow, we must form a clear picture of what to do about all the *structure* that is attached to the various type-nodes and individuals: the parts and sub-parts, each with its own description, and the network of statements that connect these parts to one another, to the owner, and to various external nodes. Most existing knowledge-base systems (and the early versions of my system) handle these problems with varying degrees of success using an assortment of techniques, but they lack any clear, unifying view of what is going on. After fighting with this problem for a couple of years, I hit upon a way of looking at it that -- to me, at least -- made it much clearer what ought to happen in any given situation. That viewpoint is the *virtual copy* concept. The basic idea of this concept can be expressed as follows:

What we really want is to create virtual copies of entire descriptions. These descriptions can be arbitrarily large and complex pieces of semantic network. When we learn that Clyde is an elephant, we want to create a single VC link from CLYDE to TYPICAL-ELEPHANT and let it go at that, but we want the effect of this action to be identical to the effect of actually copying the entire elephant description, with the CLYDE node taking the place of TYPICAL-ELEPHANT. It must be possible to augment or alter the information in this imaginary description without harming the original. It must be possible to climb around on the imaginary copy-structure and to access any part of it in about the same amount of time (speaking in orders of magnitude) that would be required if the copy had actually been made. But we want all of this for free. We just cannot afford the time or memory-space necessary to actually copy such large structures whenever we want to make an instance or a sub-type of some type-node, especially since the type-node's description may itself be a virtual copy of some other description, and so on up many levels. A description may also contain other descriptions -- the parts of an object, for example -- that are themselves expressed as virtual copies. We want all of this structure to be virtually, but not physically, present.

If, in the description of the typical elephant, there are nodes representing its hip-bone and its thigh-bone, and there is a CONNECTED-TO statement linking these two nodes, then we want Clyde to have his own hip-bone, his own thigh-bone, and his own version of the CONNECTED-TO statement. (Clyde's version of this statement might be modified in some way; if he has been injured, for instance, Clyde's hip-to-thigh connection might be very weak.) It is not the case, however, that every node to which the TYPICAL-ELEPHANT node is somehow related is therefore a part of the TYPICAL-ELEPHANT description, in the sense that we want to copy it for each elephant. If the typical elephant respects Charles Darwin, then we want Clyde to respect him as well, but we want him to respect the same version of Darwin that all the other elephants respect. We do not want every elephant to have his own copy, virtual or otherwise, of the DARWIN node. The HIP-BONE node, then, is a part of the TYPICAL-ELEPHANT description; the DARWIN node is outside this description, but is connected to it by a RESPECTS-statement.

How do we know which nodes are a part of a given description, and which nodes are not? We cannot tell this reliably from the attached statements alone, so we must state the attachment explicitly. This is done with a special link called the EXISTENCE-link, indicating that the role in question exists as a part of the description to which it is attached, rather than as a free-standing external entity. (Actually there are two kinds of existence links, and either kind can be replaced by a special wire coming out of the role-node, but we will ignore these complications for now.) These EXISTENCE-links correspond, more or less, to one sense of the word "has": "Every elephant *has* a hip-bone."

A description, then, consists of a *base-node* representing the thing itself (TYPICAL-ELEPHANT is the base-node for its description) and a set of *role-nodes*, connected to the base-node by EXISTENCE-links and representing the various things that every copy of the base-node has one of. Most role-nodes specify individual entities, but there are also *set-roles* (with attached type-nodes) for representing such things as the typical elephant's set of teeth and the typical member of this set. The links and statement-structures that attach the nodes within a description to one another or to nodes outside the description are also considered to be parts of the description, and therefore parts of the structure that is virtually copied. When a statement connects nodes in two different descriptions, as in "the typical elephant hates the typical aardvark", it is considered to be a part of *both* descriptions, and to be copied whenever either type-node is copied. We will see the details of all of these things later; for now, it is only important to understand in a general way what is going on.

Of course, we do not actually create nodes to represent all of the roles in the virtual copy; if we did, it would be a *real* copy. In fact, to do so would be impossible, because the roles and sub-roles that are virtually present within a description often form an infinite set. Consider the PERSON node. One of its roles is the node MOTHER (every person has one). But the MOTHER role-node is itself a virtual copy of the PERSON node (perhaps indirectly through WOMAN) and therefore has a MOTHER of her own, and so on. All of the nodes in this chain are virtually present -- we can refer to someone's mother's mother's mother to any level without talking nonsense, and we know that this is so because of the structure of the PERSON description -- but the point is that we only create actual nodes to represent those roles about which we have something to say. The rest of the role mappings are left implicit. We may know that every elephant has an appendix, but we only create the node representing Clyde's appendix if, for instance, we want to say that it is infected. When we do create such a node, called a MAP-node, we tie it to its owner (CLYDE) and to its parent role (ELEPHANT-APPENDIX) in such a way that it inherits all of the information attached to or inherited by the parent, and adds its own attached information to this description. All of this will be explained in more detail later.

The idea of roles within a description can be expressed in another, more mathematical form. A type-node like TYPICAL-ELEPHANT works more or less like a universally quantified variable in logic. When we attach a property P to TYPICAL-ELEPHANT, we are saying that for all X such that X is an elephant, $P(X)$ is true. The creation of a role-node is, in this view, like an existential quantification: for all X such that X is an elephant, there exists a hip-bone Y such that $P1(Y)$, $P2(Y)$, etc. The predicates on Y, of course, are the properties and descriptions that are attached to the role-node. When I speak of a description this way, as a bag of existential quantifications tied to a common variable, the relation of all this to the partitioned semantic networks of Hendrix [1975a, 1975b, 1976] becomes obvious. He uses his partitions as a means of delineating the boundaries of a single description tied to some quantified variable. (He also uses them in other ways.) Philip Hayes, in a recent paper [1977] has extended Hendrix-type networks even further in the direction of creating virtual copies.

As I said, people have been doing virtual copying in knowledge-base systems for years, with varying degrees of success, but they have not been talking about it in exactly these terms. The whole point of Winston's [1975] network-learning scheme, for example, was to build up the description of an arch (or whatever) so that new instances of this type could be described with a single statement instead of many. He doesn't develop this idea very far in his thesis, but it is constantly lurking in the background. Logic-based systems provide virtual copies of a sort, but most of them force you to build up the structure surrounding any part of the virtual copy that you want to look at, and many of them are very inefficient at this task.

Since Quillian's work, a number of semantic network systems have appeared, each with its own distinctive set of features and emphases. All of these systems employ some mechanism for the inheritance of properties but, as Woods has pointed out [1975], all of the early systems suffer from some degree of vagueness in their semantic representations. None provides the kind of precise control over quantification that is necessary for implementing true virtual copies of the kind I have been describing. Included in this group are the systems of Simmons [1973], Carbonell and Collins [1973], Anderson and Bower [1973], and Rummelhart, Lindsay, and Norman [1972]. My own earlier efforts [Fahlman, 1975] suffered from similar imprecision in the semantics. One of the early systems, that of Shapiro [1971], avoided such ambiguity by staying very close to the language of mathematical logic and by representing the quantifiers explicitly in the network. The resulting system, however, represents much of its knowledge in the form of rules for altering and re-copying parts of the network; this makes it a poor candidate for use in a large, performance-oriented system -- especially a parallel network of the sort proposed here.

Later semantic network systems, notably those of Scragg [1975a, 1975b] and of the TORUS group at Toronto [Mylopoulos, *et al*, 1975], developed better solutions to many of the problems of representational precision, but left other problems untouched. Only in the network systems of Hendrix and the subsequent work of Hayes, Cercone and Schubert [1975], Schubert [1975], and Brachman [1977] do we at last see sufficient quantificational power to implement virtual copies of descriptions with interesting internal structures: parts, subparts, and a network of internal relationships among these parts. Even these systems, however, lack a clear unifying principle that I believe the virtual copy idea could provide. (For a more extensive review of the evolution of semantic network systems, see Brachman [1977].)

Schank, in his conceptual dependency networks [1973], has explored the question of what the descriptions of various verbs and actions must contain, and how this information can be used, but he makes no attempt to represent these descriptions as *virtual* copies; when he wants to represent some action, Schank makes a *real* copy of that action's full definition, in terms of his dozen or so primitive action-types. The steps telling *how* an action was accomplished may be omitted, but the description of *what* happened must be fully specified if the action's implications are to be found. This leads to certain problems: not only is it wasteful of space and effort to represent statements in their fully-expanded form, but it leads to some difficulty in finding those implications that result from the combination of actions rather than from the constituent primitives. To use Bob Moore's example, the action of kissing has implications that are not evident when it is decomposed into a set of PTRANS operations involving the lips of two people. With a virtual copy system it is possible to define an action-type like KISS once and for all in terms of more primitive actions, and to have both the inherited implications and those from KISS itself be virtually present whenever an instance of KISS is created. KISS, in turn, can be used as a primitive in defining even more complex concepts, and so on through any number of levels. A virtual copy system would thus provide a way of implementing some of Schank's ideas more effectively. (In some of the newer work on "scripts" by Schank and Robert Abelson [Schank 1975, Schank & Abelson 1975, Abelson 1975], there does seem to be a move toward a certain limited kind of action-type hierarchy, or at least a packaging of the basic primitives into larger structures, but there is still very little discussion of the role that inheritance plays in this hierarchy.)

Minsky's frames [1975] are classic examples of virtual copies, or at least of the need for them. Though Minsky had a different, more procedural implementation in mind, I would claim that *in their intended effect* his frames are essentially what I have been calling descriptions, and his slots correspond closely to what I call roles. (I have deliberately chosen a different set of terms to avoid confusion, since in the wake of Minsky's paper people have adopted his terms for a variety of uses, not all of them compatible with what I am trying to express.) To me, the principal contribution of the Frames Paper is that it re-focussed everyone's attention on the need for some way to create virtual copies (or something like them) in a knowledge base. This issue had been neglected too long in favor of work on other areas of intelligence. The numerous frame-related systems currently being developed share this general point of view though, as I mentioned in Section 1.2, their view of how the frames are to be accessed tends to be more procedurally-oriented than my own. These systems face a common set of semantic problems, and some of their ideas (especially from KRL) have influenced the evolution of NETL.

If all of this work is going on already, what difference does it make whether we think of the knowledge-base as implementing virtual copies, frames, inheritance, or something else? What's in a name? All I can report is my own experience. As long as I was thinking in terms of property-inheritance and symbol-mapping, OF-links and IN-links, contexts and owners and areas of attention, things kept going wrong, and it was very apparent that they were going wrong because I did not really understand what I was trying to do. Which properties were to be inherited and when? What, if anything, did a part inherit from its owner? What did I really mean by context -- was a person the context for his hand or just its owner, and what did that imply about the set of statements to be activated? What kinds of exceptions made sense and which ones were illegal or useless? And so on. All of these issues became much clearer (as, I hope, will be evident in the description of NETL) once I started thinking in terms of virtual copies. If the goal is to make the network behave as if a well-defined piece of it had been copied, it is clear what needs to be done in almost any situation. In a few words, we have captured a very powerful idea. All of this may be idiosyncratic, of course -- it may be that the type of confusion that I was suffering from was a manifestation of my own mental processes and prejudices -- but I doubt it. I have seen too many other people falling into what appear to be the same set of traps. The virtual copy idea, when it is made explicit, adds a sort of global clarity of purpose to a knowledge-base system, and even a little bit of added clarity can sometimes be important.

2.3 Nodes, Links, and Set Intersections

Now that we have some idea of the kinds of operations that we want the knowledge-base to perform, it is time to take a closer look at the elements from which the network is built and how they can be used to implement deductive search. In particular, we will see how such networks can be used to find the intersections of certain kinds of sets in essentially constant time, and why this is important. We will cover here only those details that might be of interest to the general reader; sample circuit diagrams of the node/link units and some discussion of the possible techniques for making the node-to-link connections are included in appendix A.

The knowledge network is built from simple hardware node and link units, connected together to form the patterns of knowledge that are present in the knowledge base. The whole network is controlled by an external control unit -- a serial computer of the familiar sort -- that is able to communicate with all of the node and link units via a single party-line bus. The node units contain internal flip-flops for representing the dozen or so distinct marker-bits that are propagated through the system, over the connections formed by the network of link units, according to the dictates of the external controller.

Each link unit has a number of distinct terminals or *wires* that can be connected to the various nodes in the system. Each node unit has a single terminal to which these link-wires can be tied. In order for the marker propagation to proceed in parallel, these node-to-link connections must be private lines -- actual wires of some sort. To use the common bus for this intercommunication would mean that only one link could be propagating a marker at a time, and would destroy the desired parallel speed advantage. While the pattern of marker distribution and the contents of the control computer registers contain a certain amount of short-term information, all of the system's permanent knowledge is represented in the form of node-to-link interconnections. It is therefore necessary to alter these interconnections as the system learns new things, though this alteration may proceed very much more slowly than normal look-up operations: a few new link-connections per second ought to be adequate for human-like performance. (The psychologists have amassed a considerable body of evidence that people can only assimilate a few facts per second into their long-term memories.)

Each node unit has a permanently assigned, unique serial number by which the controller can address it directly. Usually, however, a command is broadcast to an entire class of nodes on the basis of their type and current marker content. A command might be addressed, for instance, to all individual-nodes with marker M1 on and marker M2 off. (As we will see, a number of bits are required to fully specify the type of a node or link. These can be represented as special read-only marker bits within the unit or as certain bits of the unit's serial number.) Sometimes the controller will merely be testing to see if zero, one, or many nodes fall into the specified category. Sometimes the command will specify that the selected nodes are to report their serial numbers over the bus to the controller. (If many nodes are selected, they will have to queue up and report in one at a time. This can be accomplished by a daisy-chain arrangement, or by a bitwise scan of the serial-number space -- see appendix A for details.) Usually, however, the command will specify that all of the selected node units are to set or clear certain of their markers. A typical command might order all nodes with M1 and M2 set to clear these and set M3. One possible format for these commands will be presented along with the circuit descriptions in appendix A.

The link units have a serial number but no internal storage for markers. Commands to them may be direct, using the serial number to specify the target link, but this is rare. Normally, the controller wants to order all links of a certain type to examine the markers of the attached nodes and, if the desired pattern is found, to set or clear specified markers on other attached nodes. The controller might, for instance, order that all VC links examine the node attached to their A-wire (as in "A is a virtual copy of B") for an M1 marker and, wherever this is found, to set the M1 marker-bit in the node attached to their B-wire. This operation propagates all the M1 bits in the system one level up the VC hierarchy in a single parallel step. To propagate bits all the way up the hierarchy, we would want to address our command to every VC link with an M1 bit on the A-node and no M1 bit on the B-node. If any such links are found (the controller can sense this over the bus) the propagation is performed and the process is repeated. When, finally, no links respond, the propagation-scan is complete.

        Actually, the situation is a bit more complicated than this. To actually allow the link units to sense, in parallel, the entire marker-state of a node or to alter that marker-state would require that the node-to-link connections consist of a bus many bits wide. Since these connections, and not the node and link units themselves, are the most costly part of the network-system, we want to keep each connection down to a single wire. To do this we connect the link-wire in question through the node's single terminal to an internal flag-bit in the node unit, called the SELECT flag. Using this flag for node-to-link communication, the controller can make the appropriate node units examine and alter their own marker-states. The single-step propagation operation described above would now be completed in several cycles, an increase by a small *constant* factor. First, the controller would call all VC links to attention. Next, it would order all nodes with the desired marker pattern (in this case, an M1 mark) to set their SELECT flags. All of the links at attention would then sense whether the node connected to their A-wire is among those selected: if so, the link remains at attention; if not it drops out. This process is repeated for any other attached nodes that are to be examined in the current step. Finally, the links still at attention are ordered to set the SELECT flag of the attached B-node, and these selected nodes are ordered (by the controller) to set their M1 marks. This may sound complicated, but it is still possible to propagate any number of bits one level in four or five bus-settling cycles, and all the way through the type-hierarchy in a time that is acceptably short, even for very slow processing elements.

There is one more complication to add before we go on to see how all of this works. I have spoken of the node and link units as separate entities, and will continue to do so, but the difference is largely one of emphasis. It has proven to be convenient (though not really necessary) to implement nodes and links identically in the current version of NETL. The reason for this is that every link has an associated *handle-node* that represents the statement that the link implements. To this node we can attach any modifications or meta-information that we want to apply to the statement, for instance to say that it is a mere default that can be cancelled with impunity, or that it is sacred and should never be cancelled. The marker-bits of the handle-node are also a convenient place to flag which links are to be considered active in the current context and which of these are cancelled in the virtual copy under consideration.

The nodes, in turn, sometimes need a few link-type wires for special-purpose connections to other nodes. Any connection that represents an arguable or deniable statement of fact should be represented by a full link, so that we can attach cancellations or qualifications to the handle-node, but connections that form a part of the identity of the node have no need for such attachments. The connection of a type-node to its set-node, for instance, is a part of the definition of the type-node, rather than a deniable statement: it makes no sense to argue over whether TYPICAL-ELEPHANT is the type-node for ELEPHANT-SET -- by definition, it must be. This connection is therefore represented by a special set-wire coming out of the TYPICAL-ELEPHANT node, rather than by a true link. Other specialized attachments of one node to another are also represented in this way, as we will see in the description of the various node and link types defined in NETL.

Since every true link has a handle-node and every normal node has a few special link-wires, it seems only natural to use the same piece of hardware to represent them both. I call this piece of hardware an *element* when I want to refer to it without indicating whether it represents a node or a link. An element has the marker-bit storage and the single terminal of a node (the handle-node if it is representing a link) and a set of connecting wires that it uses in the manner of a link. The interpretations that are placed on these wires and the number of wires that are actually used depends on the type of node or link that the element is representing. Some nodes use only one or two, while a link with its handle-node may use six or so. The maximum number of wires that is allowed is, of course, a parameter of the hardware (or simulated hardware) implementation; generally, it is possible to use more links with fewer wires per link, or fewer links with more wires. It would be difficult, however, to get along with only two wires per element, and impossible with only one. Three wires would appear to be the practical minimum. In general, in this thesis, I will continue to talk about links and nodes as though they were distinct hardware entities, because that seems clearer to me.

Now, how can these nodes and links be combined into a network that represents knowledge and performs certain deductions at high speed? Let's forget, for now, about virtual copies and just consider old-fashioned property inheritance. Suppose someone asks the system what color Clyde is. The system's knowledge about this subject might be stored as a COLOR-OF link from TYPICAL-ELEPHANT to the node GRAY. It so happens that the ELEPHANT node, where COLOR-OF is attached, is only one or two levels up the VC hierarchy from CLYDE, but such a property could be attached anywhere in the hierarchy, and the hierarchy could be very large. It might be necessary, therefore, to look individually at a great many superior nodes in order to locate the desired property-link. The parallel hardware network can, in effect, look at many nodes at once. An M1 marker is placed on the CLYDE node, and is then propagated *up* the network of VC links by the method described above. This marks all of CLYDE's ancestors in the network -- in other words, all of the nodes to which properties that CLYDE should inherit might be attached. A command is then broadcast to all COLOR links that are tied to *any* of the marked nodes, telling them to mark the associated color node with M2. This is done in a single step. The controller then asks all M2-marked nodes to report in and, if all has gone well, the single node GRAY does so. Note that this process does not tell us where in the tree this property was attached, but it doesn't matter: the scan takes the same amount of time to find any of Clyde's simple properties, regardless of their position in the hierarchy. There is much to add to this picture -- exceptions, for example -- but the basic idea remains the same.

The time required for this marker scan is proportional not to the total number of nodes that appear in the lattice of CLYDE's superiors, but to the length of the longest path through the lattice. Actually, the time can be shorter still, since the propagation up some long path will be terminated whenever it rejoins a path that has already been marked by some shorter route. The length of these paths for most real-world knowledge domains does not seem to exceed ten or so links; the longest naturally-occurring chain of "is a" relations that I have seen comes from the formal taxonomy of animals, and even here the length is less than twenty levels, depending on exactly what is counted as being a level. If any single branch grows unusually long, it can be short-circuited by installing some redundant VC links that skip over several intermediate levels -- straight from ELEPHANT to ANIMAL, for instance. Consequently, it is possible to treat the time required to mark upwards or downwards in a type hierarchy as being a small near-constant, regardless of the number of nodes that become involved due to branching. We can treat the operation of marking a type hierarchy, with an arbitrarily large number of nodes, as a simple primitive -- one that we can use as freely as, say, CONS or SETQ in LISP.

When we mark downward from a node in the type hierarchy, the branching can be even more serious, but the parallel hardware works just as well. Suppose we have an OWNS-statement linking KING-ARTHUR to EXCALIBUR (his famous magical sword), and we are asked whether any ROYAL-PERSON is known to own a WEAPON. Marking downward from ROYAL-PERSON with mark M1, we mark every type of royal person (queens, princes, czars, etc.) and all individual members of these sub-types. Marking downward from WEAPON with M2 we get all the types and subtypes of weapons and eventually all known individual weapons that are represented in the system. Finally, we broadcast a call for any OWNS-statement that has an M1 mark on one side and an M2 mark on the other to report in. In would come the ARTHUR OWNS EXCALIBUR statement, along with any others that the system might happen to know. As you can see, the trees marked by M1 and M2 in this example are rather large, but they still would only take a few cycles to mark.

Examples such as this are useful for conveying the general idea of what the network is good for, but to really understand its strengths and weaknesses we need a more abstract characterization of its abilities and how they differ from those of a serial machine. I would claim that the key difference is that the network can very quickly intersect two or more sets whose elements are already present in memory, while a serial machine can do this only very slowly if the sets are large. If, as I hope to demonstrate, the knowledge-related areas of intelligence depend heavily on the operation of intersecting large, pre-stored sets (perhaps because the human brain itself has some special hardware or other tricks for getting intersections done quickly) then it is not too surprising that we have had trouble in duplicating this kind of intelligence on our serial machines.

Of course, the intersection of known finite sets is Turing computable, so we can do it in principle on any computer, but we are talking about huge differences in speed: the parallel machine might do in a constant few dozen cycles a task that the serial computer would do in time proportional to the size of the sets, which could be very large (the set of all animals, for example). Even so, the very great speed of our serial machines might save the day, but there is the constant temptation to resort to special-case tricks to avoid or cut down the searches. These tricks generally involve making premature assumptions about the structure of the knowledge and how it will be used, and they have a way of coming back to haunt us.

In assuming the existence of the parallel network hardware, then, we are postulating a world in which set intersection is a trivial operation. This frees us to concentrate on the more substantive issues of representational theory, without the constant distraction of worrying about whether we are creating unmanageable search and intersection problems. Later, when we understand what we are doing, we can decide whether to actually build the hardware or to do the intersections by some software method. The knowledge-base problem is thus divided, and I would argue that this particular division has a substantial effect in clarifying the representational issues that are our main concern.

It is important that we clearly understand what sort of set-intersection is being discussed here. Sets can be represented in many ways. They can be *implicitly* represented by generator-functions or predicates; they can be represented *explicitly* by a list of members or a set of membership assertions in a hash table; or they can be represented *semi-explicitly.* By a semi-explicit representation, I mean one in which all of the elements of the set are explicitly represented, as well as all of the statements from which set-membership can be deduced in a straightforward mannner, but in which there are not necessarily single-step links from the set to each of its members. A type hierarchy of the sort we have discussed would be an example of a semi-explicit representation of a set: from every type-node there is an uninterrupted set of VC links down through the various sub-types, and eventually to all of the known members of the type-node's set. It is the explicit and semi-explicit sets that the parallel network system can intersect quickly. In such networks, any semi-explicit set can be marked in time proportional to the length of the chain of deductions that is necessary to reach the

farthest element of the set -- as we have seen, in the type
hierarchy this distance is only a few steps -- and the
intersection-set of any two (or more) marked sets can be marked
in a single cycle. ("All nodes with M1 and M2 on, turn on M3
as well.") This newly marked set is then ready for subsequent
processing; only if it is to be read out must it actually be
scanned node by node.

Even if we confine our attention to fully explicit sets, a
serial computer is much slower. It is very inefficient, in the case
of large sets, to use the obvious algorithm of scanning one set
and, for each element, scanning the other set to find a match. A
better approach is to scan one set, marking the elements or
remembering them in a hash-table, and then to scan the other.
As each element of the second set is found, its membership in
the first set can be checked at unit cost. The time spent is thus
proportional to the sum of the lengths of the two sets. If every
set is recorded once and for all when it is first created, it is only
necessary in performing any specific intersection to scan the
shorter of the two sets. If one of the sets is short this is an
obvious advantage, but if both are large there is still a serious
time problem. And if the sets are not static entities but are put
together on the spot (as would be the case if the sets were stored
semi-explicitly), we are back in the situation of having to scan
them both.

In general, then, to intersect sets on a serial machine
takes time proportional either to the sum of the sizes of the sets
or to the size of the smaller set, depending on the circumstances.
I don't know of any proof that this is minimal, but it certainly
seems unlikely that there is any way to intersect two sets without
looking at least once at each of the nodes in one of the sets. Of
course, once an intersection has been performed on two sets, the
result can be saved for future use if we ever need the same
intersection again. If we are not very careful about this,
however, we can easily fill up all of the available memory-space
with intersection sets. There is also a serious problem in keeping
all of these intersections up to date if set-membership is ever

allowed to change. And, of course, it buys you nothing if the two sets are being intersected for the first time. It is sometimes useful to store the intersection sets of certain commonly-encountered subsets of the sets that we are really interested in, and to splice together an intersection out of a collection of these pre-intersected subsets. In some cases this approach can lead to a significant improvement in performance (see McDermott [1975] for some examples of this), but the amount of savings depends in very complex and subtle ways on the exact structure of the knowledge and on the order in which it is accessed.

In view of these problems, there is an understandable temptation among AI researchers to insure that, whenever an intersection is performed, one or both of the sets to be intersected is very small. This can seriously distort one's view of what constitutes a reasonable representation strategy. A good programmer, when faced with the task of intersecting two million-member sets, will want to try every special-purpose programming trick in the book to avoid actually doing the work, and the tricks chosen may seriously limit the future generality of the system (not to mention their effect on the system's elegance and understandability). By postulating a fast-intersecting parallel hardware system, and by working with a simulation of such a system, we can effectively eliminate this temptation.

The hardware system will obviously not be built soon. At best, we will need to simulate these networks for a few years to see if they are what we really want; at worst, it might never be possible to build a large system of this sort at a reasonable cost. But, as I argued in section 1.3, the parallel network system has its uses even as a gedanken-machine. By providing us with a particularly clean and precise way to envision a world in which set-intersection is fast, this system can free us from the constantly distracting problems of search-efficiency and can let us consider in isolation the question of how to represent what we know and how to use this knowledge once we have found it.

2.4 Exclusive Splits and Clashes

We have seen, in general outline, how the parallel network system of Section 2.3 can implement a fast form of property inheritance. In the remainder of Section 2 we will see, in the same very general sort of way, a number of other knowledge-base functions that such networks can perform. In reading this, I would urge you not to become overly concerned with details or with marginal cases and counter-examples. To the extent that such details have been worked out (almost entirely in some areas, only sketchily in others) I will present them in Section 3, the detailed description of NETL. My purpose here is to convey a broad overall picture of the system's operation so that the details, when they appear, will have a context to fit into. Nothing presented in this section should be taken too seriously: in order to convey the clearest possible explanation of the big picture, I will occasionally have to mangle a detail or two, and present the corrected version later.

Just as we want the knowledge base to perform certain obvious deductions for us, we also want it to detect certain obvious inconsistencies between new information and old. I am not talking here about inconsistencies which can be detected only by a difficult process of reasoning or mathematical proof -- these are the responsibility of the problem-solving system. What I am talking about are the kinds of inconsistencies that are immediately obvious to any human who tries to assimilate certain descriptions or concepts. I call such obvious contradictions *clashes*. A clash would occur, for instance, if I told you that Clyde, in addition to being an elephant, was a cabbage. I could have said that he was a herbivore or a male or a quadruped, and that would have been all right, but cabbages and elephants are not compatible descriptions. A similar, if somewhat more complex, type of clash occurs if I refer to a green idea or a hungry rock. It is possible to make such descritions mean something by a process of metaphorical description and analogy, but first it is necessary to determine that the straightforward literal interpretations of these phrases don't make sense. This testing of appropriateness or consistency seems to be one of those effortless operations that the knowledge base ought to handle.

I believe that most such clashes arise from the structure of the knowledge base and the operation of the inheritance mechanism. We could, of course, state the fact that no elephant is a cabbage and, when the situation arises, retrieve and use this fact. This is obviously not the right answer; to store assertions about all the things that an elephant is *not* would be ridiculous. A better approach is to split the LIVING-THINGS class into PLANT and ANIMAL and somehow indicate that these sub-classes are disjoint, that they contain no members or non-empty subsets in common. Whenever an attempt is made to create such a member or subset, the system should notice the violation and complain to the process calling for the creation. The complaint might be handled in any of several ways: the operation might be aborted, the caller might replace the literal statement with some metaphorical interpretation, or the complaint might be overruled and an exception created (as in the case of a Euglena, for instance). Whatever action is taken, the important thing is to notice potential conflicts of this kind as they arise, but without wasting too much time in the process.

To see how this clash-detection process might be implemented in the network, consider the example in Figure 4. The key to this is the SPLIT statement between the type-nodes ANIMAL and PLANT. A single SPLIT statement can be tied to an arbitrarily large number of type-nodes, indicating that the classes in question are mutually disjoint. It is therefore not possible to represent this statement using a single link, since links must have a fixed number of wires, but we will treat it as a single link for the present -- the effect is the same, in any event. Now, suppose that CLYDE is already tied to ELEPHANT as shown, and we want to add a new VC link to CABBAGE (dotted in the diagram). Whenever a new VC link is added to the network, the system checks to see if any SPLIT statement has been violated.

This is done by propagating M1 markers up all the pre-existing VC-links and propagating an M2 marker upward across the link just created (or about to be created). M1 thus marks the node's original set of ancestors, while M2 marks the new ones; some nodes will have both marks. Then a call is broadcast to all SPLIT statements that have M1 but no M2 on one attached type-node, and M2 but no M1 on another node: all such statements are to report their existence over the bus to the controller. Any statement-nodes that report in are the ones being violated by the new VC link; in this case we would find the SPLIT statement splitting ANIMAL from PLANT. Note that the clash will be found regardless of where it occurs in the node's hierarchy of ancestors. If we want to overrule the clash, we can cancel it (using a CANCEL-link) for the particular node in question. This will keep the clash from bothering us again, but we will now have to sort out any possibly-clashing properties of the two descriptions, and decide for each property which description should predominate.

A similar type of clash-checking, suggested to me by Jon Doyle, can be used to look for individual exceptions whenever a new VC link is added to a type-node. Suppose that we have a type-split between the SMART-PERSON and STUPID-PERSON categories, which are sub-types of the PERSON type. If we then try to add a VC link from AMERICAN to STUPID-PERSON -- that is, if we want to say that all Americans are stupid -- we would like the system to complain if it knows any individual Americans who are in the SMART-PERSON category. If such exceptions are found, we must either state explicitly that they are exceptions to the general rule, or we must reject the newly added node as contrary to the facts at hand. Like the clash-checking that we saw earlier, this search for exceptions is easily handled during the digestion of the new link: with mark M1 we mark everything below the AMERICAN node; with mark M2 we mark everything below the type-nodes that clash with STUPID-PERSON; then, in a single command, we ask all nodes

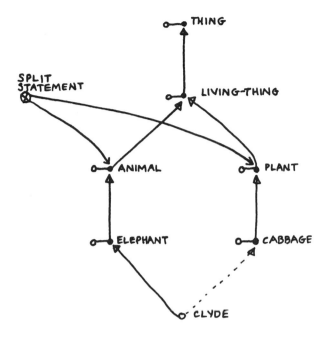

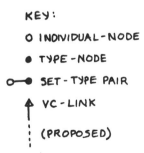

KEY:

O INDIVIDUAL-NODE

● TYPE-NODE

O—● SET-TYPE PAIR

↑ VC-LINK

⋮ (PROPOSED)

Figure 4: Partition of LIVING-THINGS into PLANT and ANIMAL.

with both marks to report themselves. If any such nodes are found, they represent the exceptions to the new statement that we are trying to digest.

This clash-checking might seem like a lot of work to do every time we create a new link. In fact, however, it is very fast. As we have seen, the upward marker-sweeps are not very costly, and the parallel call for the violated SPLIT statements is a single operation requiring only a few bus cycles. This speed results from the fact that the clash-test is, in effect, one of the semi-explicit set intersections described in Section 2.3. To see that this is so, consider this slightly altered description of what happens in the clash-test: first, we mark the set of old ancestors of the node being tested by performing an upward propagation; then, by propagating a mark through the SPLIT statements, we mark the set of type-nodes corresponding to forbidden sets for that node; finally, we intersect this forbidden set with the set of the node's new superiors to find the clashes. The method described above is a slight improvement over this, since the intersections occur on the SPLIT node itself, but the effect is the same. The key point is that these sets must indeed be semi-explicit: the ancestor nodes and the SPLIT statements must actually be present, as well as the VC links that tie the ancestor-sets together. If this is not the case -- if some of these items are not really present but must be deduced -- then the clash can only be found by more conventional serial deduction methods.

Even if the search were slower, however, it would not necessarily be disastrous. In this system, the creation of a new link or node is a relatively rare and costly event compared to normal accessing operations, and to add a bit of checking to this (within reason) is not very significant. In fact, the system performs several such checking operations when new information is added, all of which activity is referred to as the *digestion* of the new link. The most important of the digestive operations, like the split-test, can be performed by fast parallel mechanisms. Other digestive operations require some linear search, and thus become slower as the knowledge-base increases in size, but this set is somewhat open-ended. If the linear digestion processes must be terminated prematurely, the only harm done is that some possible deductions will go undeduced and some subtle absurdities may sneak into the knowledge-base. In a conventional logic-based system we would have to be very careful about this, but in this system the effect of a contradiction or two is strictly local. Complex digestive processes of this type form a continuum from the trivial deductions of the knowledge base to the complexities of full-blown problem-solving. The amount of work that is actually done for any new piece of information depends on how much time the system can afford to spend on that piece at the time of its arrival, but the few most-critical tests are fast enough to be run for every new item. We will look at these processes more closely in Section 3.

A given class can be partitioned into exclusive split-sets in a number of different ways. Figure 5, for instance, shows two distinct ways of cutting up the class of people: by age and by sex. The tangles in the tangled hierarchy arise not because we have illegally rejoined sets that were divided by a SPLIT statement, but because we allow a node to claim membership in *one* compartment of *each* of the splits under a given type-node. The type-node BOY, for instance, is under both CHILD and MALE, but an attempt to combine CHILD and ADULT would result in a clash. The creation of a re-joined node like BOY not only gives us a way to pick up MALE and CHILD properties with a single link; it also gives us a place to attach properties that are characteristic of objects in the intersection-set of the two classes, but of neither parent class -- elegibility for membership in the Boy Scouts, for example.

Because of the clash-detection mechanism, a VC link serves two functions. First, it allows the node being described to inherit properties and memberships from its parent-node, if such properties and memberships are not already known. If the offspring-node already has some descriptive links attached to it, however, the VC link serves as a *restriction* mechanism as well as

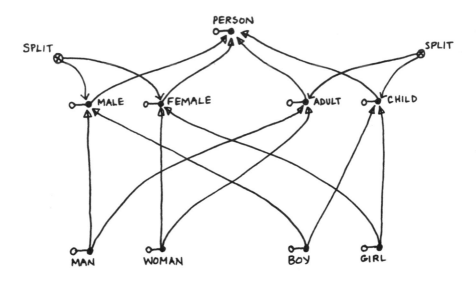

Figure 5: Multiple partitions of the PERSON class.

a property-inheritance link. If the newly-inherited memberships are inconsistent with the pre-existing ones, the creation of the VC link will be disallowed or at least flagged with a complaint. This restriction mechanism is especially important when a role in some node's description is about to be filled by some other node. (This is done with an EQ-link rather than a VC, but don't worry about that for now.) If the type-node PERSON has a role-node FATHER, and there is a VC link from FATHER to MAN, then any attempt to fill this role (or a map of it) with a node known to be a WOMAN will generate a clash at the MALE-FEMALE split. A restriction of this sort is more powerful than the semantic-marker systems of the linguists (Fodor and Katz [1963]), since any type-node in the system, from the most general to the most specific, can be used. The green ideas and hungry rocks mentioned earlier are examples of this kind of restriction: in a literal description, only physical objects (PHYSOBs) and light have a COLOR property, and an idea can be neither of these; only a living thing can be hungry, and a rock is non-living. (We will see in Section 2.5 how an object can be placed in a class on the basis of its properties.)

The set of exclusive subtypes created by a single SPLIT statement may or may not be declared to be *complete*. (We will see how to represent this declaration in section 3.6.) If the split is complete, every member of the parent class must fit into *exactly one* of the sub-classes. This means that if we have an entity which is known *not* to fit into all but one of the sub-classes created by such a split, we have the right to place it (by creating a VC link) into that final sub-class. (Of course this does not apply to entities that do not belong to the parent class.) If the class of VERTEBRATES is split completely into BIRDS, MAMMALS, REPTILES, AMPHIBIANS, and FISH, and I tell you that some vertebrate is not a member of the first four groups, then you are justified in assuming it to be a fish. Of course, if we do not yet know where the object fits, we can leave it hanging under the parent type-node, but this represents a state of partial information, not a belief that none of the existing sub-types is appropriate. The search for complete splits that are ripe for further processing is a part of the digestion process of any links stating non-membership in a class, either directly or through some other exclusive split. A parallel search can find candidates for this process, but in the current NETL it is necessary to check each candidate individually. This inefficiency does not worry me too much, since people are not very good at this sort of reasoning by the elimination of alternatives -- if there are more than two or three alternatives in the set, we tend to mumble and count them off on our fingers. Grossman [1976] has developed a system which handles complete exclusive splits more elegantly, if we ever really feel the need to do this.

Note that if the set of subtypes created by an exclusive split is not complete, that does not alter the exclusivity of the subtypes; it simply means that there may be other subtypes besides those listed. A list of the individual members of any set may be declared to be complete or incomplete, depending on whether we believe we know all of the members. The completeness of any given set or type-split is arguable and deniable, and it may be different depending on the context. In this respect, completeness is no different than any property-value assignment, and it is dealt with by the general context mechanism to be described in Section 2.6. Collins and his colleagues [1975] have studied the relationship between the completeness of a set or a type-split and the way it is used in reasoning and answering questions.

2.5 Matching and Recognition

The research described in this report is primarily concerned with representing knowledge of various sorts and with retrieving it in such a way that it can be useful to programs implementing the other parts of intelligence. I have not been able to devote much time and attention to how these other parts would work, or even to get very far into the interfaces between these parts and the knowledge base. There is one area, however, in which the facilities provided by the parallel network system can be so useful that I feel some discussion is warranted, even if it is of a rather incomplete and speculative nature. That area is what I call *symbolic recognition*. This was, in fact, the original area of my thesis research, before I had even begun to consider parallel networks and all of the representational issues that they raise. A large part of my motivation in moving from classical, procedurally-oriented frames to parallel networks was the difficulty I was experiencing in setting up an adequate search system for stored descriptions, a problem which is neatly circumvented by the networks. This section can be read, then, partly as a set of suggestions for applying the knowledge-base system and partly as an added argument for the usefulness of a parallel implementation.

By symbolic recognition I mean something considerably more powerful than the brittle, localized kind of pattern matching that goes on in a data-base of the familiar sort. Viewed abstractly, the recognition problem is to take an incoming symbolic description, which I call the *sample*, and to find the best match to this sample from among a large set of stored symbolic descriptions. This serves two purposes: it provides us with a compact way of representing the sample by creating a virtual copy of the matching description and noting any differences between it and the sample; it also supplies us with a considerable body of information, not directly observed in the sample, that can be reasonably assumed to apply to it. (In most real-world domains of interest, the things encountered fall into reasonably stable categories. This means that if certain features have appeared together in the past, they will probably appear together again in the future. One could imagine artificially created domains without this kind of regularity, in which case recognition would be useless and probably impossible.)

Both the sample and the stored descriptions may be symbolic structures of considerable size, and not all of the features present will have the same importance or degree of certainty. The features may differ in their degree of specificity: some may be very precise while others are identified only by their general categories in the hierarchy of types. Some features of the sample may even be wrong. Usually, too, the sample and the stored descriptions will differ in extent: the sample will contain only a small and unpredictable subset of the information in the stored descriptions.

Perhaps the clearest example of this type of symbolic recognition is the problem of medical diagnosis, given a set of symptoms and findings that are already in some symbolic form. (See Rubin [1975], Pople et *al.* [1975], and Shortliffe [1976] for a variety of approaches to this problem.) I believe, however, that symbolic recognition also plays a large role in domains such as vision and speech understanding which work with raw, noisy sensory input. At some point, these systems will have beaten their inputs into an internal symbolic form and will want to know what, if anything, that form matches. I am not saying that the two levels are cleanly separable -- there might be much interleaving of effort and communication between the symbolic system and the peripheral processes -- but that some symbolic matching and indexing facility must exist. The more powerful and flexible the symbolic portions of the system are, the easier life will be for the peripheral systems -- at present, the people working on these systems can only guess about how good their output will have to be. Marr and Nishihara [1977] describe some current ideas about what the intermediate language for vision should look like.

In problem solving, too, symbolic recognition has a role to play. Often we do not really want to solve a problem, but to remember a similar past problem whose solution might apply to the case at hand, perhaps with some slight modifications. (See, for example, Sussman [1973].) Of course, we will seldom see exactly the same problem twice, so our matcher must look instead for a sort of family resemblance between the new problem and the old ones. Those features of a problem that determine the overall course of its solution must be taken into account in this search, but minor, inconsequential differences should be ignored. Obviously, a requirement of this kind will rule out any straightforward hashing or indexing scheme for the library of descriptions, and we will ultimately need a library that will be too large to search item by item.

Initially, I divided this problem into two components: testing a hypothetical match once you have one and finding reasonable hypotheses in the first place. The hypothesis tester was responsible for weighing the various degrees of evidence, arbitrating any conflicts, and for explaining away certain discrepancies on the basis of context (a purple cow in the vicinity of a paint factory explosion, for instance). This part of the system contained many interesting problems, but the general process of description comparison was well understood, due to the work of Evans [1968], Winston [1975], and many more-recent contributions. The really hard problem, in my opinion, was in locating a reasonable hypothesis to test from a very large body of stored descriptions, given such an uncertain set of features to match on. The problem of indexing descriptions to allow quick location of the best partial match to a probe has been solved for certain very neat cases (see Rivest [1974]), but I could see no way of applying these results to the rather amorphous descriptions that appear in most real-world recognition problems.

The hypothesis-finding system that I first considered was the one advocated by Minsky in the Frames Paper [1975]. The idea was to select certain prominent features from each of the stored descriptions, and to create a network of suggestion demons to look for these triggers in any incoming sample. If a proposed match fails, another set of demons was to analyze the nature of the discrepancy and suggest a neighboring description to try. Of course, this involves the creation of a tremendous number of demons, but the hope was that by partitioning the description-space, the number of demons that are active at any one time could be kept within manageable limits. Another idea was to place the demons at various levels of the type hierarchy so that the more general demons could be shared by many descriptions.

This approach has several problems beyond the obvious one of creating and herding the demons. The most serious of these, for a domain like vision, is the brittleness of the triggering system. It is often hard enough to find *any* usable features of an object, let alone the precise set of features that was anticipated by the system designer, in exactly the proper format to trigger the appropriate demons. The search must be able to use whatever set of features the peripheral system can find if the recognitions are to be consistently successful in scenes with noise and occlusion. The fast-intersecting parallel network provides us with exactly this capability. That is why I set aside my work on demon-based systems to explore this new approach.

The basic description-finding operation is really very simple in a network system. We start with a list of features that are present in the sample. For each of these, we mark (with separate marker bits) the set of stored descriptions that possess this feature, either directly or by inheritance. We then broadcast a call for any node that has collected all of the appropriate marks. These are our hypotheses, ready for any further, more detailed checking that we might want to perform. If I am in the Everglades and see a greenish, six-foot long, four-legged animal swimming toward me, I simply intersect the sets of Everglades inhabitants, greenish things, four-legged things, swimming things, and animals, and out pops a winner. (The need for a reasonably fast intersection process should, at this point, become evident.) This strategy would be ridiculous for a serial system, but for a parallel network it is perfectly natural and very fast.

If we run out of distinct marker-bits for the feature sets, we simply intersect those sets marked so far, freeing all but one bit, and proceed as before. If the intersection set is empty, it probably means that one of the features on the list was spurious. In this case, we just look for the node that has collected the most marks. We might accomplish this by adding hardware to the node units to count the bits present or to compact them to one end of the bit-register. Probably, however, this added expense would not be justified: unless we are intersecting a great many features all at once, we can simply try various subsets of the given feature-set until we find a winner. Often we will know that certain of the features are unreliable, and can try throwing these out first. We might have to try several subsets before we find one that is not empty, but each test takes only one cycle.

To understand the power of this network-based matching system, you must understand several points. First, a matching description can be found given *any* set of features that uniquely describes it, even if these features are obscure ones. We do not have to pre-select the sets of features that we are looking for and hope that these are the ones that arrive. Feature descriptions at various levels of specificity are not a problem: we obviously get a smaller set of possibilities if we specify a snout rather than a nose, but each will play its appropriate role in the intersection process. Features, of course, do not actually have to be present in the descriptions being sought; inherited features work just as well. The only real restriction is that the features be represented in some semi-explicit form and do not have to be deduced during the search; obviously, if we were to ask the system for a prime number between some specified limits, it would have to abandon the parallel search and use some linear problem-solving method. Finally, the match can cover any arbitrarily large portion of the network surrounding the node we want to find. If we ask for a person whose last name starts with Q and whose grandfather's mistress was left-handed, and if the system knows of such a person, it will be able to find that person's node just as if we had indexed this particular set of features. Serial-computer indexing systems must index much more selectively, usually confining themselves to indexing within a single assertion. (For a discussion of what such systems can be made to do and the difficulties involved, see McDermott [1975].) With great care and effort, we might be able to approach this level of indexing performance on a serial machine, but the parallel network gives us the whole package in a very clean and simple form.

If we want to model human matching ability, the parallel network system may be *too* good. Many people, for instance, would have trouble remembering all of the animal-types whose names start with the letter N, while the network would do this easily. On the other hand, the procedural demon-based system does not seem to be nearly good enough to model human performance: even if we could make it less brittle, it would still involve a lot of computation to produce what people call a "flash" of recognition. I think that some sort of parallel matching is required, but perhaps of a more restricted, less powerful type than I have described here. In section 3.7 we will encounter some limitations of the parallel network system which bring its performance more into line with that exhibited by the human memory, and in section 5 we will briefly consider some other factors which might be responsible for the remaining disparity. Of course, it is also possible that the human memory operates in some fundamentally different way.

In all of the above we have assumed that there is something called a *feature* that is found by the low level routines and is passed to the hypothesis-finder as a tidy package. Sometimes this will be the case. Often, however, the features themselves will have to be recognized from their sub-features, and so on through many levels. This would not be so bad if the features could be recognized in a context-free way, starting with the most local and primitive of them and combining them into larger and larger packages, ending eventually with whole scenes and other global structures. Unfortunately, this is not always the case. Many features can only be properly identified in the context of the larger structure of which they are a part. This leads to a kind of circularity: we want to find the identity of an object or scene by intersecting its features, but to identify these features we may need to know what the object is. Which comes first, the elephant or the trunk? This apparent paradox is one of the favorite arguments of Hubert Dreyfus in his criticisms of the classical AI approaches to recognition [1972, 1976], and the argument is not without some validity. I believe, however, that we can escape the trap by identifying the object and its features simultaneously. To be more precise, we want to gradually refine the descriptions of the object and its features in an alternating pattern, making both appear to emerge at once. Intersections play an important role in this process.

To see how this might work, it is important to understand a few points. First of all, we do not have to choose between completely context-free methods and those that require a fully-specified context. A partial identification of the context, corresponding to some type-node farther up the tree than the one we ultimately want, is often enough to establish a framework for sorting out the features. If, for instance, we know that some object is an animal -- perhaps it has moved or is in a cage in a zoo, or perhaps because *some* animal-feature is clear and unambiguous -- we can begin to look in the appropriate places for legs, a tail, a head, and so on. Objects which before had only intrinsic, geometric descriptions (long vertical cylinder) can now be matched with role-nodes in the animal description (left front leg). Once this is done (and after clashes are checked for) we can decide what kind of leg we are looking at and on this basis can perhaps reclassify the animal to a lower, more specific category. This, in turn, will help us to identify still more features, and so on. Obviously, this depends heavily both on the matching process and on the structure-inheritance mechanism of the underlying knowledge base. The animal and its parts thus emerge together, little by little, like the solutions to a set of simultaneous equations or the junction-labels in the mutual constraint system of Waltz [1975]. Of course, once things start to converge, the process may be completed very quickly. We are not creating new network structure at this point; we are just moving pointers from high-level descriptive nodes to lower ones. Since we need distinct pointers for the object itself and for each of its features, I call this process "two-finger" recognition.

It is also important to note that the matcher can find an identity for an object even if no one of its features, by itself, can be unambiguously identified. Since I do not want to discuss all of the issues invloved in representing shapes and how they are positioned in space, let me illustrate this point with a linguistic example. Suppose, in a single context, I happen to mention the following words: base, diamond, pitcher, bat, plate, run, ball, and slide. Obviously I am talking about baseball. Any one of these words (and some pairs of them) could appear in a number of different contexts, but baseball is the only context in which *all* of them are likely to appear. Each word has a set of likely contexts, and baseball is the only member of the intersection of these sets. We find this intersection as we have found all the others, by marking the sets and looking for the node that has collected the most marks. Note that when we select baseball as the probable context, we are also selecting the appropriate meaning for each of the words. An analogous process would allow us to see a face, even though the individual features by themselves are ambiguous. Norman and Rumelhart [1975] expess a view of recognition very similar to this, and they illustrate this point about face recognition in their book (page 296).

The fast-intersecting network, then, is not a recognition system in its own right, but it is a valuable tool for building recognition systems. Much more work needs to be done on these feature-finding strategies, on the hypothesis evaluation process, on the intermediate-level representations for vision and speech, on the peripheral processes themselves, and on the techniques for cooperation between these peripheral components and the symbolic levels of the system. To me, however, the overall problem looks considerably more manageable once the intersection problems have been cleared away.

2.6 Assorted Other Uses for the Network System

The preceding three problems -- inheritance, clash detection, and recognition -- are the ones that motivated my current interest in fast-intersecting parallel networks, but these networks can solve (or help to solve) some other problems as well. In this section we will take a quick look at three such problem areas: the maintenance of multiple world-models or contexts, the monitoring of certain classes of objects or situations by demon programs, and the completion of implicit chains of causal relations. I will not try to explain the details of these operations here, since they require some of the machinery that will be developed in Section 3; I will just try to give you some general idea of how parallel intersection can be used in the solution of these problems.

It has long been recognized that a knowledge base must have some way of represesenting multiple world-models without confusing them, and of sharing the information that two such world-models have in common. This latter ability is essential in systems with a lot of real-world knowledge: we obviously can not afford to re-copy everything that the system knows whenever some local change of state occurs in the knowledge base. (This is one aspect of the "frame problem" discussed by McCarthy and Hayes [1969] -- no relation to Minsky's frames.) This kind of sharing ability in a general-purpose data-base was first implemented in the CONTEXT mechanism of the CONNIVER language [McDermott & Sussman, 1972]. Each assertion (the statement of a single fact) in the data-base is tied to (or "resides in") one or more *context-layers*, and it can be cancelled in other layers. A *context* consists of a set of context-layers, built up according to certain rules. At any given time, one of the contexts is declared to be active: only those assertions residing within one of the layers of the active context and not cancelled by any of these layers will be seen by the accessing mechanisms; the rest will be invisible and will take no part in any deductions while the context in question is active. Since a given

context-layer can appear in any number of contexts, the desired
sharing can be implemented by storing common information in
one of these shared layers; information that is not to be shared
is kept in a private context-layer. Hendrix [1975a, 1975b, 1976]
has applied a similar scheme to semantic networks, with one
interesting difference: in his system, the nodes (atoms) as well
as the links (assertions) are tied to partitions (contexts). This
makes it possible to use his partitions to model quantification as
well as multiple states of knowledge.

    This context mechanism has a number of uses. The
obvious one is to represent changes of state in the world being
modeled. This, in turn, gives us the ability to represent events
and actions as transitions from one world model to another, with
the unaffected parts of the universe occupying a context-layer
that is shared by both the before and after contexts. A context
might also represent a hypothetical world, some person's beliefs
or fantasies, or the world-model created by a novel. Logical
disjunction can be viewed as the creation of several distinct
world-models, one of which must be the true one. In all of these
applications, it is only necessary to record the differences --
additions and cancellations -- between the world being created
and the "real" world, whose information can be shared by all the
others. Some of the assertion-patterns in the data base may in
fact be the triggers of demon programs. These, too, may be
attached to context-layers within which they are active or
inactive, and may be shared by several contexts in the same
manner as assertions.

    Unfortunately, on a serial machine it is very hard to
implement a context system that will run reasonably fast when
both the number of layers active at once and the number of
assertions matching a given probe is large. Once again, we are
caught in an intersection: we want to intersect the set of items
matching the probe with the set of items residing in any of the
currently active context-layers. In CONNIVER this was handled
by indexing the assertions without regard to context; when an
access request produced a list or "bucket" of matching items, this

bucket was filtered, item by item, to eliminate any elements that did not reside in currently-active layers. As CONNIVER was implemented, this layer-check itself involved an intersection, but it would be possible in principle to reduce it to unit cost. This was an adequte solution for knowledge bases of the size appearing in typical CONNIVER programs, but it would be quite slow if the match-buckets were large. Another possible approach, useful when the number of active layers is small compared to the typical bucket-size, is to hash items into different buckets according to their layer-membership; an access would thus involve many calls to the data-base indexer, one for each currently-active layer, but no further filtering would be needed. McDermott [1975] discusses some other strategies that fall between these two extremes and which, *under the proper conditions,* speed thing up considerably. In general, however, the need to filter data-items according to their context-layer membership imposes a substantial additional cost on every access request handled by the knowledge base.

Since this problem is an intersection of semi-explicit sets, it is not surprising that the parallel network solves it. When a new context is activated, we can propagate a marker-bit trough the tree or tangled hierarchy of inclusion-relations to all of the nodes representing layers within that context. This process is very similar to the marking of the nodes in a type hierarchy, and it runs just as fast. Then, in a single step, we mark the handle-node of every link that resides in a marked layer. Cancellation marks can be placed as well. In any subsequent propagations or accesses, a part of the controller's command will specify that only those links marked as being active and non-cancelled are to respond; the rest simply ignore the command. Changing contexts is thus very fast, and no cost at all is added to other kinds of data access.

I might add, at this point, the observation that a scheme I suggested in an earlier paper [Fahlman, 1974b] for the fast inheritance of properties through a type-hierarchy by replacing the superior nodes with context-like "packets" of information is in fact a non-solution. Where previously we had to intersect (in some sense) the set of nodes with the desired property with the set of nodes superior to the node in question, the packet-based system would have to intersect an equivalent set of property-assertions with the set of currently-active packets. Since there will be one active packet for each of the node's superiors, the intersection is computationally identical. The packet system may have some psychological importance in organizing the problem of demon-control, but it does not buy us any speed. Because of my experiences in using CONNIVER, I had come to think of context-filtering as a free operation, even though on some level I knew that this wasn't true. Of course, in a fast-intersecting network system, the inheritance problem is solved without any gimmicks of this kind.

Though a parallel network system can perform the normal kinds of information storage and retrieval without resorting to the use of demon programs, it may still be desirable to use some demon-like mechanism for interfacing the knowledge base to the problem-solving system. We might, for instance, want the system to be constantly on the lookout for certain classes of objects, events, situations, and proposed goals: whenever some member of one of these monitored classes is noticed, the system is to initiate an appropriate action. An example for humans would be a rattlesnake or a burning building: if we see one of these items, we want our recognition processes to interrupt our current train of thought and initiate (or at least consider) certain special actions; a blade of grass or a car going by would not normally cause this sort of interrupt in normal situations, though they would do so on the moon. A more AI-flavored example of set-monitoring would be found in Asimov's Three Laws of Robotics [Asimov, 1950], which inhibit the robot from performing certain broad classes of actions and specify high-priority goals to be pursued in several broadly-defined situations. Obviously, if the robot is going to obey these rules, it must have monitors watching its own goal-proposing and situation-analyzing systems, looking for the cases in question.

Monitoring operations of this type have a lot to do with the phenomena that we call "awareness" or "common sense". Each individual monitor may be invoked only rarely, but there are a lot of them; taken together they can have a large effect on the system's behavior. The problem, of course, is to detect the monitored cases as they appear, but not to bog the system down by making it repeatedly check the triggering conditions for thousands of individual monitors.

The usual solution is to use demons: for each item that we want to monitor, we put a separate demon-program in the data base. We speak of these as though they were independent, constantly-running processes, but of course they are not really implemented in this way on a serial machine. Instead, we associate the demon program with a pattern in the data base, and we look for a matching demon pattern whenever the system encounters a new object, proposes a goal or action, or makes an addition of any sort to its knowledge -- in short, whenever it encounters some entity that might be monitored. The ongoing process is thus being constantly interrupted by demon checks, but this is tolerable since each of the checks is very quick -- just one call to the data-base. We must, however, be very careful not to do anything that would slow down these checks in any significant way.

Unfortunately, that is exactly what happens when we try to use monitors in a human-like way. The problem is that we want to monitor *classes* of items, but the demons must be triggered by *individual members* of these classes. Asimov's First Law prohibits the robot from performing any action that might harm a human; it says nothing *explicitly* about the act of sticking a knife into John Smith. Again, we are faced with a substantial intersection: we must intersect the set of all possible descriptions of the proposed action with the set of all action-types that are prohibited or otherwise monitored, and we must do this for every action that the system wants to perform, every object that it recognizes, every new fact that it deduces, and so on. Obviously, then, the intersection must be a fast one.

Unfortunately, the set of all possible descriptions for a given action is not available in any explicit or semi-explicit form in the knowledge-base. To be perfectly safe, then, we would have to consider each monitored class separately and check whether the action in question can somehow be made to fit into it. It appears, however, that for human-like performance we do not have to be infallible in this matching, and that we can confine ourselves to considering only those monitors that are attached to the new item's *explicit* superiors in the type hierarchy, after the item has undergone the usual kinds of digestion and analysis. Demon inheritance, then, involves the same kinds of processing that we have already seen in the inheritance of properties. If the tree of superiors is large (but not deep) the parallel network will have a substantial advantage over any serial machine.

The sort of exclusive-split clash detection that we saw in Section 2.4 can be viewed as a special case of type-monitoring. Whenever we add an item to one class in a type-split, we must in effect create demons to prevent it from being added to any of the other classes in the same split. We must check for such demons whenever a new VC-link is added to an entity that already is being described in some other way. The clash-checking scan described earlier takes the place of all these demons. Other particularly important demon-types can be implemented by comparable special-purpose digestive mechanisms. Usually, though, it is sufficient just to tie the demon to a type-node somewhere in the network, and to run it whenever an instance of that type is created.

Another use for fast intersections is in the completion of chains of causal relations in a story or in a real-life situation. This problem has been investigated by Charniak [1972], and more recently by Rieger [1975a, 1975b], Bullwinkle [1975a, 1975b], and Rumelhart [1975]. Schank's group also has been active in this area [Schank, 1975; Wilensky, 1976]. In general, these problems consist of a situation from which a number of possible actions might be predicted, each with a large set of possible sub-actions, and a specific observed action that might be occurring for any of several possible reasons. The task, then, is to find the simplest chain of goals and sub-goals that connects the observed action to some goal related to the given situation.

An example of this, taken from a lecture by Schank, is the following: "John wanted to be chairman of the department. He bought some arsenic." Most readers seeing these sentences together would assume that an assassination is in the works, but it is not clear how deductions of this type can be made so easily. It cannot work purely by prediction, since there are many thousands of other steps which could just as easily have followed the premise: John might have decided to shine his shoes, or to get another cup of coffee and return to his typewriter, or to buy a revolver instead of arsenic. Since each of these statements makes sense, and there are thousands more like them, it would be very difficult to create predictions for all of them. Nor can we work only backwards: the arsenic might be for moles in John's garden, for bumping off rich Aunt Agatha, or for doping semiconductors. It would be impossible to list all of the situations in which a person might buy arsenic and then try to find becoming a department chairman in this list. The best solution, probably, is to expand the tree of predictions out a few steps, to expand the tree of possible reasons for the observed action back a few steps, and to hope that something connects. (Of course, if we know *in advance* which paths are going to be important in a given set of examples, we can make sure that those paths appear among the predictions. This is cheating, though it may be useful temporarily as an exploratory technique.)

This is, of course, an intersection problem: we are intersecting the set of action-types which might be predicted from the given situation with the set of possible descriptions of the observed action; to put it another way, we are intersecting the set of possible reasons for the action in question (given its various alternative descriptions in the type-hierarchy) with the set of predictions emanating from the situation. (As we will see, actions and situations live in a hierarchy of types just as objects do.) The general strategy, then, is to mark the set of superior descriptions of the situation and of the observed action. Then, a few levels at a time, we propagate markers from the situation to its predicted actions and sub-actions and from the action to its possible reasons and super-reasons, looking for a connection. Each of these expanding networks is potentially huge, of course, but that is no problem for a parallel system of this sort. When a connection is found, we must check it to see whether it makes sense in the situation at hand, but each of these candidates has a high likelihood of success: since we are carefully controlling the general direction of the propagation, we will not find the kind of totally irrelevant paths that would plague a less-disciplined system like Quillian's.

The big question in all of this is whether the system contains enough *explicit* information about goals and subgoals, plans and expansions, for the intersection to proceed entirely by propagation, or whether new descriptions will have to be created as the search proceeds. In other words, are the sets to be intersected represented in the necessary semi-explicit format, or are they merely implicit in memory? I have not worked on this enough to have a really good answer, but I think that in most cases the necessary path will actually be present at some level in the network. The key to this expectation is the observation by Rieger [1975b] that, except for the indexing strategy used (and in this system there is no indexing), the same body of knowledge is needed to plan actions as to recognize and record them. If, whenever we see, produce, or read about an action we save it in memory, and if the record includes not only the action's type, but also the reason for it and the list of sub-actions that were used to carry it out, then we will very quickly build up a library of explicit plan-types linked together along the dimension from cause to effect. When we want an action capable of producing a desired goal we can find it, and if we want a list of actions that have some other type of action as a step, we can find that too. It is this network of action-types and expansions that the marker bits can crawl around on in the search for causal connections. Of course, if the chain to be recognized is novel in some way we

will not find a connection, but that is true of humans as well; if
a dead end is reached, we enter a much slower mode in which we
build up new descriptions for the items we are trying to connect.
All of this is just a plausibility argument, of course: there is a
great deal of work to be done before a system of this sort can
deal with any but the simplest cases of causal connection. Still,
it does seem to give us one way around a problem that would
involve a tremendous amount of search on a serial system.

The point of all of this has been to demonstrate the
surprisingly large number of explicit and semi-explicit set
intersections that must be performed by an intelligent system,
especially in those areas of intelligence which have traditionally
been the most difficult for researchers in AI. Any serial
machine will have trouble with these intersections: it will either
have to perform them very slowly or resort to complicated
heuristic techniques to avoid or reduce the problem. A parallel
network, on the other hand, can solve such problems very quickly
and cleanly. The parallel technique requires no cleverness in
designing indexing systems or heuristic guidance programs, no
canonical formats to aid the matcher, and it involves none of the
problems of arbitration and mutual intelligibility that afflict the
more familiar kinds of parallel systems. If intelligence (in the
sense that people use the word) is indeed built in large part from
such intersections, then the serial computer is a rather poor tool
for attacking the problem, both as a piece of hardware and as a
metaphor. Too many operations that ought to be very easy are
made to seem very hard by our use of this tool, especially in the
critical area of representing and using knowledge. Whether or
not it is ever actually built, the parallel network system gives us
a better way of thinking about these problems.

3. The NETL System

3.1 Overall Goals of NETL

If the fast-intersecting network system is to be useful to us as a knowledge-base, it must be supplied with an appropriate body of representational conventions and the procedures to exploit them. NETL is my attempt to create such a system. The tangible part of NETL consists of three sets of procedures: one set translates incoming knowledge into pieces of network structure, performing various kinds of checking and digestion along the way; another set accesses pre-existing structure in response to queries or match-requests; the final set performs a variety of housekeeping tasks when the system is not otherwise occupied. These housekeeping functions include the completion of any complex digestions that were interrupted by the flow of ongoing events, the massaging of portions of the network into equivalent but more efficient forms, and the creation of new intermediate-level descriptions by an extension of the learning methods developed by Winston [1975]. The intangible portions of NETL include the representational conventions themselves and the more general representational principles and ways of looking at things that gave rise to these conventions. This integrated collection of viewpoints and attitudes is the real substance of NETL; the decisions about whether to name a link VC or IS-A, and whether it should have two incoming wires or three, are rather arbitrary and unimportant. Still, without a few trees it is impossible to build a forest.

NETL might be thought of as a language for representing knowledge and a processor for that language. A certain base-load of knowledge is assumed by the system -- facts about sets and membership, areas and sub-areas, numbers, statement types, and so on -- but specific knowledge about any particular problem or domain is not a part of NETL. There is thus a boundary (though in places a rather fuzzy one) between the representational system itself and the knowledge it contains. There is a difference in philosophy between NETL, *a language for representing knowledge*, and KRL [Bobrow & Winograd, 1977], which is advertised as a language for *creating knowledge-base systems*: in KRL many of the decisions about the strategy for representing and accessing a given piece of knowledge are left to the user's discretion; in NETL these decisions have, for better or for worse, already been made; the user supplies only the knowledge itself. The reason for this difference is that, given the power of the parallel network system, I do not see any real need for hand-tailoring the processing strategy to the domain under consideration -- domain-specific tricks are not needed to achieve acceptable search-speeds. In this respect, NETL combines the advantages of the slow but general logic-based approaches to knowledge representation and the fast but highly specialized procedural approaches.

NETL was designed with five basic goals in mind:

(1) Compatibility with the parallel network implementation.

Not all network systems have this property. Shapiro's system [1971], for example, represents its deduction rules as patterns for the replacement or copying of portions of the network. It might be possible to convert such a system into a propagation-based format, but it could not be used directly. NETL is the first comprehensive system of which I am aware (since Quillian) to have been designed from the ground up with a parallel marker-propagation strategy in mind. Of course, NETL can also be used on a system that simulates the parallel hardware, and many of the ideas in NETL are equally applicable to systems that handle search in other, more traditional ways.

(2) Completeness: the system should be able to represent anything that people can.

This is, of course, a goal to be approached, not an absolute requirement to be met. There are many areas of human knowledge for which the representational machinery has not yet been built in NETL. So far, however, I have not encountered any particular domains or problems for which the representational ideas of NETL are *fundamentally* unsuited -- NETL is not, for instance, confined only to verbs or only to single-state static descriptions. Note that I am referring here to the NETL representation, not to the parallel network system: as we saw in previous sections, there are many problems for which the fast marker-propagation scheme is no help, but NETL is still able to represent the knowledge involved in these areas. As new domains are explored, it is likely that problems will be encountered which will invalidate some of NETL's basic ideas, but I see no signs that this is imminent.

At present, NETL can represent most of the things that I would like to tell it in a fairly natural way, and can represent most of the remainder in *some* way, however clumsy and awkward. The general area that causes the most trouble is the use of multiple contexts and descriptions to describe the interaction of space, time, subject area, and various hypothetical states. This is not too surprising, since these areas have been troublesome for everyone else, and I have only recently been able to give them my full attention. Some basic mechanisms exist for these things, but they are far from being fully developed. This is a high priority goal for future work, since the proper handling of multiple contexts is essential in many applications, especially in the areas of problem-solving and natural language.

All things considered, I am encouraged by the breadth of coverage that I have been able to get from the relatively compact set of mechanisms in NETL. If one concentrates *only* on verbs or physical objects or static descriptions, the rest of the world can provide an awfully large rug to sweep things under -- any problem that becomes embarrassing is simply banished from the domain of interest. NETL is denied this tactic by the goal of completeness. This has made it a harder and slower task to develop NETL, but I believe that the resulting system is much more useful because of this goal.

(3) Semantic precision.

As Woods [1975] pointed out, many of the early semantic networks suffered from problems of semantic imprecision: it was not always possible to assign a clear meaning to a link, especially when quantification was involved. My own early attempts at creating a network-based semantic system [Fahlman, 1975] suffered from most of these same problems. I believe that the current NETL avoids most of the problems noted by Woods, though it was a difficult struggle to reach this point while maintaining the speed advantages of parallel search. The key idea in clarifying the semantics was the concept of a virtual copy, as explained in Section 2.2.

(4) Simplicity and intuitive clarity.

It should be a relatively straightforward process to stuff new information into the system. That means that the representations being used should be natural and intuitive for people, and the representational philosophy behind the system should also be reasonably intuitive. There should be no agonizing decisions involved in deciding how an idea should be represented: if there are two possible ways of expressing a given concept (as there often are in NETL), and it is not immediately obvious which one is appropriate, then both representations should produce essentially the same results. Ideally, NETL's ways of looking at the world should be so simple and intuitive that they become invisible, at least until they are compared with older, more awkward representational schemes. To some extent, of course, simplicity and intuitiveness are in the mind of the beholder: notions of how some idea ought to be expressed are probably very different for an English speaker than for a native speaker of Chinese or Navajo. All I can say, then, is that *to me* NETL seems very intuitive in most respects, and the places where it is not intuitive yet -- I will point these out as we go along -- are in general the parts that have not yet been fully developed.

The mapping from English into NETL is, in many respects, surprisingly direct. This was not a design goal, but it started happening anyway; after a while, I began to actively encourage these linguistic parallels to develop. If a certain way of expressing an idea seemed natural in English, I tried to find some analogous way of expressing that idea in the network. In many cases, this search was successful. Again, this was a heuristic guidance mechanism for my own use -- a way of deciding where to look and what to look for -- not an attempt to do serious linguistic research. I'm not sure that this aspect of NETL will make it any easier to write a natural language interfacing program, but it does seem to aid one's intuitions when deciding how to express a given idea in nodes and links.

The danger here, of course, is that a system which parallels some aspect of natural language without really capturing the whole idea will often cause more confusion than one that is completely alien. I don't know how serious this problem will be in the case of NETL, but by exposing it to a diverse audience I hope to find out. If necessary, I can disguise these quasi-linguistic aspects of the system so that they resemble nothing at all. (McDermott [1976] presents some of the arguments in favor of such a step.) Until such problems appear, however, I have decided to let these parallels develop freely in NETL, and even to encourage them, in the hope that the resulting system will be more intuitive and easier to learn. It is interesting to speculate about the extent to which our language reflects the inner structure of our mental representations, but NETL is much too new and its relationship to human psychology is much too unclear for it to play a role in these speculations.

(5) Economical representation.

We would like the representations used by NETL to occupy the smallest possible number of nodes and links, and to run in the minimal amount of time. We would also like the node and link elements to be as simple as possible, and we would like to keep the number of node and link types reasonably low. Obviously, we can optimize some of these factors at the expense of others; the best trade-off depends on the precise nature of the implementation technology and the nature of the tasks it is being used for. In general, all of these goals have been assigned a rather low priority, since the system is already very fast compared to serial systems, and the number of nodes and links is also small -- no space is wasted by redundant storage of potentially-inheritable facts, no space is used for indexing-structures, and very little space is used by the programs responsible for searches and simple deductions, since these are handled in a uniform way. I have tried not to actually *waste* time or space, but I haven't fought too hard to eke out that last ten percent. In this stage of the system's development, clarity is more important than parsimony. One thing that I have tried to avoid is any unnecessary lengthening of the tree branches, since that does translate directly into added marker-propagation time. A few compromises have been made for the sake of the simulator, such as the arbitrary decision to limit all node and link-types to a maximum of six attached wires, but I have tried not to do anything for the simulator that would actually hurt the ultimate hardware implementations.

Of the existing representational systems mentioned in section 2.2, none was satisfactory by all of these criteria. Each system had its strong points, however, and NETL has many features in common with each of them. Where some feature of an existing system has been adopted directly, I will of course note the source, but there is a real problem in properly crediting the original source of features that are either very common in representational systems or that only bear some indirect relationship to the forms used in NETL. The problem is that notational conventions of this kind are extremely sensitive to the context within which they are used: two systems may use some piece of notation that looks identical on the surface, and even in its formal definition -- an IS-A link, for example -- but if these constructs are not used in identical ways, their *effective* meanings could be very different. On the other hand, two ideas which look very different on the surface could be very closely related in spirit. Also, some of these ideas are floating around loose in the language we use every day, and will thus be independently captured any number of times before exactly the right combination of ideas clicks together into a stable form. I am afraid that it will take a better scholar than I to sort out this tangle in a way that is fair to everyone.

3.2 Creating Basic Descriptions

As I mentioned earlier, NETL represents both nodes and
links with a single type of hardware device (real or simulated)
called an *element*. Each element contains storage for some
number of marker-bits (currently a rather generous 15) and for
some set of type-flag bits (currently a rather generous 20). The
type-flags may be thought of as permanently-set marker-bits or as
address bits on the bus connecting the element to the controller.
One flag-bit indicates whether the element is a node or a link;
others specify what *type* of node or link the element represents;
still others are used to specify particular options or properties
within those basic types. All but a few of the flag-bits are
redundant, specifying properties of an element that could be
established by a normal marker-propagation through the links of
the network. Since certain sets of elements would be marked
rather frequently, it is easier to leave the markers in place
permanently in the form of flag bits. The number of flags and
markers currently used by the system has been influenced by the
word-length of the PDP-10 on which the simulator runs -- in a
hardware implementation, speed and economics would determine
the mix, but the total number of markers and flag-bits would
probably be somewhat smaller.

In an attempt to minimize confusion, I will begin the
names of the various node and link *types* with a single asterisk:
*VC link, *INDV node, and so on. Those flag-bits that *modify* a
node or link without changing its basic type will be written with
two asterisks: **NOT, **LIKE, and so on. It is just a matter of
taste whether a given modification is serious enough to be spoken
of as a new element-type or whether it should be treated as an
option within a type. I have tried to make these choices in the
way that will cause the least confusion for the reader. The
system, of course, sees only bit-patterns and doesn't care what
names we give to one pattern or another. Occasionally in the
following examples I will refer to some relationship like "hates"
as though it could be represented by a single link, though in

reality it would take several nodes and links to represent "A hates B". The asterisk notation, however, will always be reserved for true NETL primitives.

Each element-unit has a set of wires coming out of it, and a single terminal to receive incoming wires from other elements. The number of wires in use and the meanings attached to the various wires depend on the type of the element in question. Most types use only two or three wires, but the system allows up to six. Internally, the system refers to the various wires of an element by neutral labels (the letters A through F), but in this report I will normally use the type-specific labels indicating what the wire is used for: parent-wire, owner-wire, or whatever. Link-elements normally use the wires A and B for their primary connections, as in "A is a virtual copy of B". A table of the currently-defined node and link types in NETL, along with the wire assignments and flag-bit modifiers relevant to each, is included in Appendix B. Most of the entries will be rather cryptic until we complete our discussion of how these nodes and links are used, but it might be useful to glance over this table before going on, just to get a feel for what it contains.

In the following sections, I will describe a series of increasingly complex representational examples and how they would be handled in NETL. The mechanisms of NETL -- the node and link types, the modifiers, and the procedures for digestion and for accessing portions of the network -- will be introduced gradually, as they are needed. I will also try to point out, as we go along, why certain choices were made and what the problems were with the alternatives. Since, in a system like this, everything depends on everything else, there will have to be a few forward references and some hand-waving use of structures that have not yet been fully explained, but I will try to keep this to a minimum. If the usage of some node or link type becomes confusing, consult Appendix B.

For clarity in earlier sections, I often referred to *TYPE-nodes as TYPICAL-ELEPHANT or whatever; from now on, I will drop the "typical" and just refer to the *TYPE node as

ELEPHANT. If I want to refer to the associated set-node, I will call it ELEPHANT-SET.

3.3 Creating a Free-Standing Individual

In creating simple descriptions we will need four basic types of nodes. An *INDV node represents some specific individual entity that exists within some universe (real or imaginary), or an individual *role* within some type-description. (These individuals are not necessarily *physical* objects, but could be individual places, events, statements, etc.) A *TYPE node does not represent any particular individual entity, but serves as a description for a whole set of individuals which inherit its structure and properties through *VC (virtual copy) links. Each *TYPE node is associated with another node (an *INDV) that represents the *set* of individuals that the *TYPE node describes. When a virtual copy of some description is created, the roles within that description are *mapped* into the new copy (see 3.5 for details). Such mappings are left implicit until we have something to say about the new version of the role in question, at which point we create a *MAP node to represent the new version. If we map a *TYPE node into a new description, we want the new version to behave as a *TYPE node also. This is represented by the use of a *TMAP (type-map) node. NETL contains a few other, more esoteric node types, but we will save them for later.

Let's begin by creating the description for a free-standing individual: we will create a description for the individual Clyde, an elephant that (we will claim) exists in the real universe. We begin by finding a virgin *INDV node (or a virgin element that can be turned into an *INDV node by setting the proper flag-bits). This node is to represent the *concept* of Clyde -- the *name* "Clyde" is another *INDV node, a descendant of the WORD type-node, and is associated with the CLYDE node by a PROPER-NAME statement. In general, the concept-node will be referred to as CLYDE and the word-node as "CLYDE". A word-node can have many meanings, and a concept-node can have many names. We will see later how the sequence of letters or phonemes that make up a word are represented, and how the parallel network system can help us to disambiguate multiple word-meanings. In the current simulated version of NETL, each node has a unique internal name hidden inside it, but this is a debugging and developmental aid that will go away when a natural-language interface for NETL has been developed. External programs that must communicate with NETL will generally bypass the names altogether and use pointers to directly access various nodes in the network.

Having created the *INDV node CLYDE, we must do two things: we must indicate what kind of individual the node represents, and we must indicate the universe or area within which that individual exists. We can perform the first of these tasks by creating a *VC link from CLYDE to some *TYPE node -- in this case, the ELEPHANT node. Every *INDV node, and every *TYPE node except the top-level THING node, has at least one *VC link to a superior *TYPE. If we have nothing to say about the type of an *INDV, we can place it directly under the THING node, which is so general that it tells us essentially nothing about the entity in question. Usually, though, we will have at least some broad idea of what we are dealing with -- a physical object, a place, a set, or whatever.

Notice that the *VC link does two things: it makes the CLYDE description a virtual copy of the ELEPHANT description, and it makes CLYDE a member of the set that is associated with this *TYPE node -- in this case, the node ELEPHANT-SET. The set-member relationship is implicit between a set-node and its *TYPE node, and is considered to be inherited by any instances of the *TYPE node. This convention is rather arbitrary: we might instead have required an *INDV to have explicit connections both to the *TYPE node and to the set, but this would have wasted links. We might also have made membership relation between the individual and the set explicit, and have left the virtual-copy relationship to be inherited. This option in some ways seems more intuitive -- it is somewhat easier in English to talk about class-member relationships than about virtual copies -- but it would double the length of all scans through the type hierarchy, since the markers would have to pass through the set-nodes as well as the *TYPE nodes. In this case, I opted for speed rather than intuition. Since the two forms are so closely related, I doubt that the choice of one or the other makes any real difference.

To cut down on the number of links the system uses, every *INDV comes equipped with a *parent-wire* with which it can be attached to *one* superior type-node. This parent-wire connection functions exactly as a real *VC link does, except that it lacks a handle-node of its own and therefore cannot be cancelled, modified, pointed at, or tied to a context. The idea here is to use the parent-wire to represent the *INDV node's most fundamental (and presumably immutable) identity -- for CLYDE this would be ELEPHANT -- and to use real *VC links to represent any other, less secure class-memberships that the object might possess. In the unlikely event that the elephantness of Clyde becomes the subject of controversy, the parent wire connection from CLYDE to ELEPHANT should be cut and replaced with a real *VC link that can be argued about explicitly. For the vast majority of *INDV nodes, however, the fundamental identity will never be questioned, and this parent-wire mechanism will save the system many links.

The parent-wire mechanism is not really necessary, since every parent-wire could be replaced by a *VC link. I have included it both for economy and for symmetry with certain other node-types which do require a direct parent-connection of this kind. It also seems very intuitive, somehow, to indicate an object's *fundamental* identity in a way that sets it apart form other classes to which the object just happens to belong. Let me make it clear, however, that NETL does not use this distinction, as many systems do, to control or limit the inheritance-search machinery. In a parallel network system all of the upward paths can be explored at once, so there is no need to confine the search to some special path of primary identities. In almost all cases, then, the marker-propagating procedures of NETL treat parent-wires and *VC links identically.

We can indicate the universe or area within which the individual is considered to exist by the use of an *EXIN ("exists in") link from the *INDV node to the node representing the area. As with the *VC links, we can replace one *EXIN link with a wire coming out of the *INDV node, called the *existence-wire*. The existence-wire, like the parent-wire, should only be used in stable, non-controversial situations. If we want to refer directly to the statement that the object exists, to deny that statement, modify it, or make it dependent upon some context or set of conditions, then we should replace the existence-wire with a full-scale *EXIN link possessing its own internal handle-node. In this case, we want to place CLYDE into the current "real" universe, which NETL calls REAL-U, so we simply connect the existence-wire from the CLYDE node to the REAL-U node. (I am not going to get into a discussion of what "real" means -- read as much or as little into this term as you like.) Figure 6 shows the resulting configuration. As in all the examples we will see, the figure only shows some tiny portion of the knowledge network; even so, these figures have a way of becoming hopelessly crowded.

In NETL, an individual exists within some specified *area*, which is represented by an *INDV node descended from the AREA *TYPE-node. Areas are also used to indicate the scope within which a link or other statement is considered to be valid. (We will see more clearly the difference between scoping and existence in section 3.6.) An area can represent a certain portion of space, of time, or of subject-matter; neutrinos, for example, exist within the area of particle physics. An area can also represent some combination of other areas: Massachusetts in 1775 or Physics in the Nineteenth Century, for example. Most areas are parts of other areas -- in fact, the PART-OF relation can form a tangled hierarchy of areas that is similar to, but distinct from, the type-hierarchy. Unlike the type-hierarchy, however, the hierarchy of areas and sub-areas does not spring from a single, all-inclusive root node. There are many areas that are not parts of other areas, and these outermost areas are given

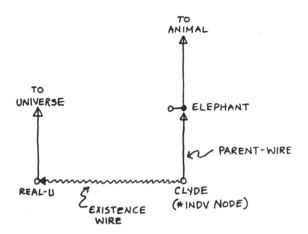

Figure 6: *INDV node for CLYDE, an ELEPHANT in REAL-U.

the special name of *universes.*

A universe is represented by an *INDV node that is descended from the UNIVERSE *TYPE-node, which in turn is a sub-type of the AREA *TYPE-node. In addition to REAL-U, there are universes representing various imaginary or hypothetical realities, such as are often created in works of fiction or in exploring possible solutions to a problem. Most of these universes begin life as virtual copies of REAL-U (not *parts* of REAL-U) and local changes are then made within them. As a general rule, if some individual exists in an area A, it also exists in all areas of which A is a part, up to and including the universe that contains A.

(As individuals, the universes must exist somewhere, so the system contains a special universe called META-U within which the other universes exist. META-U exists within itself. Note, however, that universes are individual entities that exist within META-U, not parts or sub-areas of META-U. Guy Steele has suggested that META-U is NETL's representation of itself -- I am not sure about this, but it is an interesting idea.)

The interaction of multiple universes and areas -- of space, time, and alternative versions of reality -- is, as you might imagine, an extremely complicated subject, and one which I have only begun to explore in the context of NETL. I do have some interesting ways of using these things, however, and we will see them in section 3.9. For now, let's forget about the time dimension altogether and confine our attention to two rather tame static cases: we will allow an individual to exist either directly within some universe like REAL-U, or to exist within *one* sub-area of some universe. We might, therefore, have said that CLYDE exists in AFRICA, which is a sub-area of REAL-U; this would of course imply CLYDE's existence in REAL-U as well.

This explicit existence-connection serves three purposes. First, it allows us to answer direct questions about what exists where. Second, it makes it possible for the system to mark all individuals that exist within a certain area and its sub-areas. This can be of great use to the recognition system in filtering out possible matches: if I am trying to recognize someone that I pass on the street, I do not want the matcher to find face-descriptions from mythology or leading figures of the French Revolution. Finally, if we state (with a **LIKE *VC link, but never mind that for now) that one universe is to be a virtual copy of another, we want the new universe to begin life containing everything that the old one did. The existence links in the old universe show us which individuals are to be included in the virtual copy. Of course, most of these individual mappings remain virtual: we only create *MAP nodes for those individuals that we want to say something about. It is this ability to virtually copy a structure without doing much real work that makes it possible to copy whole universes at a time, contents and all.

The usefulness of the existence-connection can be seen more clearly if we consider the use of an *INDV node to represent an individual role within some *TYPE-node description. Such a description can be thought of as a sort of mini-universe, with its own individuals, sets, and interrelations among them. Consider the circuit-description of some particular variety of radio, and an individual resistor, named R23, that appears in that circuit. R23 would be represented as an *INDV node with the existence-wire (or equivalent *EXIN link) connected to the *TYPE node around which the circuit-description is built. That description *is* R23's universe: R23 exists there and nowhere else. While we are working *within* the circuit description -- to analyze how the circuit works or to calculate the voltage at some point -- we want R23 to behave in all respects as an individual. If we are asked which individual resistor in the circuit dissipates the most power, R23 would be a perfectly acceptable answer. If, however, we look at the circuit from the *outside*, R23 is not a real individual at all, but a role to be mapped when we make individual copies of the circuit-type in question: each radio we make from this plan will have its own distinct version of the resistor R23. Individuality, then, is a somewhat more elusive quality than we might have imagined. It is a function not of the node itself, but of the universe from which it is viewed. That is why it ,is so important to tie an *INDV node to the proper universe.

Before we go on to discuss type-descriptions and roles in more detail, there are a few options relating to *INDV nodes that we should cover. The first of these is the **SPLIT flag. As we will see in later sections, two *INDV nodes can be equated by placing an *EQ link between them. This link says that the two nodes in question represent the same external entity, and that any descriptive information that applies to one is to apply to the other. The **SPLIT flag on an *INDV node says that this node is *not* to be equated with any other *INDV node in the same area that also is marked with a **SPLIT flag. In other words, a **SPLIT node represents a true, distinct individual within its area or universe, one that we feel certain is not equivalent to any other such individual. Any attempt to create an *EQ link, directly or indirectly, between two such individuals causes a clash-alarm to be raised. (It is possible, of course, to ignore this clash-warning and create the *EQ link anyway.) Once again, there is a choice of whether to use a link or a more compact form for representing a certain option: the **SPLIT flag on an *INDV node is equivalent to a *SPLIT *link* running along that node's existence-wire from the node itself to its area of residence. If there is some question about whether the split is valid, the full-scale link should be used, so that it can later be denied or argued about.

If the **SPLIT flag (or the equivalent link) is not present, we speak of the *INDV node as representing a *pseudo-individual.* A pseudo-individual can function perfectly well as an individual, and can have any amount of descriptive information attached to it, but it does not complain when it is equated to other pseudos or to a single real individual (assuming, of course, that the things being joined do not clash for other reasons). With this pseudo-individual mechanism we can, for example, create a complex description of the suspect in a crime, and can later try to equate this suspect-description to various real individuals. Note that the existence of a proper name is not really the issue here, though real individuals often have one and pseudos usually do not. Jack-the-Ripper is a pseudo, a mere description that is equivalent to some existing real person; my notebook, since I have not bothered to christen it, has no name, but is still a true individual, equivalent to no other notebook. The issue, then, is whether or not we want to commit ourselves to believing that some new individual is distinct from any true (non-pseudo) individual that we already know about.

We can indicate that some group of pseudos are distinct *from one another* by the use of the DISTINCT statement-type, which will be described in detail later. We might, for example, want SMITH, JONES, and ROBINSON to be real individuals within the universe of a particular puzzle, and to let THE-ENGINEER, THE-BRAKEMAN, and THE-CONDUCTOR be a set of *distinct* pseudos within the same universe. No clash is caused when we equate JONES with THE-CONDUCTOR, but any connections within either of the two distinct sets is forbidden. This general approach to the use of pseudo-individuals is similar to, and was to some extent inspired by, the "manifestation" mechanism of KRL.

The other option-flag that ought to be mentioned here is the **EXTERN flag. In the NETL simulator, this indicates an *INDV node that represents a legal LISP-object: a number, an atom-name, or an S-expression. This LISP-object is hidden inside the node in the internal name field. When the system is preparing an answer to some question that it received from an external LISP program using the knowledge-base, these **EXTERN objects are of particular interest: they represent the legal, meaningful answers that can be passed back to the external program. A pointer to some anonymous *MAP node would not be a very useful answer to an external query. As the system develops, the need for such canned answers will probably disappear, but it might still be useful to mark the nodes that represent legal interfaces to other portions of the intelligent system: phonemes, muscle commands, or whatever. Again, KRL has a structure comparable to this in its "direct" descriptions.

3.4 Creating a Type-Description

In the previous section, we created an individual member of an already existing type; in this section we will see how to create a type-description, a sub-type of some already existing, more general type. (Don't worry about creating the first one -- NETL comes with the top-level THING node and several other high-level types already built.) Whenever a *TYPE-node is created, the corresponding set-node must be created as well. The central example in this section will be the creation of the ELEPHANT *TYPE-node and the *INDV node that represents the set of elephants in REAL-U. ELEPHANT will be a subtype of the existing MAMMAL *TYPE-node.

The set-node is created first. We simply obtain an unused *INDV node from the stock of free elements, connect this node's parent-wire to the SET *TYPE-node, and connect the existence-wire to REAL-U. It would be possible to use a flag-bit to permanently mark set-nodes as a distinct node-type, but I have not yet found any real need for this. If desired, we can connect the set's parent-wire not to the SET *TYPE-node itself, but to some sub-type of SET: NON-EMPTY-SET, LARGE-SET, etc. The area in which the set is said to exist is normally the area in which the set's individual members exist -- if the members are scattered, the set's area should be chosen to include them all. An attempt to create an individual member outside the range of its set will create a mild (easily dismissed) clash. If the set of unicorns is defined for some mythical universe, we want to notice that something is amiss if we try to create a unicorn in REAL-U, but we might decide to go ahead with the creation anyway.

For the ELEPHANT node itself, we need an unused *TYPE-node. This has a parent-wire, identical in purpose to the parent-wire of an *INDV node, which is connected to the MAMMAL *TYPE-node. It also has a *set-wire* which, not surprisingly, is connected to the ELEPHANT-SET node. It does not have an existence-wire, since the *TYPE-description does not really exist anywhere as a real individual, and in fact behaves rather like a universe itself. The name "ELEPHANT" can be represented as another *INDV node, a descendant of the WORD node, which is connected to the ELEPHANT *TYPE-node by a TYPE-NAME statement. (The names ELEPHANT and ELEPHANT-SET may be hidden inside the new nodes by the simulator, but these are just debugging aids and will not be seen by any natural-language interface.) Figure 7 shows the final configuration of the ELEPHANT node and its set-node.

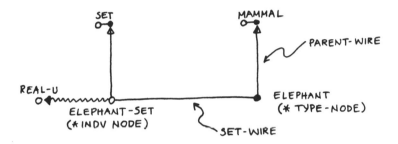

Figure 7: *TYPE node for ELEPHANT, a subtype of MAMMAL, with its set-node.

As we noted earlier, the parent-wire or *VC-link connection from ELEPHANT to MAMMMAL creates an implicit MEMBER-OF relationship between ELEPHANT and MAMMAL-SET. In addition, a parent-wire or *VC-link connection between two *TYPE-nodes creates an implicit PART-OF or SUBSET relationship between the corresponding set-nodes. To find the subsets of a given set S, we simply mark the *TYPE-node attached to S, propagate this marker down to all *TYPE-nodes below, and mark the set-nodes of these sub-types. To mark the supersets of S, we do the same thing, but propagate

the markers upward. There may also be explicitly-stated subsets
or supersets of S, represented in the usual role notation (see
section 3.5), which should be added to the implicit subsets or
supersets found by the scan through the type-hierarchy.

At this point we might also want to create an explicit
statement of the SUBSET relationship (a special type of PART
relationship) that holds between the new ELEPHANT-SET node
and the old MAMMAL-SET node. This relationship is implicit
in the *VC connection from ELEPHANT to MAMMAL, but it
is sometimes useful to put it in explicitly -- certain propagations
are speeded up and it gives us a useful place to hang certain
type-split information. I will save this for later, however, since
we have not yet developed the machinery for stating relationships
of this kind. I will not usually include subset relationships in
the diagrams, since they clutter things up tremendously.

The reason for using two separate nodes for a set and its
typical-member description should be obvious: their properties
behave differently during inheritance. The properties and
structures attached to the *TYPE-node are inherited by each
individual member of the class, while the set-node's properties
belong to it alone. The most important property attached to the
set is its member-count or cardinality; if we don't have the exact
count, perhaps we have upper or lower bounds. In fact, useful
subclasses of the SET class exist to make it easy to specify the
most commonly used count-bounds: empty sets, non-empty sets,
few, many, pair, and so on. As new individual members are
added to a set, the bounds are checked and a clash is reported if
a violation is detected. (This is done during the digestion of the
new member, along with other kinds of clash-checking.) If we
have an exact count for a set, and that many members are
already represented, the set is placed in the COMPLETE-SET
category and no new members can be added. The membership of
the set in COMPLETE-SET also makes it possible for us to
reason by eliminating all but one of a set of alternatives. (See
section 2.4.)

Many other properties, usually thought of as meta-information, can be attached to the set-node. Taxonomically, we might speak of mammals as being a *class*. This, clearly, must refer to the MAMMAL-SET, since we don't want CLYDE to be a class by inheritance. The ELEPHANT set has a GEOGRAPHIC-DISTRIBUTION covering substantial parts of Asia and Africa; again, we do not want this to be inherited, since the AFRICAN-ELEPHANT subset has a smaller GEOGRAPHIC-DISTRIBUTION. One of a set's subsets may be the largest, the most popular, the most widely scattered, the first to be identified and named, or the set that has grown the fastest; none of these things necessarily apply to that subset's individual members.

In some cases, there seems to be a weak form of inheritance from a set to its members: if the set of dogs is more popular than the set of snakes, this probably means that the typical dog is more popular than the typical snake. Perhaps this is a default at work: if a statement is made about a set that would normally make sense only when applied to its individual members, that statement is treated as applying weakly to each individual member, as though it had been attached to the *TYPE node. ("Weakly" here means that the statement serves only as a default and that exceptions are freely allowed.) This sort of inheritance would be handled by serial processes outside of the normal marker-propagation mechanism, either when the statement is made or perhaps at access-time. Effects of this sort need to be studied more closely if NETL is to be brought into line with human usage. In general, though, we will not consider a set-node's properties to be inherited by the members of that set.

In case there is some confusion, let me emphasize that I am using the word "set" here in the normal, intuitive sense, not in the mathematician's sense: it is *not* the case in NETL that if two sets have the same membership, they must therefore be the same set. Since every set has an attached *TYPE-description, the empty set of unicorns is a very differnt entity from the equally empty set of gryphons, and the two sets are represented by different nodes. Both of these set-nodes are members of the EMPTY-SET class.

I should also point out that a *TYPE node of the normal sort *describes* the typical member of a set, but does not *define* that set. It is not the case that any individual fitting the *TYPE node's description *must* be placed in the set. A *TYPE-node's set contains only those things that we say it contains, and these things then inherit the *TYPE-node's description.   There is another mechanism, the *EVERY node, for representing defined sets -- the set of *all* purple mushrooms in North America, or whatever -- and we will consider this mechanism in a section of its own (3.8).   The recognition system is allowed to examine *TYPE-node descriptions and to *suggest* which type-set a new individual fits into best, but this works by a sort of weighted average over the available features, not by satisfying a formal definition.   The *TYPE-node sets are very similar in spirit to the exemplar-based sets that, according to Rosch [1975, Rosch & Mervis 1975], dominate much of human recognition and thinking.

.We will see how to divide a given type into a split-set of exclusive subtypes in section 3.6.

3.5 Creating and Mapping Roles

As we saw in section 2.2, a *TYPE-node is intended to serve as the nucleus or *base-node* of a description, consisting of an arbitrarily large portion of the semantic network. Whenever we create an instance or subtype of that *TYPE-node, by attaching a *VC link or parent-wire to it from below, we want the entire description associated with that *TYPE-node to behave as though it had been copied. In particular, we want the role-nodes within that *TYPE-description to be *virtually* mapped into the new description; the *MAP-node representing the new version of a given role is only created when we want to say something about that new version that does not apply to the original. In this section, we will explore the mechanics of role-creation and mapping, and will see in a general way how the virtual-copy inheritance mechanism is implemented.

A role is simply an *INDV node, representing either a single entity or a set, whose existence-wire (or link) is attached to a *TYPE-node rather than to some individual area or universe. We will refer to this *TYPE-node as the *owner* of the role. Regardless of whether it represents a single individual or a set, a role-node functions as a description in its own right, with its own set of properties, identities, and statements linking it to other nodes. In addition, a role-node representing a set (and therefore descended from the SET *TYPE-node) will have an associated *TYPE node of its own, describing the typical member of the set; this *TYPE-node may have its own set of roles, and so on down any number of levels. We will look at the individual roles first, since they are simpler.

An individual role (or a set-role, for that matter) may be either an *IN-role* or an *OF-role*. The issue here is whether the owner node can in any way be viewed as representing an *area* within which the role-node's referent exists, or whether we just want to indicate that for each copy of the owner, a corresponding map of the role-node exists *somewhere*. Both IN and OF roles establish this one-to-one correspondence, but only the IN-role implies that the role exists within the area defined by the owner. The OF-role relationship is therefore a weaker version of the IN-role relationship, and it is included in the IN-role's meaning. This distinction between IN-roles and OF-roles is not a particularly critical one in the operation of the system, but it is useful in bringing NETL into line with human intuitions about area-inclusion, as reflected in the way we construct natural-language descriptions. Consequently, it seems reasonable to follow the form of English expressions rather closely in deciding what is OF and what is IN. If a case seems to be on the borderline, it probably doesn't matter which form we choose.

ENGINE, then, is an IN-role within CAR, since it is both "of" and "in" the car: the car defines an area -- in this case, a certain volume of space -- and the engine exists inside this area. MOTHER is an OF-role tied to the PERSON description: every person has one, but there is no sense of area-inclusion. We can say that every person *has* a mother, but we would not say that the mother is *in* the person. Some examples of other IN-roles would be the CONDUCTOR in an ORCHESTRA, the FIRST-ELEMENT in a SERIES, the YOLK in an EGG, the BEST-TEXTBOOK in a SUBJECT-AREA, the OUTPUT-TRANSISTOR in an AMPLIFIER-CIRCUIT, and the SHORTEST-DAY in a YEAR. As you can see, the sense of "area" in use here is a very broad one, including time, space, subject-area, and the area defined by a set or grouping of elements. Some examples of strict OF-ROLES, with no sense of area-inclusion would be the NAME of a PERSON, the HOME of a FAMILY, the LENGTH of a STICK, and the OWNER of a PET. The fact that some *TYPE-node clearly represents an area does not imply that *all* of its roles are IN-roles. An area can have properties that are not inside the area, just like any other *TYPE-node. We might, for instance, speak of the LENGTH *of* a SERIES, the CIRCUMFERENCE *of* a CIRCLE, or the PRINCIPAL-EXPORT *of* a COUNTRY. None of these roles could reasonably be expressed with the word "in".

To represent an individual IN-role, we simply create the *INDV node for it, and connect an *EXIN link (or the node's existence-wire) from the role-node to the *TYPE-node of the owner. This, of course, is exactly the notation we developed for stating the existence of a free-standing *INDV in an area, except that here the area is a *TYPE-description rather than some individual area within a universe.

An OF-role relationship is represented by a different link, called the *EXFOR ("exists for") link. An *EXFOR link from *INDV-node A to *TYPE-node B says that *for* every member of type B, there exists a map of individual A. In other words, every B *has* exactly one A. Note that this does *not* say that every A has exactly one B: every person has a mother, but one mother may fulfill this role for many offspring. If we really want to indicate that every person has a *distinct* mother, we can set a special flag, called the **RSPLIT flag, on the existence-link creating the role (or on the role-node itself if the existence-wire is used). This flag causes a clash to occur if some individual, is assigned to play the given role twice in the same context, for two distinct owners. This is detected during the digestion of the second assignment.

If we want to use the role-node's existence-wire instead of a full-scale existence-link, we use the **EXIN option-flag to indicate which sort of existence the wire stands for: if the flag is on, the wire acts like an *EXIN link; if the flag is off, it acts like an *EXFOR. Figure 8 shows the ELEPHANT description with a HEART IN-node and a WEIGHT OF-node. Note that both of the existence-wires are represented as wavy arrows, but that the stronger *EXIN connection is drawn with a heavy solid arrowhead. This is just an illustration, of course. In actuality, both of these roles would be created at some higher level in the type hierarchy and mapped down into the ELEPHANT description: HEART would be created at the VERTEBRATE or ANIMAL level, and WEIGHT would be created far up the tree at PHYSOB (physical object).

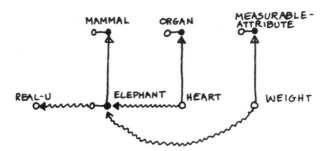

Figure 8: The HEART IN-role and the WEIGHT OF-role of the typical ELEPHANT.

If an individual OF-role does not exist within the area defined by its owner, where does it exist? This is a rather tricky question. We might at first imagine that the OF-role exists in whatever area the owner exists in, but this is not always the case. We might want to say that every famous scientist on earth has a namesake-crater on the moon. We might even want to represent the statement that for each of his relatives in real life, Tolkien created a corresponding orc in *Lord of the Rings*. (As far as I know, this statement is false.) Each relative has an orc, but the relatives and the orcs exist in entirely different universes. I think that in general we will have to explicitly indicate where an OF-role exists by the use of an *EXIN link, pointing to the desired area, in addition to the *EXFOR. It is not clear what default, if any, should be used if this *EXIN link is absent. If I say that every ELEPHANT has a MOTHER, is it fair to allow some ELEPHANT's mother to exist only on Alpha Centauri or in some completely imaginary universe? If we allow this, the original statement becomes rather meaningless. Until a good answer comes along, I will use the universe (not the specific area) that the owner occupies as the default in such cases, but I am not claiming that this is right.

Now, as soon as we have created the *VC link saying that Clyde is an elephant, we can begin referring to his inherited roles: his heart, his trunk, his mother, and so on. As long as we are just asking for information, we do not need to create the corresponding *MAP-nodes; the role-nodes in the ELEPHANT description will respond to our queries as though they were a part of the CLYDE description. If, however, want to make some statement about CLYDE's version of one of these roles, we will have to create the *MAP node to which this new information can be attached without altering the original. In creating the *MAP-node, we have two wires to worry about: the *map-wire*, which is attached to the role-node being mapped, and the *owner-wire* which is attached to the mapped version's owner -- in this case CLYDE. This *MAP-node will henceforth function as a pseudo-individual description, and we can say anything we want to about it. Figure 9 represents the statement that Clyde's mother is Bertha. Figure 10 represents the statement that Clyde's mother is the same as Ernie's mother, whoever she might be.

Notice how this works: First, we create the *MAP node that represents *by definition* the mother of Clyde, or whatever. If Clyde has a mother, this *MAP-node represents her, whoever she may be. Then we attach arguable assertions, in the form of links and statement-structures, to this node. Among these assertions may be an *EQ link stating that the MOTHER-OF-CLYDE *MAP-node and the BERTHA node represent the same entity in the real world. This statement can be argued about, tied to a particular context, or even denied. While the *EQ link is in effect, the descriptions attached to the two nodes are effectively merged -- anything we know about one applies equally to the other. If however, this link is cut or cancelled, or we are operating outside of its area of validity, then the two nodes become separate once again, and each retains its own description. This is the normal procedure in NETL for assigning an individual player to a role or, to use the more familiar

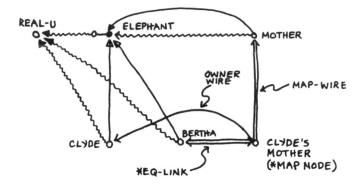

Figure 9: "Bertha is the mother of Clyde."

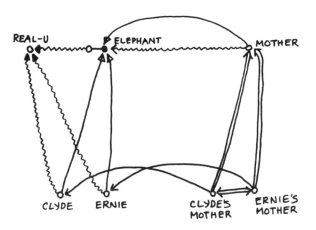

Figure 10: "Clyde's mother is Ernie's mother."

vocabulary, for assigning a value to a property or filling a frame-slot.

What if Clyde, unlike other elephants, has no mother? Perhaps he is a clone, created in a (rather large) test-tube. In this case, we simply run a *CANCEL link (which will be described in detail in the next section) from the CLYDE node up to the original MOTHER role-node. (The *CANCEL link could also be connected to the MOTHER node's existence-link, if it has one.) This will have three effects: first, if we ask whether Clyde has a mother, the answer will be that he does not; second, if we try to create a *MAP node to represent Clyde's mother, the discrepancy will be noticed and a complaint will be issued; finally, if we want to spend a bit of extra time to check for this, every reference to an already-existing *MAP node for Clyde's mother can be made to issue the same complaint. In the system's normal, non-careful mode of operation, discrepancies of the latter sort would not normally be checked for, and some might slip by.

(A similar condition might hold in an example like "The present king of France is bald" -- a favorite example in Epistmology and the Philosophy of Language. (See, for example, Strawson [1971] and several other papers in the same collection.) The problem, roughly, is in explaining how a property like baldness can be ascribed to this non-existent entity, and still have some sort of apparent meaning. In a system like NETL, there might well be a node for the king of France, an individual role within the France description, a descendant of the MAN node, and a node whose existence-link happens to be scoped in some past area of. time. In the current universe, this entity does not exist, but *the node* is still there. If we refer to the king of France, we will find this node, though possibly with a warning message that its referent does not currently exist. Still, if we ignore the warning we can refer to the king's hair or fingers, or attach any reasonable human properties to him without any further clash appearing. If we refer to the king's gills or say that he is a cabbage, we will get a clash -- non-existent the king may be, but his node is still descended from the MAN node, with all that that implies. Of course, this only explains how such an example might *work* -- what it *means* is a problem I gladly leave to the philosophers.)

If a role is mapped from one *TYPE-description down into another, it still functions as a role. It may then be mapped down again, and so on until it reaches a free-standing *INDV description -- normally the bottom of the tree. Figure 11 shows the NOSE role being created in the MAMMAL description, and being mapped down through ELEPHANT into the CLYDE description. (The NOSE role's parent wire would be connected to the *TYPE-node of the PART set-role, defined somewhere above MAMMAL, but this need not concern us at present.) At the ELEPHANT level, this role picks up a great many new properties, including a new role-name: TRUNK. From ELEPHANT on down, either the term TRUNK or the inherited term NOSE can be used to refer to this role. Figure 12 shows how a role's role can be mapped: the ELEPHANT's TRUNK is described as a CYLINDER, and every CYLINDER has a LENGTH. The LENGTH of the ELEPHANT's TRUNK is equated to a node representing the quantity 1.3-METERS. This quantity is the length of the typical elephant's trunk, and is the default to use if no other length is specified for an individual elephant. Moving down to CLYDE's level, we see the *MAP nodes for his trunk and its length, ready to have more properties attached. Note that if we equate CLYDE's trunk-length with some other quantity, not equal to 1.3-METERS, we must cancel (for CLYDE only) the *EQ link on the ELEPHANT level so that the two quantities do not both try to answer any question about Clyde's trunk-length. If NETL gets two conflicting answers to a question, it will try to find and return the more local answer, but it is much better to eliminate the conflict before it happens.

Now, finally, we have built up enough structure that we can begin to examine how the inheritance process works for virtual copies. To look at some mapped role within a

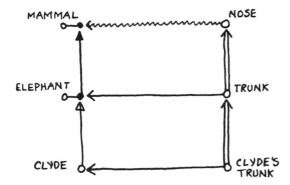

Figure 11: The NOSE role mapped from **MAMMAL** to **ELEPHANT** to CLYDE.

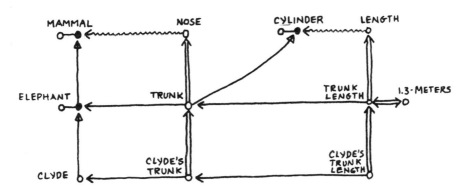

Figure 12: "An elephant's trunk is a cylinder, with a typical length of 1.3 meters."

description is a two stage process: first, we must *activate* the description in question; then, with a different marker-bit, we can explore whatever role it is that concerns us at the moment. Suppose, for example, that we want to look at the properties of "the trunk of Clyde". First, we activate the CLYDE description by choosing a free marker-bit, placing it on the CLYDE node, and propagating it upward through the hierarchy of *VC links and parent-wires. These markers are also propagated across all *EQ links in either direction, since the intent of an *EQ link is to merge the descriptions of the two nodes it is joining. Cancellation markers are also placed at this time on all those links and statements that are not to play a role in the CLYDE description, but we will not worry about the details of this for now. The result of this activity is to place activation markers on all of the superior descriptions of which CLYDE is supposed to be a virtual copy, directly or by inheritance.

Now for the tricky part: *Every *MAP-node whose owner-wire is connected to a node that we have marked as being active will behave as though its map-wire were an *EQ link.* Any marker placed on the *MAP-node will be propagated up the map-wire to the node above; any marker placed on the role-node will be propagated down this wire to the *MAP node. In other words, while we are working within the activated CLYDE description, all of the nodes representing some particular role and its maps are effectively merged or shorted together -- if we mark any one of these nodes, within a few cycles we will have marked them all. (This discipline is enforced by the scanning programs in the controller, which still govern all propagations.) In effect, this means that a property attached to any of these nodes will behave as if it were attached to all of them. When we are attaching information to the node representing CLYDE's trunk, we still want to use the *MAP-node in the CLYDE description, but for accessing purposes it is wrong to think of any single node as representing Clyde's trunk -- all of the shorted-together nodes represent this concept jointly. Notice that if we ask for the trunk of some other elephant, a different set of trunk-nodes is shorted together, and the information pertaining only to Clyde's trunk will not be accessible.

To find the LENGTH of the TRUNK of CLYDE, then, we proceed as follows: First, the CLYDE description is activated by an upward marker sweep of marker M1. Then, marker M2 is placed on the TRUNK role-node which, as it happens, is found in the ELEPHANT description, and is propagated up all *VC links, across all *EQ links, and across all M1-activated map-wires. This will mark all the nodes in the system that might carry information relating to "the trunk of Clyde". At this point we are done with the M1 marks, but we may want to leave them in place in case we later want to find out something else about CLYDE. The M2 marks can now be used as an activation set to find the properties of Clyde's trunk. If we are looking for the length, we place another mark, M3, on the LENGTH role (found in the M2-marked CYLINDER description), and we propagate these within the M2 activation. Figure 13 shows the diagram of figure 12, with the M1, M2, and M3 markers in place. The M3-marked description-set, representing the length of Clyde's trunk, can be used for subsequent processing, or it can be returned as an answer. In returning an answer, we want to return an *INDV node from the marked set that will make sense to the outside world -- that is, a node marked with the **EXTERN flag. In this case, the 1.3-METERS node would be chosen. (If there are several nodes with the **EXTERN flag set, any one of them will probably be an adequate answer.) We will need to add a few complications to this picture later, but that is the general idea.

This might seem a rather strange and indirect way to implement virtual copies. Why allow the *MAP nodes to propagate markers in both directions? Why not just treat them as *VC links, propagating only upwards during property-inheritance scans? There are two advantages to the scheme I described above: first, it allows us to skip over unimportant levels as we map roles through the hierarchy; second, and more important, it makes it possible for us to create

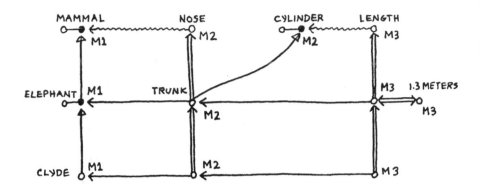

Figure 13: Marking to find the LENGTH of the TRUNK of CLYDE.

virtual copies of descriptions that themselves contain virtual-copy relationships between some of their roles.

To see why we might want to skip levels in the mapping process, consider the following case: Suppose we have a role for HEART in the MAMMAL description, and want to create a *MAP of this for CLYDE. Suppose, too, that we have nothing at all to say about the HEART of the typical ELEPHANT. In this case, we would like to connect the *MAP-node in the CLYDE description directly to the HEART-role in MAMMAL, skipping over the ELEPHANT level, as shown in figure 14. If at some later time we do want to create the ELEPHANT-HEART node and hang some properties from it (also shown in figure 14) a unidirectional inheritance scheme would force us to scurry around reconnecting all of the heart-nodes of individual elephants so that they will appear below ELEPHANT-HEART, and thus inherit its properties. In the NETL scheme, however, we can leave the configuration of figure 14 as it is, since whenever we are within an elephant description, ELEPHANT-HEART and MAMMAL-HEART will be merged by the map-wire joining

them, and both sets of properties will be found. If the
role-definition and the map are widely separated in the hierarchy,
this can save us many intermediate nodes.

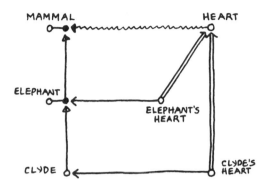

Figure 14: Level-skipping by a *MAP-node.

The value of this is clearer if we look at its global
effects. The solid directional backbone of the system is provided
by the tangled hierarchy of virtual-copy links. You will recall
the importance of always sending markers either upward or
downward through this hierarchy: if we do both at once, we
eventually mark everything and the scan in question is worthless.
If we were to handle role-mapping by the same sort of
unidirectional inheritance, we would end up with many copies of
the type-hierarchy, one for each role that we want to map. The
system described above avoids this by letting the role-maps make
a sort of parasitic use of the solid, directional type-hierarchy
connecting the owner-nodes. Since the activation scan follows a
path that is directional and orderly, the network of map-links
that are activated by this scan can get away with being
fragmentary and undirected.

To see why we might want to virtually copy a description that contains a virtual-copy relationship between some of its roles, we must consider the case of set-roles. A set-role is just like an individual OF-role or IN-role, except that it is descended from the SET node and therefore has a *TYPE-node of its own attached to it. In figure 15, we see that every ELEPHANT has a set of four LEGS, and that the typical leg in this set is a CYLINDER. Either the set node or the *TYPE-node for this set or both may be mapped down into the description of some individual elephant; figure 16 shows the *MAP nodes representing CLYDE's set of legs and CLYDE's typical leg. Since the map of a *TYPE-node is to be treated as a *TYPE-node in its new description, we use a *TMAP to represent it instead of a regular *MAP; the connections are identical and the *TMAP node works like a *MAP node during inheritance. Of course, we would not normally map these nodes until we have something to say about them in the CLYDE description. Note the difference between *creating a virtual copy* of a *TYPE-node and *mapping it into an existing description*: the former creates a *new* individual or sub-type of this type; the latter just makes explicit the version of a type that *already logically exists* within some virtual copy.

If we now create LEFT-FRONT-LEG, an *INDV role within the ELEPHANT description, we want to indicate that this is a *VC of the TYPICAL-ELEPHANT-LEG *TYPE-node. This creates exactly the situation mentioned above: a *TYPE-description in which one mappable role is a virtual copy of another. Figure 17 shows what happens when we map both the typical elephant leg and the left front elephant leg down into the CLYDE description. Assume, now, that we say something about the typical leg of Clyde -- perhaps his legs are extra-long for an elephant. This property must somehow be made to apply to CLYDE's left front leg as well. Fortunately, this falls out of the propagation rules described above. If we ask about CLYDE's left front leg, we activate the CLYDE description with marker M1, then begin marker M2 on the LEFT-FRONT-LEG node

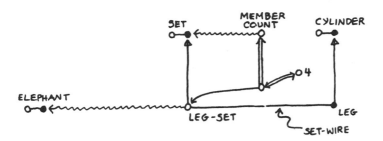

Figure 15: The set of four LEGS of the typical ELEPHANT, that set's typical member.

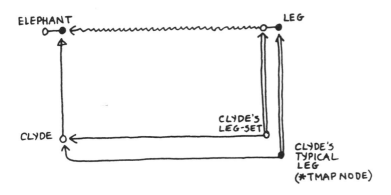

Figure 16: CLYDE's typical leg and set of legs.

defined in ELEPHANT. This marker will travel down the map-wire to CLYDE's version of LEFT-FRONT-LEG, giving us access to the properties there. It will also go up the *VC link to ELEPHANT's TYPICAL-LEG, and from there down to CLYDE's TYPICAL-LEG. The properties on all of these nodes, as well as nodes above them like CYLINDER, would be available for use. Note that the markers must flow both up and down at once to achieve this effect, an impossible situation without the activation step. Such cases have been very hard for previous

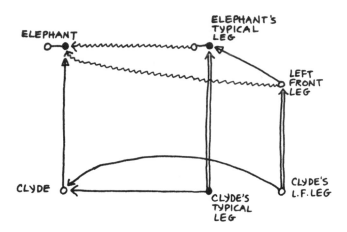

Figure 17: CLYDE's typical LEG and LEFT-FRONT-LEG, mapped down from ELEPHANT.

semantic networks to handle, if they allowed them at all.

Notice that we do not have to create the *MAP node for CLYDE's typical leg in order to create a random individual leg for CLYDE: we can run the new leg-node's parent-wire to the ELEPHANT description's TYPICAL-LEG node instead. If, later, we do create the map of this *TYPE-node for CLYDE, the two TYPICAL-LEG nodes will be shorted together whenever we are working within the CLYDE description, so the individual leg will inherit from both nodes. Notice, too, that if we have several individual legs represented, they will all inherit from the TYPICAL-LEG node, but they will not inherit from one another: the virtual copy links still only allow *upward* propagation during inheritance scans.

If a single role-name is used for many roles, each of which is in a different description, NETL can help the natural language system in disambiguating the reference. Suppose the word "HEART" is used both for the blood-pumping organ in the

ANIMAL description and the central part of an ARTICHOKE. If we ask for "Clyde's heart", we will activate the CLYDE description, including the ANIMAL node, mark all of the roles within the active descriptions, and then see if any of these is associated with the role-name "HEART". Presumably, we would find the ANIMAL-HEART role-node and not the one associated with ARTICHOKE. If two HEART-roles are within the activated description-set for CLYDE, then we have a more interesting problem. In general, this must be solved by looking at what is being said about the heart in question -- if we are lucky, one interpretation will clash and the other will not. If we ask for some role which is not present in the CLYDE description, the system could do one of several things: create the role, asking for more information about it; find some class into which Clyde could fit that *does* contain the role in question, and place Clyde there; or complain to the user.

In addition to their primary function of mapping roles into copy-layers, *MAP nodes can also be used to represent the description of some individual within a given area. We might, for instance, have some special set of properties to attach to our description of Abraham Lincoln, but want these only to apply to Lincoln in the year 1860. We could represent "Lincoln in 1860" by creating a special *MAP-node whose parent-wire is connected to the basic ABRAHAM-LINCOLN description, and whose owner-wire is connected to the node representing the temporal area that we call the year 1860. This *MAP-node functions almost exactly as a normal *MAP-node functions in a description: when the 1860 node is marked as being active, the LINCOLN-IN-1860 node is merged together with the basic ABRAHAM-LINCOLN node, and both descriptions are accessable. When we are operating outside of the 1860 area, the connection is broken. Also, if you want to look at the description represented by the LINCOLN-IN-1860 node, you must first activate the 1860 area. The area-activation procedure is slightly different from the procedure for activating descriptions -- for one thing, markers propagate across PART-OF relations as well as *VC links -- but the general idea is the same. We will see more of this when we look at the context system.

One final topic should be covered before we go on to other things: a phenomenon that I call *role reversal*. In most situations, the use of the indefinite article to express some idea in English indicates that a virtual copy is being (or has been) made. Clyde, for instance, is *an* elephant, and every elephant is *a* mammal. The definite article, on the other hand, refers to some existing individual, often an individual role within some description. (It can also refer to the typical member of some existing set, as in "The elephant has a long nose.") The reason you can refer to *the* heart of Clyde is that somewhere above Clyde is a description containing the assertion that every whatever-it-is *has* a heart, and Clyde inherits this. Similarly, we can refer to *the* legs of Clyde, meaning the set of Clyde's legs. No rule in English is ever without qualifications and exceptions, but this seems to serve as a fairly reliable rule of thumb for determining whether a given case is a virtual copy or a mapped role. Often, of course, the possessive form is used instead of the phrase "the A of B".

Typically, then, we refer to an animal and its heart, a person and his or her mother, a car and its engine, and so on. Sometimes, however, we refer to a heart or a mother or an engine as an entity in itself, as though these things were *TYPE-descriptions rather than roles to be mapped. We could, of course, translate "a heart" into "*the* heart of *an* animal" and represent that instead -- in other words, to create an arbitrary copy of some role, we create an arbitrary anonymous individual for this role to belong to. For some cases, this seems to be the right approach: it is hard to think about a circumference without its circle or a last-element without its series. In other cases, however, it seems clear that the entity in question is able to exist independently of its normal owner: if we see a row of hearts in a butcher shop, there seems to be no overwhelming compulsion to describe these in terms of some now-defunct animal -- they are just pieces of meat of a certain type.

It seems clear that in cases like this there are two nodes for HEART, one representing the physical object-type that we speak of as a heart, and the other representing the role of heart within some animal. These two nodes are distinct, but they are intimately connected: the HEART role-node has a *VC-link up to the HEART *TYPE-node; the *TYPE-node for HEART has an individual role in its description for the animal of which it is (or once was) a part. (In general, if the role-node has the **RSPLIT flag set, the *TYPE-node will have an individual owner-role; if the **RSPLIT flag is not present on the role-node, there may be a set of owners.) Given a role, we can always define a class that includes all of the players of that role in a given context-area. To do this, we need an *EVERY-node, as we will see in section 3.7.

3.6 Statements and Links

In the preceding sections we saw how to build up various kinds of nodes in NETL; in this section, we will consider in detail the techniques for saying things about the concepts that these nodes represent. The basic unit of declarative information in NETL is the *statement*. Some statements are represented as link-elements; others are represented in the form of individual statement-descriptions, built around an *IST-node* (for Individual STatement) in much the same way that an individual object's description is built around an *INDV node. The statement itself is represented by the internal handle-node of the link element or the *IST-node in the statement-description. In general, the word "statement" will be used here to refer either to a link or to an *IST-node description, and the word "handle" will refer either to a link's internal handle-node or to the *IST-node within a statement.

Through its handle-node, a statement can be treated as an object, with properties and class-memberships of its own. We might, for instance, want to create role-nodes for the SOURCE of a statement or its set of SUPPORTS -- the set of other statements that it depends on. (Doyle [1977] shows how such support statements might be used in a deductive system.) We might want to indicate that a statement is a mere DEFAULT, easily overridden if contradictions arise, or that it is SACRED and is never to be cancelled or doubted. All such meta-information about the statement is attached to the handle or *IST node, just as it would be attached to any *INDV-node description.

Each individual statement is an instance of some *statement-type*, just as an individual object is an instance of some object-type. This class-membership is indicated by a *VC-link running from the statement's handle to the appropriate *TYPE-node. As in the case of *INDV-nodes, each *IST-node and link-element has a parent-wire which can be used instead of a *VC link to indicate its principal class-membership. The statement-types are represented by *TYPE-nodes which are descendants of the STATEMENT *TYPE-node. The *IST-node representing the statement "Rockefeller owns Standard Oil" will have its parent-wire connected to the OWNS-STATEMENT *TYPE-node; the *VC-link representing "Clyde is an elephant" will have its parent-wire connected to the *VC-LINK *TYPE-node.

For the links, this explicit connection to a particular statement-type is redundant, since the link's type is indicated by flag-bits in the link-unit, but the connection is made anyway. There are two reasons for this: first, it makes the representation of link-statements and *IST-node statements more uniform; second, it makes it possible for us to split up the basic link-types defined in NETL into sub-types on the basis of their source, degree of certainty, or any other property. The *VC-LINK *TYPE-node will appear somewhere above every *VC-link, but it does not have to be the *immediate* parent. Regardless of what the parent-wire says about the type of a link, the link-unit's internal type-flags govern how it operates during marker propagations. It is important to remember that the parent-wire of a *VC-link indicates the parent of the *VC statement itself, not the parent of the node that the statement is about.

An individual statement is declared to be valid within some area (space, time, subject-area, etc.), which is called the statement's *scope*. When the system is working within that area, we want the statement to be *active* and to take part in marker-sweeps, deductions, and other activities; when the system is not working within a statement's scope-area, we want the statement to play dead. A *SCOPE-link is used to connect the statement's handle to the desired area. Most statements have only one scope, but it is possible for a statement to have many: the statement is active if *any* of its scope-areas are. Each link-unit and *IST-node has a *scope-wire* which can be used to replace any single *SCOPE link coming into that node. As in other such cases, this wire should only be used in static, non-controversial situations; if there is a likelihood that the system will want to refer to the scope-relation of a statement directly or modify the scope-relation, the full-scale *SCOPE link should be used. If some statement A has its scope-wire connected to another statement B, instead of an area, it means that A is to be active whenever B is, and A is to share in any cancellations coming into B.

The scope connection of a statement is analogous to the existence connection of an *INDV-node -- in fact, an *IST node can be thought of as an *INDV node with a scope-wire in place of the existence-wire. The difference is an important one, however, since the two types of area-connection behave differently during inheritance through the hierarchy of areas and sub-areas. As we noted in section 3.3, this hierarchy is distinct from the type-hierarchy, since it follows the transitive PART-OF relationships rather than the IS-A or *VC-links. (There is some overlap in the two hierarchies, as we will see shortly.) Both hierarchies are tangled, but the type-hierarchy has a single root-node, while the PART-OF hierarchy terminates in a number of outermost universe-nodes.

If an object is said to *exist* within an area, that means that it exists *somewhere* within the area; if a statement is said to be *valid* within an area, it means that it is valid *everywhere* within the area. If coyotes *exist* within NEVADA, they also exist within the larger areas, like WESTERN-USA, of which NEVADA is a part; they do not necessarily exist within any given part of NEVADA, like DOWNTOWN-LAS-VEGAS. If the statement "defenestration is legal" is true in NEVADA, then it is true in DOWNTOWN-LAS-VEGAS as well (unless there is an explicit local exception), but it is not necessarily true in WESTERN-USA as a whole. This means that there are two distinct kinds of marker sweeps that can be performed through the PART-OF hierarchy. To mark all of the individual entities that *exist* within a given area A, we mark A and propagate markers to all of its parts; we then mark the individuals whose existence is tied to any of these marked areas. To activate all of the statements that are *valid* in area A, we mark A and propagate the marks in the other direction, to all of the areas of which A is a part; we then mark the statements that are scoped within these selected areas. This difference in the behavior of existence and statement-scoping came as something of a surprise to me -- I am told that the logicians have known something of this sort all along, but they tend not to express it in these terms. This difference caused a lot of trouble until I understood what was happening.

The PART-OF relation between two *INDV nodes, X and Y (which may be areas, physical objects, or whatever), is represented not by a special PART-OF link-type, but simply by creating a PART set-role for Y (the owner) and stating that X (the part) is a *VC of this role's *TYPE-node (or *TMAP-node). Figure 18 (omitting the dotted links, which will be explained in a moment) shows the PART hierarchy for various parts of the EARTH area-node. The principal reason for treating PART as a normal set-role is to allow all of NETL's inheritance machinery to function in the normal ways: we can now state things about every PART of some entity, and these statements will be inherited by the players of the PART-role. In addition, we can divide the parts of an object into various classes and sub-classes, while still allowing members of these sub-classes to inherit membership and properties from the PART-role of that object.

The PART-OF relationship is transitive: a part of a part of X is a part of X. This means that there are implicit *VC links between some of the *TMAP nodes representing PART-roles, as shown by the dotted *VC-links in figure 18. Anything that we know about the typical PART of the EARTH must also be inherited by RENO (unless there is an explicit exception). Furthermore, in marking the areas that RENO is a PART of, we must find the EARTH and the USA areas, as well as NEVADA. As we saw earlier, it is possible to inherit implicit *VC links from a higher level through the virtual-copy mechanism. We could, therefore, state at the level of the original PART-role that these implicit *VC-links exist, and allow them to operate by

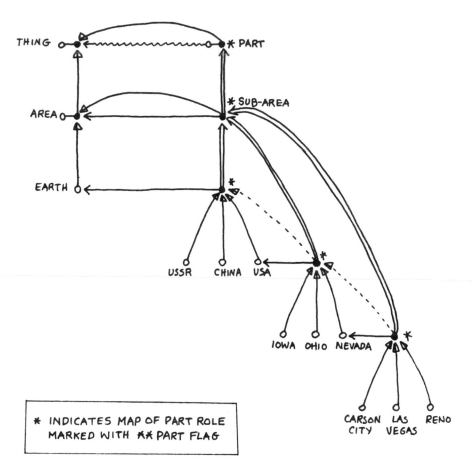

Figure 18: A section of the PART-OF hierarchy, with added explicit *VC links.

inheritance. This approach works well enough for the inheritance of a few isolated *VC links, as we saw in the LEFT-FRONT-LEG example, but in cases like this one, where the inherited *VC links are numerous and chained together, it could slow down the system's marker propagations tremendously: crossing an inherited *VC link requires a marker to travel all the way up the type hierarchy and back down again, in place of the single step that would be necessary if the link were physically present. Even worse than this is the fact that during a part-to-owner scan through the PART-OF hierarchy, markers normally enter *TMAP-nodes whose owner-nodes have not been activated. Following the normal *MAP-node procedures, the only way to tell whether a given *TMAP-node represents a PART-role is to individually activate its owner's set of ancestor-nodes and then see if the *TMAP has been shorted to the PART node within this activation.

To avoid these inefficiencies, NETL treats PART-roles specially in two ways. First, the original PART role-node and all of its maps are marked with a special **PART flag-bit. Whenever a new *TMAP node is created, the system looks for the **PART flag on the parent-role and, if it is found, adds a **PART flag to the new *TMAP node as well. In figure 18, these **PART nodes are marked with an asterisk. Second, whenever a **PART role is mapped for an owner that itself has a **PART-node among its ancestors (that is, if the new *TMAP node is a part of a part), then the implied *VC-link from the new *TMAP-node to the **PART-node above its owner is added explicitly to the network. With these *VC links explicitly in place, the inheritance system works properly and efficiently, and it becomes easy to mark the parts of node X or the things of which X is a part. To mark the parts or sub-areas of USA, we simply activate upward from USA, then send a mark down from PART within this activation, crossing all *VC-links from top to bottom. To find all the areas of which RENO is a part, we mark up the network of *VC links from RENO with one mark; then, for every **PART *TMAP node in the activated set, we send a second mark across the wire to its owner-node.

In effect, we have incorporated the PART-OF hierarchy into the type-hierarchy, and we can now scan in either direction easily. Also, we have specially marked those *TMAP nodes that are to function as PART-OF links between their descendants and their owners, in addition to their usual duties as *TMAP-nodes. It is admittedly rather inelegant to treat the PART role in this special way, but its function in establishing the important hierarchy of areas and sub-areas seems to justify this exceptional treatment. This mechanism may in the future be generalized to handle the transitive closures of other selected role-types.

A statement must somehow be connected to the nodes that it is about. The manner of this connection is the principal difference between links and *IST-node statements. The link-units have two special wires, designated A and B, which are connected to the argument-nodes. (It would be possible to allow links with more than two argument-wires, but this option is not currently needed and has not been included in the current simulated version of NETL.) Figure 19 shows the *VC-link representing "Clyde is an elephant", with all of its wires connected and labelled. In most diagrams, the handle-nodes, parent-wires, and sometimes the scope-wires of the links are uninteresting and are therefore omitted.

The *IST nodes use a more flexible method: for each type of *IST statement certain IN-roles are created, representing the various arguments that the statement might take. These argument-roles may be defined at any level of the statement-type hierarchy, and are mapped down through the lower levels into the individual statement-descriptions. There, the *MAP-nodes representing arguments are tied to the aprropriate *INDV-nodes by *EQ-links. Figure 20 shows the statement "Rockefeller owns Standard Oil", which is scoped in the 1890's time-area. Note that this mechanism allows us to define any number of arguments for a statement-type, and to add whatever we want to each role in the form of properties and class-membership restrictions. In these two respects, the *IST-node format is more powerful than

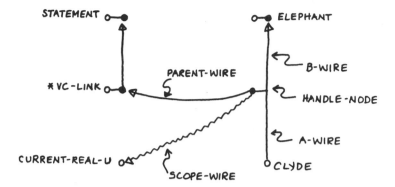

Figure 19: Detailed view of a *VC-link connection.

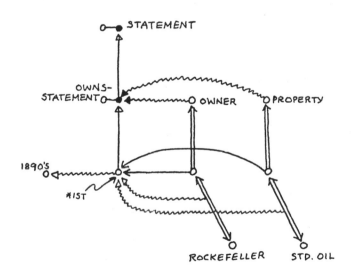

Figure 20: "Rockefeller owned Standard Oil in the 1890's."

that of the link-units. The *EQ-links connecting the role-nodes
to their players usually have their scope-wires tied to the
statement's *IST-node, since the statement itself and the
argument-bindings are normally intended to be used as a unit. It
is possible, however, to tie some of the *EQ-links to other
scope-areas. We might, for example, want to state that some
unspecified person owns Standard Oil in the 1890's, and to *EQ
this owner-role *MAP-node to several person-nodes in different
hypothetical universes.

In addition to the IN-roles representing the arguments of
a statement, the statement-description may contain OF-roles
representing the things we know about the statement itself. A
statement, for instance, may have OF-roles representing its
SOURCE, its DEGREE-OF-CERTAINTY, and so on. These
roles may or may not be filled, or they may be filled only with
an inherited default value. Links, as well as *IST-node
statements, may have OF-roles of this sort. I am not altogether
convinced that the IN-role/OF-role distinction is the proper one
to use here, but so far it has not caused any trouble -- there does
not seem to be any other reasonable interpretation for the use of
a statement as an area. People sometimes speak of their
confidence "in" a certain statement, but this feels like a linguistic
anomaly to me.

As we move downward through the hierarchy of
statement-types, the categories become more specialized and carry
more information. Usually this specialization takes the form of
restrictions (class-membership statements) on the roles in the
specialized statement-type or stated relationships that must hold
among the various roles. In figure 21, for example, we see the
definition of the OWNS-SLAVE statement-type, a specialized
form of the OWNS statement-type in which the PROPERTY role
is constrained to be an instance of PERSON. In addition to the
information inherited from the basic OWNS description, this
subtype has some properties of its own: the PROPERTY role is
given the added role-name SLAVE, and the relationship itself is
declared to be illegal in the CURRENT-USA context area.

There could also be specializations of OWNS for property that is land, stocks and bonds, inanimate objects, and so on. Similarly, the subtype of OWNS in which the owner is an instance of NON-PROFIT-ORGANIZATION has certain special properties with regard to the tax laws.

A statement-type can also be specialized by filling one of the argument-roles, rather than merely restricting it. Each such assignment has the effect of reducing the number of freely-assignable arguments of the resulting statement-type by one. In figure 22, we see the two-place HATES statement-type specialized into a one-place HATES-CLYDE predicate by the assignment of CLYDE to the role of HATED. Note that we can define restricted statement-types that do not have particular words associated with them in English.

Actually, the above examples are somewhat oversimplified, since they provide us with no way to distinguish between the restrictions that *define* a new statement-subtype (the PROPERTY being a PERSON), and those statements which are *incidentally true* of that subtype, but do not help to define it (the OWNS-SLAVE relationship being an ILLEGAL-RELATIONSHIP). We will see in section 3.8 how this distinction between defining and incidental properties can be represented and how this information is used by the system. Note that even if *all* of the argument-roles in a statement-type are filled, that statement-type is still a mere template; in order to actually *assert* something, an individual instance of the statement must be created.

So far, we have seen individual statements connected only to individual arguments. It is also possible to say things about a *TYPE-node, meaning that the statement is meant to apply to all individuals of the specified type. Figure 23 shows the statement that Clyde hates all snakes. This statement is inherited by each individual snake, just as a link is inherited. To find every individual that CLYDE hates, we sweep markers up from CLYDE to all of his inherited descriptions, across any HATE relations we find there, and down from the HATED role to the

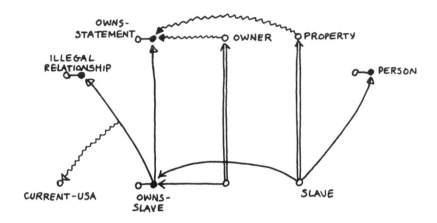

Figure 21: OWNS statement specialized to OWNS-SLAVE.

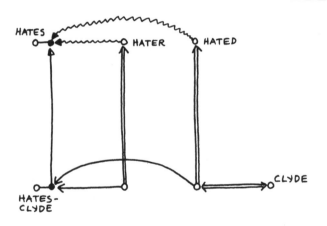

Figure 22: HATES statement specialized to HATES-CLYDE predicate.

individual. To find every individual that MONTY is hated *by*, we sweep up from MONTY, backwards across any HATE relations, and down to the individual players of the HATER role.

A statement is considered to be a part of every description in which one or more of its argument-roles resides, in the sense defined in section 2.2: if we make a virtual copy of one of the arguments of a statement, this creates a new version of the statement as well. As always, we do not actually make the *MAP node representing this new version of the statement unless we have something to say about it. Even then, we only have to map the statement's handle node; as we have just seen, the original generic form of the statement is quite sufficient to handle the functional load of passing markers through the statement, from one argument to another. Figure 23 shows the *MAP node representing Clyde's hatred for the particular snake named Monty -- a mapped version of Clyde's hatred for all snakes. This new version of the statement inherits all of the properties of the original, and may add some new properties of its own. We might, for instance, want to indicate that the INTENSITY of Clyde's hatred for Monty is VERY-GREAT.

If we have two type-nodes among the arguments of a statement, we can create a map of that statement for individual argument-instances on either side; the *MAP-node on one side can then be mapped for individuals on the other side to create individual-to-individual relationships. It does not really matter which side is mapped first in such a chain. Figure 24 shows all elephants hating all snakes, with *MAP nodes for Clyde's hatred of snakes, the hatred of all elephants for Monty, and the specific hatred of Clyde for Monty. To access the version linking CLYDE to MONTY, we mark CLYDE and his ancestors with one mark, MONTY and his ancestors with another, and allow either or both of these marks to activate a map-wire. Then, if we start at the parent HATES-relation from ELEPHANT to SNAKE, we see all of the appropriate maps of it, with whatever properties these maps might carry. This operation can be

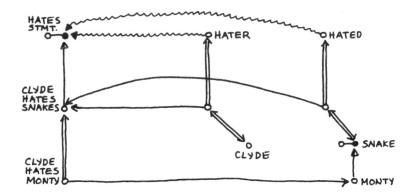

Figure 23: "Clyde hates every snake," with *MAP-node representing Clyde's hatred for Monty.

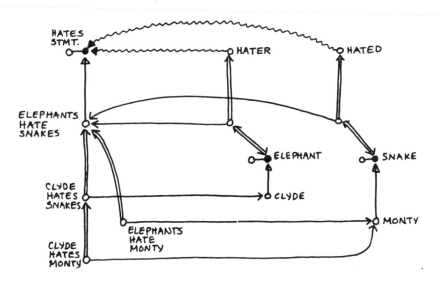

Figure 24: "Elephants hate snakes," with individual *MAP-nodes.

generalized to handle any number of type-node arguments, at
least until the system runs out of markers to activate them all.

There are two modifier flags of particular relevance to
statements: the **NOT flag which negates the statement, and the
**SPEC flag which indicates that the statement is part of the
definition of an *EVERY-node. These will be discussed in
section 3.8. In the remainder of this section we will look at the
currently-defined link types, especially those that we did not
encounter very often in the preceding sections.

Probably the most important link-type is the virtual copy
or *VC link. This, as we have seen many times already, carries
the statement "A is a B". B is always a *TYPE-node; A may
be either a *TYPE or an *INDV, depending on whether we want
to create a sub-type or an instance of type B. The *VC link also
causes A to be considered a member of the set associated with B.
A normal *VC link is never used to connect two *INDV nodes.

Sometimes, however, we want a weaker form of
virtual-copy relationship which allows a description to be
inherited without conferring formal class-membership upon the
recipient. We might, for instance, want to say that a Cadillac is
just like a Chevrolet, but with bigger fins. In saying this, we do
not want to imply that a Cadillac *is* a Chevrolet, in any formal
sense. We do this by placing a *VC link from CADILLAC to
CHEVROLET, with the **LIKE modifier set in the link-unit
body. During property-inheritance scans, this link functions just
like a normal *VC: a full virtual copy is created, which can be
modified in the usual way to account for longer fins or any
other differences. During scans to answer "is a" questions,
however, the **LIKE flag disables its link. A **LIKE *VC link
does not trigger the usual *EVERY-node digestion and
clash-detection mechanisms, both of which are triggered by
formal class-membership rather than mere inheritance of
description.

This **LIKE mechanism also allows us to state that one
individual is to inherit the description from another individual,
without in any sense equating the two. This is particularly

useful when we want to make a copy of REAL-U (or some other individual universe), so that we can make local changes and examine their effects, without messing up our view of reality. This is useful in many kinds of problem-solving activity: we might, for instance, want to create an imaginary universe in which a certain toy block is moved from one place to another, and see if the resulting structure is stable. It might seem strange to create a copy of an entire universe in order to answer this question, but in a virtual-copy system this involves the creation of only a few nodes and links.

It would be possible to set up a **LIKE *EQ mechanism, analogous to the **LIKE *VC mechanism. This would allow two descriptions to cross-inherit properties in either direction, without really equating the referents of the two nodes that are joined. Since I have not found any good use for this mechanism, it is not currently implemented.

Note that in using this mechanism, the *whole* description of the parent object is virtually copied, though the copy may then be altered. This is different from metaphorical description, in which we want to be selective about which features of the parent object are to be copied. Considerable judgement must be exercised in deciding which features should be inherited and which should be left behind. Winston [1977] has made a start toward developing criteria for making this selection, but much more remains to be done. Often, the use of a **LIKE *VC link is a temporary expedient which will be replaced later by the creation of a type-description to cover both of the objects in question.

We have already seen the *EQ link at work many times. It says that node A and node B represent the same external entity, and that their descriptions are to be merged whenever the *EQ link is active and not cancelled. This means that the A and B nodes must represent compatible views of the object in question; if the views are incompatible, and must be considered one at a time, we must use a special mechanism which will be described in section 3.7.

The closely-related *EXFOR, *EXIN, and *SCOPE links have already been described. All serve to establish the cicumstances under which a given individual or statement is considered to be present, and all can be replaced by wires in the node-unit if the handle-node of the link is not needed.

The *SPLIT link is used to create mutually distinct sets of individuals. All of the *SPLIT links sharing a common B-node form a set; the A-nodes of the *SPLIT-links in a given set are all declared to be distinct from one another. This is equivalent to, but usually cheaper than, creating a **NOT *EQ link between each pair of nodes in the set. (See section 3.8 for a full discussion of the **NOT flag.) If the nodes in the split-set are individuals, a clash will occur whenever an attempt is made to equate any two of them, either directly or through a chain of *EQ links. If *TYPE-nodes are split, it indicates that the type-descriptions have no individual instances (and thus no non-empty sub-types) in common.

The B-wires of the *SPLIT links in a set usually meet at the area-node within which the split-set exists, or at the *IST node of a DISTINCT or TYPE-SPLIT statement. Figure 25 shows the DISTINCT statement indicating that THE-ENGINEER, THE-FIREMAN, and THE-BRAKEMAN are distinct pseudo-individuals within the PUZZLE-1 area in which they are defined. This means that they can be equated to real individuals within that area, but not to one another. The DISTINCT relation is special in that it connects to its arguments by *SPLIT links instead of the usual role-map and *EQ-link mechanism. (This makes life somewhat easier for the clash detection procedures -- they can look just for *SPLIT links and do not have to treat the DISTINCT statement as a special case.)

Figure 26 shows the COMPLETE-TYPE-SPLIT statement indicating that the classes ANIMAL, VEGETABLE, and MINERAL form a complete set of distinct, non-overlapping subsets of the PHYSOB class. The COMPLETE-TYPE-SPLIT statement has two arguments: the PARENT-SET argument, which is tied to the set-node of the class being divided, and a

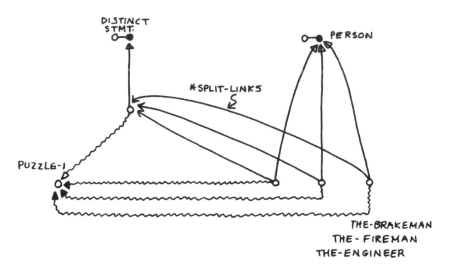

Figure 25: A set of distinct pseudo-individuals in PUZZLE-1.

type-argument named SPLIT-SUBSET into which the set-nodes of
the various subclasses are tied with *VC-links. This statement,
then, establishes a relationship between the set-nodes of the
classes involved: it is the set of PHYSOBS that is being split,
not the typical PHYSOB. The actual splitting, for the purposes
of clash detection, is performed by the *SPLIT links which run
from the *TYPE-nodes of the sub-classes to the *IST node of the
COMPLETE-TYPE-SPLIT statement. These function just as in
the DISTINCT statement. Of course, the *TYPE-node of each
sub-class must have a *VC connection, direct or indirect, to the
*TYPE-node of the parent class. If such a connection is not
present when the COMPLETE-TYPE-SPLIT statement is created,
it is added at that time. (To minimize clutter, these are not
shown in the diagram.)

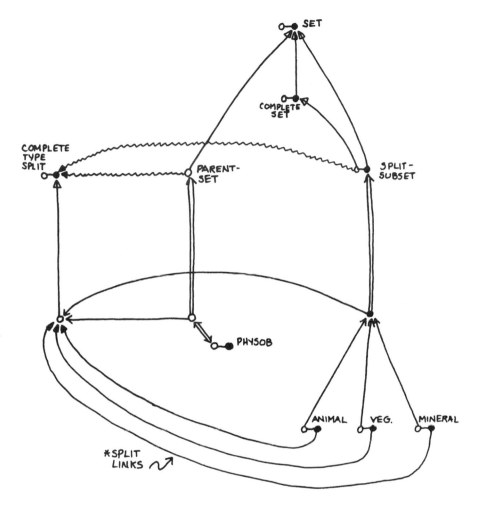

Figure 26: A complete type-split of PHYSOB into ANIMAL, VEGETABLE, and MINERAL.

The completeness of the partition is represented by the *VC connection from the set-node of the SPLIT-SUBSET argument to the COMPLETE-SET class. Note that this claims that the *set of split-subsets* is complete, not any of the subsets themselves. A regular TYPE-SPLIT statement is exactly like a COMPLETE-TYPE-SPLIT statement, but without this statement of completeness. Of course, the user of the NETL system does not normally deal with the complex internal structures shown here; there is a simple function call to create any desired TYPE-SPLIT or COMPLETE-TYPE-SPLIT.

The final two link-types are concerned with the problem of cancelling information that would otherwise be inherited. The *CANCEL link is used to cancel a statement B within the virtual-copy or context-area indicated by node A. The most common case involves the use of a *CANCEL-link to cancel some statement that is attached to a *TYPE-node above node A in the *VC hierarchy. Figure 27 illustrates the statement that elephants in general hate snakes, but Clyde doesn't. When asked if Clyde hates any other individual, the system first activates the CLYDE description by marking up from it. Then it selects a different marker to represent cancellations within this activation, and places this marker at the B-end of any *CANCEL-link whose A-end has been activated. Markers are usually used in pairs, one representing an activation and the other representing the cancellations resulting from that activation.

The presence of this cancellation marker causes the statement in question to play dead during subsequent processing. Any *MAP-nodes for which it is the owner-node will not be activated, and the statement itself will not respond to any calls for statements of its type. The HATES-statement from ELEPHANT to SNAKE, therefore, will never be found if we come in through the CLYDE description. In addition, the cancellation marker is propagated into any other statement tied to the cancelled statement by its scope-wire; as we noted earlier, such secondary statements are to share both activation and cancellation with the controlling statement. Since both the

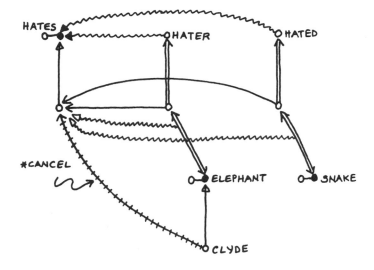

Figure 27: "Elephants hate snakes, but Clyde doesn't."

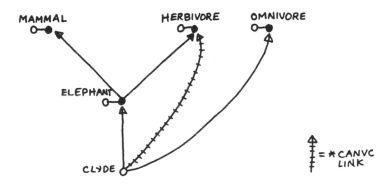

Figure 28: "Clyde is an elephant, but is an omnivore instead of a herbivore."

*EQ-link and the map-wire for the HATER role are disabled, CLYDE has no chance to inherit any of the properties of a HATER -- through this statement, at least.

What if the query enters the cancelled statement from the other direction? If we ask for a list of individuals that Monty is *hated by*, we will mark upward from MONTY and will succeed in crossing the HATES-link backwards to ELEPHANT. As we do so, however, we must notice that we have entered a class by crossing a statement-bridge that is cancelled for certain members of that class. Therefore, before marking downward to get the appropriate set of individuals, we should send a cancellation marker down the cancel-links that are attached to that bridge. A cancellation marker will be placed on CLYDE and, in the subsequent downward scan, the scanning markers will refuse to enter or pass through any node that is so marked. We will thus mark all of the individual elephants *except Clyde* as individuals who hate Monty.

Note that these cancellation-links only apply to a single statement of some fact; if a single fact is represented by several redundant statements, we will need to cancel all of these statements in order to completely eliminate that fact from some copy or context-area. This is easy to do: we simply send out a call for any uncancelled statements of the desired form, cancel the statements that respond, and repeat the process until no new statements appear. As a general rule, the system will complain at any attempt to store a completely redundant fact, but it is possible (and sometimes useful) to force it to store such facts anyway; we have seen, for instance, that a redundant *VC-link can short-cut a *VC-link chain that is becoming too long. Also, equivalent statements may be placed in different but overlapping scope areas, and where these areas intersect the statements will be redundant. It is therefore unwise to assume that a fact has been removed just because *one* statement of that fact has been cancelled; redundant cases should always be tested for.

In the above example, the statement being cancelled was attached directly to an ancestor of node A in the type-hierarchy.

It is also possible to cancel a statement that connects two roles
in the inherited description of node A, or connects one such role
to an outside entity. As we saw in section 3.5, we cannot look
at the roles of A without first activating the A-node's
description. The cancellation markers are placed just after this
owner-activation step, but before we examine any of the roles. If
a statement that would otherwise apply to a role is cancelled, the
markers examining that role will never see that statement. There
is no chance of a race developing, since the activation and
cancellation scans precede the examination of the role. If we
come into a *TYPE-node's role from outside, we proceed much
as we did in entering the *TYPE-node itself: first, we propagate
cancellation markers down any *CANCEL links attached to the
statement-bridge we have just crossed; second, we the activate
downward from the *TYPE-node that owns the role we have
entered, to get the individual owners that have not been
cancelled; finally, we propagate markers down from the
role-node in question, letting these markers cross any map-wires
activated by the owner-nodes in the set we have just marked.
This process will lead us to the individual role-players for whom
the statement in question was not cancelled.

   If a statement is scoped within area X, and we want to
cancel it within some local area, Y, that is a part of X, we
simply run a *CANCEL-link from area-node Y to the statement
in question. When the system wants to work within a given area,
it marks that area and all of its super-areas with one marker,
places a second marker on the set of statements that are activated
as a result, and uses a third marker to note which of these
statements is locally cancelled. Three markers are permanently
assigned to this context-activation duty. We will see more about
the use of multiple context-areas in section 3.9.

   A *CANCEL-link cannot be used to cancel a *VC-link or
*EQ-link that specifies a part of the A-node's own identity.
Since we first activate A and then place the cancellation markers,
this would have the effect of burning the bridges after the
activation markers have crossed them and traveled on through the

network. It would be very hard to track down and eliminate such markers once they have escaped. If we want to cancel some *identity* that would otherwise be inherited by A, we must use a *CANVC-link (cancel virtual copy) from A to the node representing the identity to be cancelled. This link cancels the identity-node itself, not the links leading to that node. The *CANVC link operates *during* an upward or downward activation-scan, to place a cancellation marker in an identity-node before the scanning markers get there. The scanning markers will not enter or pass through any identity-node that is so cancelled. There is a race created between the cancellation markers and the scanning markers, but the cancellation markers will always win: they run directly from the copy to the identity node that is to be cancelled, while the scanning markers must pass through at least one other node. (It makes no sense to connect a node to an *immediate* superior and then cancel this identity' from the same level -- both links could just eliminated.) In figure 28 we see the statement that Clyde is an elephant, but is an omnivore instead of a herbivore.

3.7 The Copy-Confusion and Binding-Ambiguity Problems

The parallel network system, while a valuable tool, is not without certain problems of its own. It is sometimes very difficult to maintain a high degree of semantic precision, while still enjoying the speed advantages of parallel search. In certain situations, it is very difficult to prevent the propagating markers from reaching inappropriate nodes as they trace out the roles and relationships within a description. Before we develop any more representational machinery, we ought to take a look at these problems and see how, and to what extent, they can be dealt with. We will consider two different problems in this section: the *copy-confusion problem*, which is caused by trying to look at two different copies of the same description at once, and the *binding-ambiguity problem*, which is caused by a shortcoming of the notational system in dealing with several arbitrary individuals of the same type. We will look at copy-confusion first.

The role-mapping scheme described in section 3.5, in which the role-node and an appropriate set of *MAP-nodes are temporarily shorted together, has the effect of temporarily cannibalizing the original copy of a description whenever we want to look at a virtual copy of it. If, while one copy of a description is activated in this manner, we activate a second copy *using the same marker-bit to represent the activation*, the roles of the two distinct copies will be tied together through the common role-node in the shared parent-description; properties that should apply only to a role in one copy will be inherited by the other copy of the same role. At first glance, it would seem to be a simple matter to avoid this condition, but in fact it crops up in a number of rather subtle and devious ways. This illegal merging of role-nodes is what is meant by the term "copy-confusion".

In most cases, when we want to describe an object in two different ways, the descriptions are *compatible* and can simply be merged by an *EQ link or by running two *VC links down to the same node. Two descriptions can be compatible even when both of them have a common parent-class: it causes no

confusion to say that CLYDE is both an
AFRICAN-ELEPHANT and a MALE-ELEPHANT. These two
descriptions both contain a virtual copy of the ELEPHANT
description, which they augment and modify in different, but not
contradictory, ways. When we tie these descriptions together at
the CLYDE node, the roles and properties of the two
descriptions will be mixed together, but *we want that to happen*:
when a reference is made to Clyde's trunk, we want to find
properties attached to the TRUNK nodes of *all* of CLYDE's
superiors in the network, and we do not usually want to know
which description a given property came from. We can, of
course, look at a particular description for Clyde in isolation --
Clyde as a MALE-ELEPHANT, for example -- by activating this
description alone among CLYDE's superiors. In normal
operation of the system, however, we want to look at all of the
descriptions of CLYDE at once, and we want all of the versions
of each role to be merged. In fact, the whole point of defining
the *MAP-nodes as we have is to fuse together all of the
inherited role-nodes into an indistinguishable blend.

Sometimes, however, we want to describe an object using
two *distinct* role-mappings from the same parent-description. In
such cases, we must not allow the mappings to be blurred
together in the usual way, though we still want to indicate that
the two descriptions share a common referent. Consider, for
example, the NECKER-CUBE drawing as shown in figure 29.
This can be represented as an instance of the CUBE-VIEW
description in two different ways: in one description, node X of
the Necker Cube plays the role of FRONT-VERTEX; in the
other, this role is played by node Y. If we were to simply tie
these two descriptions together at the NECKER-CUBE node, as
we tied AFRICAN-ELEPHANT and MALE-ELEPHANT
together at CLYDE, the system would normally activate both
descriptions at once, with a single marker-bit, whenever it wanted
to find some property of the NECKER-CUBE. This would
short both X and Y to FRONT-VERTEX, which is correct, but
it would also short them to each other, which is not correct.

The Y vertex may have properties (ROUNDEDNESS, for example) which should not be inherited by X, and vice versa.

In cases such as this, the system must do what people seem to do: think about the two descriptions and their role-mappings in sequence, but never both at once. This can be accomplished by placing the conflicting views in separate context-areas, which are arranged in such a way that they will never both be activated together. The conflicting descriptions of NECKER-CUBE then become maps of the original NECKER-CUBE node in two incompatible viewing-contexts, as shown in figure 29. In order to find which contexts to activate as views, we look in the VIEW role of the basic NECKER-CUBE description. When the system wants to look at the description of some object which has VIEW-contexts listed, it should consider the object from each of these viewpoints, one at a time, in order to get the object's full description.

Alternate-view situations like the one described above are relatively uncommon and can be handled with little trouble. I have described them here because they are the clearest example of copy-confusion in action. We will now look at two cases that are far more subtle and dangerous.

The first situation arises when a thing and one (or more) of its roles are both described as instances of a single superior type-description; I therefore call this the *recursive description problem*. Such cases are far more common than one might, at first, suspect: a PERSON has a MOTHER who is also a PERSON; an ELEPHANT is a PHYSOB, with a set of parts that are also PHYSOBS; an AMPLIFIER may consist of STAGES that are also AMPLIFIERS, and so on. The problem is that, if we are not careful in constructing our scanning protocols, we will confuse the two copies of this shared description. We might, if we are not careful, end up equating CLYDE's WEIGHT (a role inherited from the PHYSOB description) with CLYDE's TRUNK's WEIGHT.

Figure 30 illustrates how this might happen. Note that at the ELEPHANT level there are nodes for the elephant's TRUNK

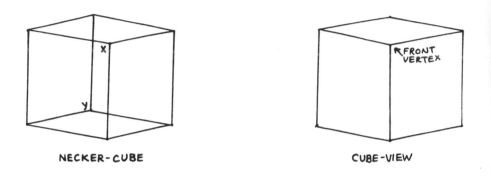

NECKER-CUBE

CUBE-VIEW

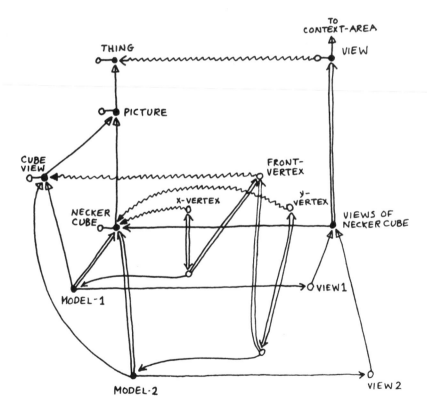

Figure 29: Two views of a NECKER-CUBE as a CUBE-VIEW.

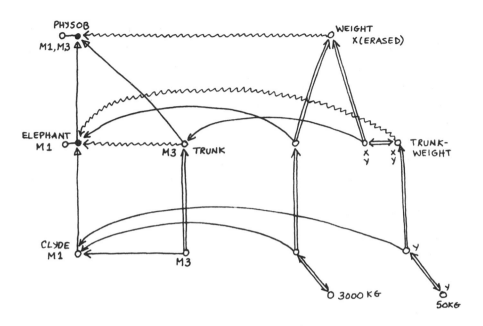

Figure 30: A recursive description: the WEIGHT of the TRUNK of CLYDE.

(a PHYSOB), the WEIGHT of the ELEPHANT, and the WEIGHT of the TRUNK. This latter node is equated to a TRUNK-WEIGHT role that is tied directly to the ELEPHANT description. (Operations of this sort are very common as a way of reducing the depth of nesting of an expression, as when we turn the BROTHER of a PARENT of a PERSON into an UNCLE of that PERSON.) Since the *EQ-link is inherited, we ought to be able to specify either the WEIGHT of the TRUNK of CLYDE or the TRUNK-WEIGHT of CLYDE with the same results; in the figure, we have stated that the TRUNK-WEIGHT of CLYDE is 50-KILOGRAMS.

Now, suppose we are asked to find the WEIGHT of the TRUNK of CLYDE. As we saw earlier in a similar example, we

first activate the CLYDE description by propagating M1 up all
*VC-links and parent-wires from CLYDE, and across any
*EQ-links. As a general rule, we use marker-bits in pairs: every
time we activate a description-copy with one marker, we want to
indicate cancellations within that copy with another.
Consequently, we now propagate M2 markers across all
*CANCEL-links from M1-marked nodes; there do not happen to
be any cancellations in the fragment of network shown, but we
can assume that there will be some elsewhere in the CLYDE
description. The next step is to activate the TRUNK description
within the CLYDE activation: we take marker M3, place it on
the TRUNK role, and propagate it across all M1-activated
map-wires, across all *EQ-links, and up all *VC-links. M4 marks
the cancellations within *this* description; again, none are shown.
The locations of the M1 and M3 markers at this point are shown
in figure 30.

Now we are ready to investigate the WEIGHT role. We
place marker M5 on the WEIGHT node (which is found in the
PIIYSOB description) and propagate this across *EQ links, up
*VC-links, and across all currently-activated map-wires. But what
exactly do we mean by "currently activated"? Should we cross
only M3-activated wires or, since we are really within both the
CLYDE description and the TRUNK description, should we
cross M1-activated map-wires as well? The latter answer must be
the right one, since it is the only way to get to the node that we
want, the one representing 50 kilograms. It also makes sense
from all that we have said about virtual copies: we are still
operating within the CLYDE description; therefore, the
map-wires within this description should still be shorted.
Unfortunately, because of confusion between CLYDE's own copy
of the PIIYSOB description and the copy representing CLYDE's
TRUNK, the M5 markers find their way to CLYDE's own
WEIGHT, 3000-KILOGRAMS, as well as to the desired
50-KILOGRAMS node. We must indeed activate both the inner
and outer descriptions, but if they share a parent (and all
descriptions do at the THING level, if not lower) we must be

sure that the roles in the two copies of this parent are not confused.

To accomplish this, we must let the ELEPHANT description and the TRUNK description use their respective copies of the shared PHYSOB description at different times, so that there will never be any confusion about which copy is in use. The first steps proceed exactly as before: CLYDE is activated with M1, CLYDE's cancellations with M2, CLYDE's trunk with M3, and the trunk's cancellations with M4. Figure 30 shows these markers in position. Now, we start M5 at the WEIGHT node, and propagate it up *VC-links, across *EQ-links, and across *only those map-wires that have been activated by M3*. If there are descriptions being shared between the inner M3 activation (Clyde's trunk) and the outer M1 activation (Clyde himself), and if M5 is marking a shared role in that shared description (as it is here), this step will make use only of the inner description's copy. This results in M5 markers on all of the nodes marked with an X in figure 30.

Next, we want to propagate the M5 markers through the connections of the outer (Clyde) description, marked with M1, *but first we must clean out from any shared parent-descriptions the M5 marks that are left over from the inner (trunk) description's use of these shared parents.* This is done by clearing (in one parallel step) the M5 mark from any role-node or *MAP-node whose owner-node contains both the M1 and M3 marks; in this example, only the M5 mark on the WEIGHT node of PHYSOB is erased. The remaining M5 markers are then propagated up *VC-links, across *EQ links, and across map-wires activated by M1. The resulting set of M5 nodes is indicated by the letter Y in figure 30. By this method, the desired 50-KILOGRAM node is reached, but the confusion of Clyde's weight with his trunk's weight is avoided.

Can this erasing step throw away useful information? Questions of this sort are hard to answer, but in this case I believe that we are safe. We are, after all, erasing only those marks which are on nodes internal to the inner

TRUNK-description, and we are not going to use that description again in this access-request. If we think of the TRUNK-description as a box, it seems evident that the outside world can only make use of markers which reach nodes outside the box, or at least nodes on the surface of the box -- the roles and *MAP-nodes that appear on the TRUNK level itself, rather than on some level above TRUNK. The erasing process will never alter any of these exterior or surface nodes (the surface nodes can never be shared), but will only remove certain M5 marks that are hidden within the box. In any event, I have not found any examples of situations in which the erasure-step causes trouble, and it seems essential for avoiding confusion among recursively-shared copies.

If we want to extend this process to four levels of role-nesting, we just activate the three outer levels with M1, M3, and M5, exactly as described above. The cancellations within these three description activations are marked by M2, M4, and M6, respectively. We then place yet another marker, M7, on the fourth-level role that we want to look at, and propagate this marker with respect to the M5 activation. M7 is then carried back out through the M3 and M1 activations, as before, erasing any possibly-confusing M7 markers as we move to each outer level. We can extend this method to handle as many levels of role-nesting as we like, though the number of activation scans required (this is the expensive step) increases more than linearly with nesting-depth; for N levels of nesting, counting both the innermost and outermost levels, the number of activation scans required is $(N^2-N+2)/2$.

Long before we encounter any difficulty with computation times, however, we will run out of marker-bit pairs. Of the current set of fifteen markers, six pairs are available for such explorations. (As we saw in the last section, three markers are reserved for the context-activation system.) Consequently, we can handle about six levels of role-nesting before we run out of markers. It is possible to handle additional nesting levels by borrowing markers form outer activations, using them for inner

ones, and then restoring them, but even at six levels we have
gone somewhat beyond the sort of trivial deduction that is
properly the concern of the knowledge-base system. It seems
unreasonable that we would have any real-world need for
statements about the nature of the A of the B of the C of the D
of the E of the F, without being able to rephrase such statements
in terms of some less-deeply-nested structure. For a roughly
human-like level of performance, then, the current fifteen
marker-bits should be more than enough.

The third situation in which copy-confusion plays a role
is even more difficult to handle. So far, we have always come
into virtual-copy descriptions through the base-node of the
description -- the *INDV or *TYPE-node around which the
structure of roles and mappings is built. To activate such a
description, we have simply started a marker on the base-node
and sent it up *VC-links and parent wires, and across all
*EQ-links. (We should also cross any map-wire whose owner is
a part of the current context-area, but we will get to that later.)
Once this activation is complete, we can investigate any roles and
relationships within it using the scanning protocols described
above. As we have seen, this leads to an orderly implementation
of the virtual-copy semantics, with little chance that any
information will be missed unless we look at a role that is so
deeply nested that we run out of marker-bits.

Sometimes we are handed a node to activate that is not
itself a base-node, but is instead a *MAP node in some
unspecified description. This case is not much harder, since we
can find the owning-description's base-node simply by following
the owner-wire of the *MAP-node. The owner can then be
activated, and the *MAP-node is investigated within the owner's
activation, just as we saw earlier. If the owner-node is itself a
*MAP-node within some still larger description, we trace back
the chain of owner-wires until, finally, we reach a *TYPE-node
or an *INDV-node. This outermost description is activated, and
we then work our way back through the nested *MAP-nodes until
we reach the original one, using the successive activation process

described above. Assuming, again, that the nesting-depth is not too great for the available set of marker-bits to handle, this gives us an orderly activation of the original *MAP-node which we can use to investigate *its* properties and roles. I call this style of processing, in which a map-wire is never crossed until the owner-node's description has been activated, *legitimate activation*: it is the approved and safe way to look at the identities and properties associated with a given *MAP-node.

Unfortunately, situations often occur in which there are many *MAP-nodes that we want to investigate at once, and we cannot afford to legitimately activate their descriptions one at a time. Suppose, for example, the knowledge-base is asked for the AGE of CLYDE. First, of course, we activate CLYDE's *intrinsic* description by marking up *VC links and across *EQ links; then we look for an AGE role within this activated description. We might find such a role, but let us assume that we do not. We are not done yet since, in addition to the usual collection of *TYPE nodes and an occasional pseudo-individual node, the intrinsic activation scan probably will have marked a large collection of *MAP nodes. These *MAP-nodes represent *extrinsic* descriptions of Clyde: roles that Clyde plays in descriptions for which he is not the base-node or the central thing being described. (The terms "intrinsic" and "extrinsic" are used here in ways that roughly correspond to their usage in the electronic reasoning system proposed by Sussman and Brown [1974].) Even though Clyde is a mere role-player in these extrinsic descriptions, any one of these roles could have an attached property specifying his age. If we want to be thorough, then, we must activate and examine all of these descriptions -- otherwise we might report that Clyde's age is unknown when, in fact, we know it.

The proper way to perform this investigation, if we could afford the time, would be to legitimately activate the description associated with each of the *MAP-nodes, one at a time, in sequence. Unfortunately, in many individual descriptions there are very many of these nodes, sometimes many times the number of *TYPE-nodes in the description. The system's representation for a person, for example, will have a *MAP-node for every action, every relationship, and every statement in which that person is known to have played a role. To activate each of these extrinsic descriptions individually would be to completely destroy the parallel speed advantage that we have worked so hard to achieve. If our knowledge-base system is to enjoy both the speed of the parallel network and the precision and elegance of the virtual copy semantics, we must find some way to search these *MAP-node descriptions in parallel.

The first solution that springs to mind is simply to mark *up* all of the map-wires at once, without bothering to activate the descriptions in which the *MAP-nodes are found. This will indeed find *most* of the description-nodes which might be associated with the property we are looking for. Unfortunately, it will miss some role-nodes that a legitimate scan would find, and it will find some spurious nodes that, in a legitimate scan, would have been cancelled. The missed cancellations occur because the *CANCEL links originate in the base-node of a description and, in this upward-only scan through the role-nodes, we never visit the base-nodes. Some description nodes are missed because, as we saw in section 3.5, markers must sometimes cross an activated *MAP-wire in the *downward* direction. This downward motion, you will recall, had two uses: it made it possible for map-wires to skip over uninteresting levels in the type-hierarchy, a useful but not essential feature; it also made it possible for us to virtually copy structures that have *VC-relationships among their roles. This latter ability is esential to the proper handling of set-roles, and to the conceptual integrity of the virtual-copy idea as a whole. The upward-only approach, then, can find most of the properties that are hidden in the extrinsic descriptions of CLYDE, but it is too unreliable to be used by itself.

Perhaps, then, we should activate the descriptions containing the *MAP-nodes after all, but all at once. By activating the descriptions in parallel, we would avoid any serious degradation of the system's speed. Since there can be an arbitrarily large number of these activations going on at once, we cannot assign a distinct marker-bit to each of them; a single bit will have to be used for all. Once the descriptions containing the *MAP-nodes have been activated, and the resulting cancellations have been marked, we can resume our original activation-scan for CLYDE, allowing the markers to flow through any map-wires that are active within the newly-created set of active extrinsic descriptions. If this leads us to still more extrinsic descriptions for CLYDE, we simply repeat the mass-activation process.

This mass-activation approach brings us much closer to the results that we would achieve with individual legitimate activations, but there are still problems. First of all, there is the problem of variable activation-depth. As I noted earlier, some legitimate activations require lengthy activation processes because the original *MAP node is not a first-level role within its description, but is nested within a set of other *MAP-nodes. It is hard to see how a parallel activation scan, handling many descriptions at once, could be made to handle such variation in levels.

In addition, we might find that the base-node of an activation has its own set of extrinsic descriptions. If we want to be really thorough, we must investigate these as well. Chains of this sort can go on indefinitely: Clyde is the brother of Ernie; Ernie is the mate of Ernestine; Ernestine is the daughter of Fred; and so on. If we arbitrarily cut this chain off at Ernestine, and if the system has stored with FRED some statement about the AGE of his daughter's mate's brother, we will miss this fact in our search. Again, it is hard to see how a mass-activation approach could handle variable-depth chains of this sort. Even an individual legitimate scan would have to give up on such arbitrarily long and bushy chains at some point -- we are, after all, trying to build a knowledge-base and not a general theorem-prover -- but it is hard to see how the mass-activation scan could cope with this chaining at all.

But the most serious problem facing the mass-activation approach is our old friend, the copy-confusion problem. If we use a single marker-bit to activate many descriptions, and if two of these descriptions are descended from the same parent-description, and if CLYDE plays a different role in the two descriptions in question, we can get some serious errors. Figure 31 shows such a situation. We have a greatly simplified version of the FAMILY description, in which there are roles only for the FATHER and a single CHILD. The assertion is made that in any such FAMILY, there is a LOVES relation from FATHER to CHILD. (The LOVES arrow here is a shorthand for the full-blown LOVES statement, as described in section 3.6.) There are two copies of this FAMILY description, F1 and F2. In F1, CLYDE is the SON of JUMBO; in F2, CLYDE is the FATHER of JUNIOR. If, in investigating the CLYDE description, we activate both of these copies of FAMILY with the same marker-bit, errors can slip in. All of the *MAP-nodes become shorted, and the descriptions of CLYDE, JUMBO, and JUNIOR are all run together. Furthermore, we can deduce incorrect results such as "CLYDE LOVES CLYDE". It would appear, then, that the mass-activation approach is no more reliable than the upward-only marking scheme: though it finds more of CLYDE's property-bearing nodes, it still misses a few; though it gets most of the cancellations right, it finds spurious nodes because of copy-confusion.

We appear to have reached an impasse: legitimate individual investigation of extrinsic-description *MAP-nodes is too slow; marking upward across all the map-wires in parallel violates the virtual-copy semantics; and activating the descriptions in parallel with a single marker-bit leads us into copy-confusion. Is there any reasonable solution to this problem? I see four possible approaches. First, we might try to use the mass-activation approach after all, but to detect and handle separately those relatively few cases in which copy-confusion might occur. This seems like an attractive solution, but after a lot of trying I have not been able to make it

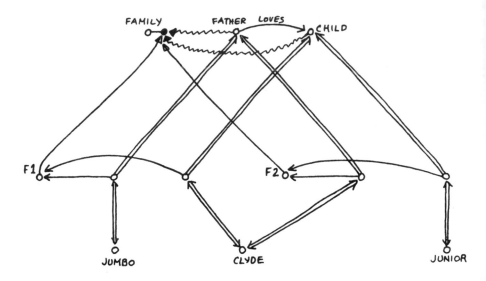

Figure 31: CLYDE as the CHILD in one family, the **FATHER** in another.

work. It is easy enough to detect the confusing situations on a case-by-case basis, but that is almost as bad as doing the legitimate scans in sequence; what is needed is a parallel method for detecting when the property or relationship about to be retrieved is coming from one of the possibly-confused descriptions. I am not yet sure whether it is impossible to do this, or just very difficult.

A second possibility is to abandon the virtual-copy semantics, at least with respect to two-way inheritance across map-wires. This would allow us to use the upward-only marking scheme, but at grave cost to the elegance and clarity of the system. Map-wires could still be skipped over vacant levels of the hierarchy, but if a *MAP-node is ever created on such a skipped level, we will have to go back and re-connect all of the map-wires for the same role that skip over this level. Also, when a copy is made of some description, the system would have to explicitly write into the copy any *VC or *EQ links that are to exist between roles of that copy; such links could no longer be inherited. Many other changes would be required in the semantics as well, almost all of them in the direction of greater obscurity. I feel that this approach should be taken only as a last resort, since it greatly increases the need for redundant storage of information, and it destroys whatever clarity was gained by the use of the virtual copy idea.

A third approach would be to use the mass-activation scheme, but to avoid the possibility of copy-confusion by marking each activation in a different way, and by using corresponding markers to explore the roles within each activation. In effect, we are performing an individual legitimate scan for each activation, but we are using separate markers instead of time to keep any possibly-confusing activations apart. The easiest way to implement this would be to replace the simple hardware elements of the network with micro-computers of some sort. These would be able to store a large number of aritrary activation-symbols at once and to match these symbols against any arbitrary exploration-marker symbols that want to pass through a given connection. The element-to-element connections in the network would cither have to be widened to accommodate marker-symbols many bits wide, or the network elements would have to break these symbols down and transmit them serially. Serial bottlenecks can develop when a number of symbols arrive at a node at once, but in most cases the resulting serial queues would be much smaller than the original set of *MAP-nodes. Grossman [1976] has investigated a system of this sort for a variety of knowledge-base and logical problems. At present, this seems a needlessly complex and economically unattractive solution, but improvements in the available technology might make it more reasonable. (Genesereth [not yet published] has extended and streamlined Grossman's system to work with single-bit markers, but in this modified form the system is unable to use the unique-label method outlined above.)

The fourth solution is the one that seems to me the most promising, and is the one that I am using in the current version of NETL. This approach uses the individual legitimate activation of a *MAP-node description in finding the final answer to a query, but it uses the other, less reliable activation methods that we have discussed as a *parallel heuristic test* to determine which of the extrinsic descriptions might contain information relevant to the query at hand. This gives use the speed and near-total coverage of the upward-only and mass-activation approaches, while filtering out any spurious responses with the legitimate confirmation-test. A few possibly relevant nodes will be missed by this approach, but it is my feeling that this shortcoming is one that we can live with. Depending on the exact trade-off that we want between speed and thoroughness, there are a number of parallel heuristic search-strategies that can be employed.

Let us assume, once again, that we are looking for the AGE of CLYDE, that we have already marked CLYDE's intrinsic superiors and equals in the type-hierarchy, and that we have failed to find an AGE property. If we are really in a hurry, we would quit at this point; otherwise, we must look for an AGE property in the extrinsic descriptions that we have found for CLYDE. We would begin with a first-order heuristic scan, the fastest and least thorough. This is simply the strategy of marking upward across *MAP-wires. As we noted above, this process finds most of the remaining description-nodes for CLYDE, but it misses some and finds a few that should be cancelled. If any of the nodes reached by this upward sweep has an AGE property, we follow the trail of markers back down from this node to its source: the *MAP-node in our original set which represents this particular role. This is the node which we want to activate legitimately, to see whether the AGE property is really there or has been cancelled. If there are several *MAP-nodes leading to roles with an AGE property, it is probably worthwhile to investigate them all until we find a winner.

If we want to spend more time and be more thorough in our search, we can use a second-order heuristic scan. This consists of a mass activation of the descriptions associated with all the *MAP-nodes in our set. This activation only goes one level deep: if some of the *MAP-nodes have owners that are *MAP-nodes, these will be marked by the upward-only method; if some of the owner-nodes have extrinsic descriptions of their own, these are ignored. Once this description-set is activated and the local cancellation markers have been placed, we send out a role-exploration marker from the *MAP-nodes in the original set. Again we test for an AGE property in the marked set of role-nodes. Again, if we find such a property, we trace the path of the markers back to the *MAP-node responsible. Again, we activate this node individually to see if we have indeed found a valid AGE property, or merely one attached to a node that we reached by confusion. More spurious candidates will be found by this method than by the first-order scan, but more genuine nodes will be reached as well.

The second-order scan finds still more of the nodes that we might want to look at, but there is still a small residue of unexamined nodes that might carry the information we need. These can be reached by higher-level heuristic scans which carry the mass-activation to greater depth: chains of *MAP-nodes are followed, as are the extrinsic descriptions of the owner-nodes. As this deepening progresses, however, we will find fewer and fewer genuine role-nodes equivalent to CLYDE, and more and more nodes that are reached by confusion. The point of diminishing returns will be reached at some level, but we will have found answers to the vast majority of queries, if indeed such answers are present. Only facts stored in terms of long role-chains will be missed by this process, and no spurious answers will make it past the legitimate-scan filter.

Note that a bit of housekeeping, performed when the system has nothing better to do, can improve the performance of the heuristic search mechanisms considerably. The network of map-wires can be rearranged to eliminate any unnecessary skipping of occupied levels, making more nodes accessible to the first-order upward-only search. Statements made about roles at the end of a long chain of other roles can, when the role is filled with an *INDV, be transferred to the *INDV node. In some cases, it is useful to create pseudo-individuals to fill roles in the middle of long role-chains; this tends to break up the chains into more manageable sections. Often a chain of relationships can be shortened by substituting other, more direct relations, as when we replace PARENT's BROTHER with UNCLE. I have only begun to develop the precise criteria for identifying cases in which such techniques can be usefully applied; much more thought and experience is needed in this area.

Note, too, that the query often gives us a hint as to which extrinsic description might contain the information we are looking for; such hints can often be used in lieu of the heuristic search techniques described above. If I ask you whether "George Washington, the boy who chopped down the cherry tree," owned a hatchet, it will be easier to answer than if I ask whether "the first president of the United States" ever, in his life, owned a hatchet. The same principle can be applied by NETL in selecting descriptions to look at.

How seriously is the system hurt by this need to use heuristics in finding roles and statements stored with the extrinsic descriptions of an object? In my opinion, the damage is not too serious. We would, of course, prefer a system with instant access to everything it knows, regardless of the form in which it is stored, but NETL still comes much closer to this goal than serial-search systems. We have, when all is said and done, a system that is still fast and parallel, that always finds those properties and relations stored with the intrinsic descriptions of an object, that finds *almost* all of the properties and relations stored with extrinsic descriptions, and that never returns a spurious answer (unless, of course, it has been fed bad information). The properties that it misses are those that are stored in terms of nested roles and other rather obscure descriptive structures, and even these can be found if the query specifies its subject in the same way as the statement being sought, or if we want to spend the time to do a thorough serial search of the extrinsic descriptions. This tendency to overlook an occasional piece of information -- to miss making an occasional connection between two different descriptions for an object -- seems rather human-like to me, and people seem to get along reasonably well with shortcomings such as this in their knowledge-accessing processes. The parallel portions of the system are not complete, in the logician's sense, but they were never intended to be; we wanted to be able to do the most important deductions very fast, and I believe that NETL still does that.

The copy-confusion problem, in its various guises, is principally a problem of properly implementing an essentially correct semantic notation in a parallel manner; the binding-ambiguity problem, on the other hand, results from a shortcoming of the semantic notation itself. Basically, the problem results from our definition of the *TYPE-node as representing "the typical member" or "every member" of some set. This is a perfectly workable definition when we are concerned only with attaching properties to the *TYPE-node, but when we want to extend the system to statements with two or more arguments, this definition can lead to ambiguous structures. The ambiguity arises when both arguments of a statement (or two arguments if there are more than two) are attached to the same *TYPE-node, or to two roles within a single type-description. It is clear that each of the arguments can refer to any individual within the class defined by the *TYPE-node; the issue is whether both connections must refer to the same arbitrarily-chosen individual, or whether each connection represents an individual choice. In other words, when is the binding of an individual to the *TYPE-description made -- once for the whole description, or once per connection?

Consider the structure in figure 32. (Once again, the HATES arrow is a shorthand for a full-scale HATES statement,

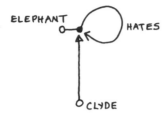

Figure 32: An example of binding ambiguity.

built around an *IST node.) This could be interpreted in two
possible ways: "Every elephant hates every elephant" or "Every
elephant hates himself." When we are looking at an instance of
ELEPHANT like CLYDE, is there a single virtual HATES
statement connecting CLYDE to himself, or is there a virtual
HATES statement from CLYDE to ELEPHANT and from
ELEPHANT to CLYDE? A case could be made for either
interpretation.

It is not really important which interpretation we choose
for the situation as shown, as long as we are consistent in this
choice; it *is* important, however, that the system include some
reasonably direct way of representing the interpretation that is
not chosen. If NETL is to provide us with a more-or-less
complete coverage of the things that we might say in English, it
must be possible to say that every elephant hates every elephant
(including himself), that every elephant hates himself, and that
every elephant hates every *other* elephant (but not himself).
Individual elephants must inherit these statements properly.
Ideally, the single HATES statement would also function
properly in reverse, to give us the assertion that every elephant is
hated by every elephant, himself, or every other elephant, as the
case may be, without our having to store this equivalent fact
separately.

Though this problem has been popping up in various forms for a while, each of its manifestations was dealt with separately; it is only recently that I have isolated binding-ambiguity as a single problem, in the terms described here. There are several possible ways of changing the NETL notation to eliminate this problem, and I have not yet made a final decision as to which of these alternatives is the best. The scheme that I will present here is the one that currently looks the best to me.

Let us establish, by decree, that the proper interpretation of figure 32 is that every ELEPHANT hates himself (or herself or itself). This convention seems to be the most natural one to adopt within the overall framework of virtual copies: it means that the descriptive links attached to the *TYPE-node all refer to the same individual at any given time. We are free to chose any individual from the type-class to bind to this type-description, but a single binding, is used for all of the connections that are made to the *TYPE-node.

That solves half of the problem; we must now find some way to connect a statement between two *distinct* individual bindings of a given *TYPE-node. In other words, how do we say that every elephant hates every other elephant? We can do this by introducing a new node-type, the *OTHER-node, which is connected to a *TYPE-node by a wire called the *type-wire*. To say that every elephant hates every other elephant, we would connect the *OTHER node as shown in figure 33. The *OTHER-node represents a single arbitrary individual chosen from the *TYPE-node's set, but it is a different individual from the one currently bound to the *TYPE-node itself. Figure 32 can be read as follows: "For every individual elephant X, X hates X." Figure 33, then, would say, "For every two distinct individual elephants, X and Y, X hates Y." Since CLYDE can be bound either to X or to Y, the statement is symmetrical: CLYDE hates, and is hated by, every other elephant.

If we want to say that every elephant hates every elephant, including himself, we must represent the self-hatred and

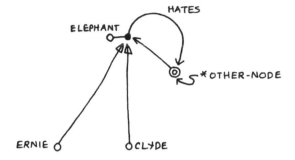

Figure 33: "Every elephant hates every other elephant."

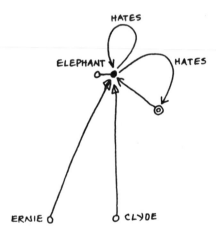

Figure .34: "Every elephant hates every elephant, including himself."

the other-hatred as separate links, as shown in figure 34. A hates link from the *OTHER-node to itself would be redundant, since each individual in the class can be bound to the *TYPE-node, and can pick up its self-hatred there. The representation of this "every-to-every" case is somewhat more awkward than the "self" and "every other" cases, but this case is also strangely awkward to express in English; perhaps something comparable is going on.

How do these changes affect the system during knowledge-base accesses? Suppose we want to compile a list of all the individuals that CLYDE hates. First, we activate CLYDE in the usual way, marking all of CLYDE's ancestor-nodes with M1. M2 marks are placed to record any cancellations relevant to CLYDE. We then send another marker, M3, across any active, non-cancelled HATES-statements that originate on M1-marked nodes. These M3 markers are then propagated in different ways, depending on what type of node they have reached. Those on M1-marked *TYPE-nodes (nodes currently bound to CLYDE) are not propagated at all, but simply cause an M3 mark to be placed on the CLYDE node. Any M3 markers on *TYPE-nodes without an M1-mark (currently unbound) are propagated down into all the individuals in their respective sets. M3 markers that reach *OTHER-nodes are propagated down into all individuals within their *TYPE-nodes' sets *except for CLYDE.* In each case, cancellation marks (M4) are sent out as the HATES statement is crossed, to block any individuals for whom the HATES statement is cancelled; the M3 markers will not enter or pass through M4-marked nodes.

We are not quite done yet: we have not yet considered any HATES statements connected from the *OTHER-nodes attached to *TYPE-nodes above CLYDE in the hierarchy. As we said earlier, each individual can also be bound to these nodes, but not at the same time that the individual is bound to the *TYPE-node. In principle, then, we should run the whole scan again, looking for HATES-statements connected to the *OTHER nodes above CLYDE. Actually, this is not really necessary: the

only case we might have missed is a HATES statement from an
*OTHER-node to its own *TYPE-node, corresponding to the
statement that every elephant is hated by every other.
Connections from an *OTHER node to itself or to a
*TYPE-node other than its own could have (and should have)
been placed on the *TYPE-node instead. We can check for the
one allowed case directly, and if it is found we can simply mark
all of the other elephants (or whatever), but not CLYDE.

This *OTHER-node mechanism can be extended to
handle three or more individual bindings chosen from a given
type-class. We might, for instance, want to say that for any
three distinct elephants, X, Y, and Z, the combination of X and
Y can defeat Z at tug-of-war. (In other words, no elephant is
stronger than any two others combined.) The *TYPE-node itself
represents the first binding (X), an *OTHER-node is used for
the second binding (Y), and the third binding (Z) is represented
by another *OTHER-node. This second *OTHER-node is
connected to the first one by its *TYPE-wire, forming a chain of
successive individual bindings. In principle, such chains can
reach any desired length, up to and including the total size of
the type-class in question; in practice, the length is limited to
the number of available marker-bits. As each individual in the
set is bound to one of the variables, a unique marker-bit must be
placed on the *INDV node of the individual and the *OTHER or
*TYPE-node to which we are binding it. If we cross a
statement-link and enter an *OTHER-node without such a
binding-marker, we are free to assign any individual in the
type-set to that variable, as long as the individual is not already
bound to some other node in the chain. The scans responsible
for all of this can become extremely complex as they try to
consider all possible bindings, but that seems reasonable: beyond
two or maybe three variables, people -- especially children -- have
trouble as well. The notation, at least, seems clear and
unambiguous, even if the associated processes are difficult to
construct and use.

My remaining uneasiness with this notation concerns the way it interacts with the use of multiple contexts. It may be necessary to state, in a much more explicit way than is possible with simple *OTHER-nodes, the exact context-area in which a given individual binding is made. Consider, for example, the subtle difference in meaning between the statements "Any player in the lottery can be a winner," and "Every player in the lottery can be a winner." In the former, we are choosing a single individual from the set of players *in the current context*, and are claiming that this arbitrary individual might, when winners are chosen, be one of them. In the latter case, we are saying that it is possible that, after the drawing, the set of players and the set of winners will be equivalent; this means that we can *then* choose any individual player and find that he is a winner. Comparable things happen when the contexts in question refer to states of knowledge or the belief systems of different people. Bob Moore [1973] has explored ways of handling such problems using an explicit lambda-binding mechanism, but I do not at present see any good way of incorporating his insights into NETL notation. This looks like a fruitful area for further research.

3.8 Defined Classes and Negation

Suppose we want to represent the assertion that every purple mushroom is poisonous. We cannot simply add POISONOUS and PURPLE as properties to the MUSHROOM *TYPE-node, since that would signify something completely different: that the typical mushroom is both poisonous and purple. Instead, we must somehow create a *defined class* that includes every purple mushroom, and attach the POISONOUS property to its *TYPE-node. Note that there are two different kinds of properties at work here: PURPLE, which is part of the definition of the class, and POISONOUS, which merely says something about the members of the class; the notation must somehow indicate which properties are part of the definition. As new mushrooms are added to the system, we must check whether they are purple and, if so, place them in this defined purple-mushroom class. Once they are in this class, the mushrooms inherit the incidental property of poisonousness.

To represent such defined classes, we need a new type of node, the *EVERY-node. An *EVERY-node is a special kind of *TYPE-node which *defines* a set, rather than merely *describing* the set's members. Some of the properties and statements attached to the *EVERY node are specially marked as defining properties; together, these defining properties constitute the *EVERY-node's *specification*. The rest of the information attached to an *EVERY-node is called *incidental information*: it plays no part in determining which individuals fit into the defined class, but it does apply to these individuals once their membership is established. During normal access operations in the knowledge-base, both kinds of properties behave identically, and the *EVERY-node is indistinguishable from a normal *TYPE-node. The difference between these node-types appears during the process of digesting new information in the knowledge-base: as new individual and type-descriptions are added, the digestion processes match the new description against each of the *EVERY-node specifications. If a match is found,

the new item is placed in the matching class by the creation of a
*VC-link from the item to the *EVERY-node. Existing
descriptions which are altered or augmented are re-checked, to
see whether the new version matches an *EVERY-node class.

An *EVERY-node has three defined wires. First there is
a set-wire which connects the *EVERY-node to the set that it
defines. The other two wires indicate a *parent* and a *scope* for
the *EVERY-node. These serve as the core of the node's
specification: if the parent is MUSHROOM and the scope is
NORTH-AMERICA, the *EVERY node would represent "every
mushroom in North America" which also meets the rest of the
specification, and the set would be the set of all such
mushrooms. Note that the scope-area is activated through the
hierarchy of areas and sub-areas just as a statement's scope is
activated: if the scope is NORTH-AMERICA, it is meant to
include *every part of North America*. If we activate a particular
context-area, we must activate all of the context areas of which it
is a part in order to find the set of possibly-relevant
*EVERY-nodes.

The parent and the scope are automatically part of the
*EVERY-node's specification. The rest of the specification
consists of a set of statements that are marked with the **SPEC
flag and are tied to the *EVERY-node by their *spec-wires*. Each
such statement is referred to as a *clause* of the specification. No
clause may be part of the specification of more than one
*EVERY-node. The spec-wire is needed because the **SPEC flag
alone is not sufficient to indicate which *EVERY-node a clause
belongs to. The spec-wire also makes it possible for the matcher
to quickly locate all of the clauses which it must check in
considering a given *EVERY-node. In addition to statements,
*INDV nodes can serve as clauses, indicating that some
individual with a matching description must *exist* if that clause is
to be fulfilled. These *INDV-node clauses serve as additional
variables to use during the matching process, much as
pattern-variables are used in standard data-base matchers.

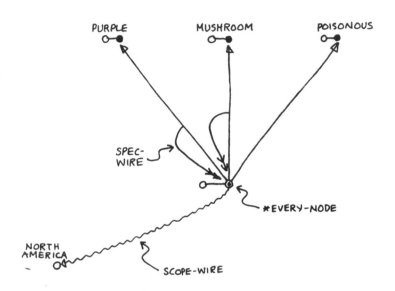

Figure 35: "Every purple mushroom in North America is poisonous."

Figure 35 shows the statement that every purple mushroom in North America is poisonous. The connections to MUSHROOM, to NORTH-AMERICA, and to PURPLE are clauses in the specification; the connection to POISONOUS is an incidental property attached to the defined class. The double-barbed arrow represents the spec-wire. (The spec-wire from the parent-wire connection is implicit, but since we draw parent-wires and *VC-links alike, we must show this implicit spec wire to avoid confusion.) Note that adjectives like PURPLE and POISONOUS are represented as *TYPE-classes -- more about this later.

With this relatively simple set of conventions, we can create arbitrarily complex class-definitions. Figure 36 shows the

*EVERY-node for "every mean dog who hates every slow mailman"; the dog, the mailman, and the act of hating all are scoped within REAL-U. If the spec-wire from the HATES statement went instead to the SLOW-MAILMAN *EVERY-node, we would have a representation for "every slow mailman who is hated by every mean dog"; if the HATES statement had no **SPEC flag or spec-wire at all, the diagram would represent the declarative statement, "Every mean dog hates every slow mailman." The connection of the spec-wire is therefore very important.

By rearranging the positions of the existence wires, we can handle various kinds of quantification. Figure 37 shows the statement that every mean dog who hates *any* slow mailman hates Fred (who is also a slow mailman). The node marked M in the diagram is an example of the use of an *INDV-node as a clause: it states that there must exist some individual who is a slow mailman, and which the dog in question hates, if this part of the specification is to be fulfilled. Figure 38 represents the statement that any person who owns a dog that hates Fred also hates Fred. Figure 39 shows the statement that any person whose father is a mailman *likes* Fred. And so on.

As we noted in section 3.6, there is a hierarchy of statement-types in NETL, ranging from very general types at high levels to more specialized forms farther down. As these specializations are made, we want to distinguish between properties that define the specialized forms and properties that are incidentally true of statements of the specialized type. This is done by representing the specialized statement-types as *EVERY-nodes instead of the ususal *TYPE-nodes. Figure 40 shows the specialization of the OWNS statement to OWNS-SLAVE, only this time done right: the PROPERTY argument being a PERSON is a part of the definition, but the statement that the relationship is illegal is not.

The *EVERY-node matcher, which is responsible for fitting newly-created items into the proper *EVERY-node classes, is really an open-ended collection of matching techniques. When

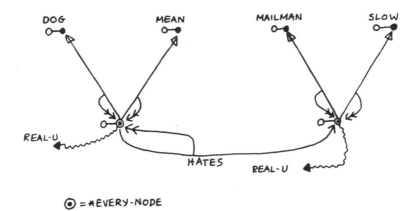

⊙ = *EVERY-NODE

↑ = SPEC-WIRE

Figure 36: "Every mean dog who hates every slow mailman ..."

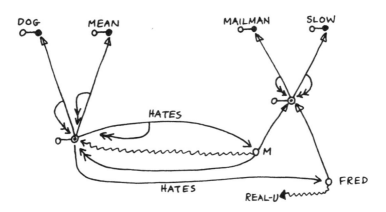

Figure 37: "Every mean dog who hates any slow mailman hates Fred."

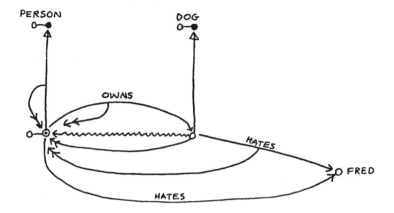

Figure 38: "Any person who owns a dog that hates Fred also hates Fred."

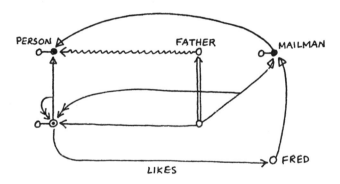

Figure 39: "Any person whose father is a mailman likes Fred."

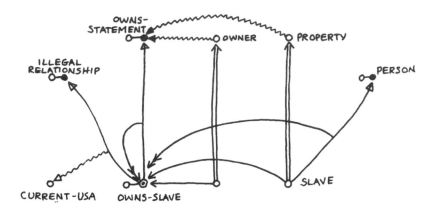

Figure 40: Every OWNS statement in which the PROPERTY is a PERSON is an OWN-SLAVE statement.

the system is in a hurry, only a minimal effort is expended to check each clause for satisfaction; if the system has more time, or is really interested in establishing whether some incidental property of an *EVERY-node class is true for some item, it might work much harder in trying to establish a given clause. The *EVERY-node matching process, then, is one of the interfaces between the knowledge-base system and the serial problem-solving components of an intelligent system. Many implication rules can be expressed clearly and unambiguously in *EVERY-node form, even though the quick parallel matcher will only find the easiest and most obvious of the matches. If a potential match is missed by the digestion processes, the system can still come back later and use the *EVERY-node in consequent-fashion (to use the PLANNER term) to establish some result that is needed at the time. If the system wants to establish that some mushroom is poisonous, and it cannot find that fact directly, it can look for an *EVERY node that would imply poisonousness; the PURPLE-MUSHROOM node would be found, and the system could try to establish that the mushroom in question is purple. That, in turn, might lead to yet another *EVERY-node, and so on. If it knows which *EVERY-node it would like to fit an item into, the system can expend much more effort in satisfying the various clauses than it could in checking an incoming item against dozens of possible *EVERY-node matches.

At present, only a rather rudimentary version of the *EVERY-node matcher has been implemented. The strategy, in general, is as follows: Whenever a new description (*TYPE or *INDV) is created, the system marks the node's ancestors in the type-hierarchy, and looks for *EVERY-nodes whose parent-wires are connected to members of this ancestor set. If we create a new ELEPHANT, we must look at *EVERY-nodes hung under ANIMAL as well as those under ELEPHANT. Only those *EVERY-nodes which are active in the new object's context-area (or an area of which the current context is a part) are considered: if we have a new ELEPHANT in AFRICA, we need not consider *EVERY-nodes for "every ELEPHANT in INDIA", but we should consider those nodes that relate to "every ELEPHANT in THE-WORLD". This initial filtering produces a set of *candidate* *EVERY-nodes which must be compared to the new description individually, clause by clause.

This clause-checking normally is very quick, and is handled by the parallel intersection machinery: in most cases, it takes only a couple of marker sweeps to determine whether the new individual's father is a slow mailman, whether the individual owns a dog, and so on. If this test fails, we must then decide whether to leave it at that, or whether to try to establish the clause in question by slower, but more powerful methods: looking more deeply into extrinsic descriptions (see section 3.7); finding and *EVERY-node that implies being a mailman, and trying to establish the father's memebership in that class; perhaps even calling up the post office in the father's city of residence. Even in the simple cases, however, each clause of each candidate-node must be checked individually.

Because they are checked individually, it is important to keep the set of candidate-nodes as small as possible. Since the parent-wire is the major factor in determining whether an *EVERY node becomes a candidate, it is desirable to tie this to the most specific *TYPE-node possible; if we have too many *EVERY-nodes with their parent-wires tied to THING, we will spend all of our time in the matching process. For the same reason, it is useful to make an *EVERY-node's scope as specific as possible, especially when the parent-wire connection of the node is not very specific -- we want one or the other of these connections to rule the *EVERY-node out most of the time, if possible. In really large systems, it might be useful to use a few of the spare type-flag bits in the *EVERY-node element to represent various levels of matching priority: always consider, consider if not in a hurry, or never consider. *EVERY-nodes of the latter sort would never be considered during digestion, but would function in consequent-driven reasoning, when the system wants to establish one of the *EVERY-node's incidental properties for some individual. For the relatively small test-systems that have been constructed so far, such priority-levels are not needed.

There are some situations in NETL which could be handled by *EVERY-nodes, but which appear so often that it is useful to give them special, more efficient representations. The most common of these, and the only one currently defined, is the *INT-node, which defines a class containing the intersection of two other type-classes (represented either by *TYPE-nodes or *EVERY-nodes). The BOY class, for example, is the intersection of the CHILD class and the MALE-PERSON class: it is impossible to be both a CHILD and a MALE without being a BOY. We could represent BOY by creating an *EVERY-node with its parent-wire hooked to CHILD and a *VC-clause to MALE (or vice-versa); instead we use a special node-type, the *INT (intersection) node. This node has two identical parent-wires, designated P1 and P2, which are hooked to the two sets being intersected. It also has a set-wire which connects it to the set-node that it defines. It does not have a scope-wire, since its scope is just the intersection of the parents' scope-areas.

Individuals and sub-types can be hung below the *INT-node, just as though it were a regular *EVERY-node. The special property of this node, however, is that any individual or sub-type description which has both P1 and P2 as an ancestor will behave as though the *INT-node were an ancestor as well, even without an upward path of *VC-links to the *INT-node. This is accomplished by a very simple process: whenever, during the activation of a single individual or type-description, the activation marker appears on both P1 and P2 of an *INT node, that marker is placed on the *INT-node as well. The *INT-node operates much like a *MAP-node, with a marker on P1 gating the flow of a marker across P2; in this case, however, both the marker being passed and the one activating the gate must be the same. The *EVERY-node matcher is thus relieved of the burden of explicitly placing new items into the proper *INT-node sets; *INT-nodes can be totally ignored by the matcher, and individuals in the intersection-set will inherit the *INT-node's incidental properties anyway. This mechanism was suggested by Michael Genesereth.

As we saw earlier, adjectives generally are associated with type-classes in NETL. The adjective "HEAVY", in its original, literal sense, applies only to PHYSOBS. We can therefore associate the word-node "HEAVY" with a HEAVY-PHYSOBS class, as a sort of alternate name. If we try to create a heavy color or a heavy number, we will get a type-clash. (We might then try to find a metaphorical meaning for the input in question, but that is another thesis.) Syntactically, these adjective-labels behave very differently from noun-labels, but they seem to do about the same job semantically. Some sets with noun-names have adjective-labels as well: HERBIVORE and HERBIVOROUS seem to point to the same *EVERY-node, a subclass of ANIMAL whose specification says that the individual's USUAL-FOOD is a member of the PLANT class. I may be missing some important distinction here which will become obvious when an attempt is made to add a real natural-language interface to NETL, but for the present it seems convenient to use adjectives as an alternative way of labelling a type-class. If this seems unnatural, feel free to read class-names like PURPLE and POISONOUS as PURPLE-THINGS and POISONOUS-THINGS.

The point of this discussion of adjectives is that the *INT-node mechanism makes it much easier to use such adjectival type-classes. We can now very easily create the set of all purple mushrooms or all purple doorknobs using an *INT-node, without adding significantly to the *EVERY-node matcher's workload whenever something purple is created. In addition, *INT-nodes make it easier to handle general-purpose modifiers like BIG or TOY which, when added to an object's description, causes a particular type-specific *INT node to be spliced into the object's description. If something is an ELEPHANT and we say that it is BIG, this causes the BIG-ELEPHANT *INT-node to be added to the object's set of inherited descriptions. This BIG-ELEPHANT node will cancel the default SIZE property attached to the ELEPHANT node and replace it with a different, somewhat larger default SIZE. If we add BIG to an object that is known to be a MOUSE, then we activate the BIG-MOUSE *INT-node, whose SIZE property is very different from that found in BIG-ELEPHANT. BIG, then, is not very useful as a class in its own right, but it is very useful as a sort of "big switch" which splices in whatever *INT node is appropriate to the type of object being considered.

What does the definition of BIG itself look like? Since it must create an *INT node for any object-type with which it is used, and since the properties attached to that *INT node depend on the properties -- in this case, the SIZE property -- of the other parent, it would appear that BIG must be defined as a procedure of some sort. One way of setting this up would be as follows: BIG is given a SIZE property, but instead of having an explicit value, the SIZE property is attached to a demon

program. This demon is to be invoked whenever the SIZE
property is accessed. Suppose that we have not yet built the
*INT-node for BIG-ELEPHANT. If we say that CLYDE is an
ELEPHANT and CLYDE is BIG, nothing out of the ordinary
happens. (Since ELEPHANTS are PHYSOBS, the two
parent-types do not clash.) The first time that we ask for the
SIZE of CLYDE, however, we will invoke the demon program.
(The SIZE value from the ELEPHANT description would also
be found, but demons take priority.) This program creates the
BIG-ELEPHANT *INT-node and gives it a SIZE property that is
near the upper limit of the sizes of known elephants, or perhaps
just adds some fixed percentage to the default SIZE for
ELEPHANTS. The demon then runs a *CANCEL-link from the
*INT-node to the default ELEPHANT SIZE, to get it out of the
way, and another *CANCEL-link from the *INT node to itself,
so that it will not be invoked again for any BIG-ELEPHANT.
Subsequent accesses to SIZE from CLYDE or any other
BIG-ELEPHANT will simply find the new SIZE value tied to
the *INT node. This is not very elegant, but "big" is a
notoriously inelegant concept in many representational systems.

The concept of negation is related to the concept of
defined sets: both require digestion-time matching to work
properly, and both can become open-ended problems requiring
serial proof methods if we really want to catch the more difficult
cases. The notation is really quite simple, at least for the simple
cases: to create the negation of any single statement, we create
the statement in positive form, then add a **NOT flag-bit to the
statement's handle-node. To say that CLYDE is not a
CIRCUS-STAR, we create a *VC-link from CLYDE to
CIRCUS-STAR and add the **NOT flag to the handle of this
link. The **NOT flag has three functions: first, it renders its
statement inoperative during normal knowledge-base accessing
operations; second, it causes its statement to satisfy certain
*EVERY-node clause-tests that would otherwise fail; finally, it
causes a clash whenever an attempt is made to add the

corresponding non-negated statement to the knowledge-base. It is this clash-test that involves the matcher: each new statement must be tested against the existing pool of **NOT statements to see if there is a conflict. The new statement does not have to match the exact form of the negated statement: any new statement that *implies* a negated statement should cause a clash, though the basic digestion-matcher only checks for class-membership and other very obvious kinds of implication. The **NOT *VC-link we created above for CLYDE will clash with any attempt to place CLYDE into a sub-class of CIRCUS-STAR in the type hierarchy. Note that a *SPLIT-link creates a form of negation, since it is equivalent to placing a **NOT *EQ link between its A-node and every other node in the split-set.

In complex statements, we have the choice of negating the entire statement or of negating only its attachment to certain arguments. If we place a **NOT flag on the handle-node of a KILLER-OF statment linking BOOTH to LINCLON, we are saying that BOOTH did not kill LINCOLN; if, instead, we place the **NOT flag on the *EQ link between BOOTH and the KILLER *MAP-node, we are saying that someone killed LINCOLN, but that it wasn't BOOTH. To state that several distinct statements A, B, and C are all false (conjunction of negations), we simply negate each of them individually. To state that they cannot all be true at once (negation of a conjunction or, by DeMorgan's Theorem, the disjunction of negations), we need to create an *EVERY-node representing any context in which all of the statements are true. We then deny that REAL-U (or whatever the scope of the negation is to be) is a memeber of this defined class of contexts. This technique of using contexts to represent logical operators comes from Hendrix [1975a, 1975b, 1976]; we will see more of this in section 3.9.

I believe that this set of representational options gives us enough power to represent any sort of negation that we might want for human-like common-sense reasoning. Note, however, that in English (and presumably in most other natural languages) the task of mapping a sentence involving negation into the appropriate underlying structure is a complicated one, depending in many cases on subtle semantic clues. See Lasnik [1972] for an analysis of this problem from a linguistic point of view and for references to other work in this area.

To state that no individual with a given description exists within a given area, we can create an *EVERY-node with the desired specification, and can state that the associated set is an EMPTY-SET (that is, one with MEMBER-COUNT equal to zero). Any attempt to create such an individual within the specified scope would be noticed by the matcher, which would try to place the new individual within the *EVERY-node's set. This would result in a clash due to member-count violation. The same end can be accomplished somewhat more directly by placing a **NOT flag on the *EVERY-node itself, indicating that the corresponding set is empty and that no such individuals exist. In this one case, it is allowable to omit the set-node altogether, since the set's properties are trivial. Under normal conditions, an *EVERY node with the **NOT flag set will never have any incidental (non-defining) properties, since there is nothing to say about the properties of a thing that does not exist.

Sometimes a clause in an *EVERY-node specification will specify that some statement must be known *not* to be true if the specification is to be met. We might, for example, want to create the class containing "every ELEPHANT in NORTH-AMERICA who is *not* a CIRCUS-STAR". This condition is represented by creating a *VC-link from the *EVERY-node to CIRCUS-STAR as part of the specification, and setting the **NOT flag on this link. The matcher will only accept this clause if it can definitely establish that the individual being tested is not in the CIRCUS-STAR class. This can be established by finding an explicit **NOT statement to that effect or by finding a split-set which implies such a statement. It might also be established by slower serial means -- proof by contradiction, for example -- but only if the system wants to pass the task to the serial problem-solver.

We might also want to say that a clause should be accepted if the truth of its statement cannot be established. We might, for example, want to specify every ELEPHANT *not known to be* a CIRCUS-STAR. This is quite different from saying that the statement is definitely known to be false. (In the context of MICRO-PLANNER this was known as the THNOT problem.) This condition can be indicated by placing an **UNK (unknown) flag on the clause in question. The matcher will try to establish the truth of the clause, and the match will succeed only if this attempt fails. The attempt to establish the statement obviously occurs within the system's own knowledge base; if we want to talk about what someone else knows, we can use the context mechanism (see 3.9), but in general this problem can become very complicated. Only the simpler cases can be handled in the current NETL.

The **UNK flag occurs only on statements in **SPEC clauses. If a statement is added to the system which violates an **UNK statement for some description, that description is removed from the *EVERY-node class associated with the **UNK statement; no clash is generated, since the added information is legal.

3.9 Events, Actions, and Multiple Contexts

In the preceding sections we developed representational techniques for static descriptions and relationships -- those residing within a single context-area. In this section, we will extend these basic ideas to cover actions and events, which we will represent as transitions between one state of the world (a temporal context-area) and another. We will also look briefly at the use of inter-context relationships to represent such things as implication, belief, expectation, and desire. I should mention at the outset that the mechanisms described in this section have not been as fully developed and tested as NETL's machinery for static descriptions. In the relatively straightforward examples that I have considered to date, the multiple-context representation seems to work rather well, but I have not yet run any large-scale tests of these techniques using the simulator, and several areas of potential difficulty remain unexplored. As the implementation and testing of NETL proceeds, I have no doubt that many of the details presented here will change, but I believe that the general approach will prove to be sound.

A context is simply an AREA of space, time, or subject matter into which we can place certain statements and in which we can.declare the existence of certain objects. When we are discussing actions and events, the word "context" will generally be used to refer to a temporal area. The term "world-model" is used to refer to the set of statements that are valid within a given temporal area or at a particular instant of time. Since time is one-dimensional, a finite area of time will be bounded by two temporal "points" or *instants*, one marking the start of the area and the other marking the end. To represent this, the TEMPORAL-AREA type-description contains two individual roles named STARTING-TIME and ENDING-TIME, both of which are members of the INSTANT class. There are two special instants, MINUS-INFINITY and PLUS-INFINITY, which are used to delimit semi-infinite areas: all of time before some instant, or all of time after it. In each universe there is one special temporal area that is infinite in both directions -- that is, it is bounded by MINUS-INFINITY and PLUS-INFINITY. This special area is named ALWAYS, and every other temporal area is a part of it. To say that a statement is true between the instants "Noon, April 15, 1977" and "3:00 p.m., December 9, 1978", we simply create these two individual instants, create a temporal area with these instants as endpoints, and scope the statement within this area.

An instant is represented as an *INDV node, descended from the INSTANT *TYPE-node. INSTANT has roles defined for its DATE, YEAR, and TIME-OF-DAY, but in many individual instants these roles will not be filled in; such instants are identified by the events that they delimit, rather than by some particular clock-time. Each instant creates a "before" context, running from MINUS-INFINITY to itself, and an "after" context running from itself to PLUS-INFINITY. These two context-areas occupy the BEFORE and AFTER role-nodes in the INSTANT description, and the INSTANT, in turn serves as the ENDING-TIME or the STARTING-TIME for these areas. Of course, if we have nothing to say about one of these areas for a given individual instant, we do not create the *MAP-node for that area, and it costs us nothing.

We may place a LATER-THAN statement between two INSTANTS to indicate their relative positions in time. If the dates and times for two INSTANTS are filled in, we have an algorithm that can compute which is the later of the two whenever this information is needed; if one or both of the clock-times are unspecified, it might be impossible to determine the proper order. Every INSTANT is known to fall after MINUS-INFINITY and before PLUS-INFINITY; these two relationships are inherited from the INSTANT *TYPE-NODE. The LATER-THAN relation thus creates a partial ordering of the INSTANTS that are present in any given universe, and the system can use a parallel marker propagation to mark all of the INSTANTS that are *known* to occur before or after some particular INSTANT. Note, however, that this scan is only able to follow LATER-THAN relationships which are explicitly stated in the network or which are inherited from higher levels in the type-hierarchy; the algorithm for comparing dates and times can only be run for one pair of nodes at once. Because of this, some potentially computable ordering relationships will be overlooked by such a scan, but this is a rather human-like limitation. At present, a LATER-THAN statement is represented by an *IST node, but it may be worthwhile to define a special link-type for this relation in order to speed up the marker sweeps through the LATER-THAN hierarchy.

Temporal areas may be grouped into type-classes on the basis of the locations of their boundary-points, the length of time that they span, or any other characteristic that such areas might share; thus, we have *TYPE-nodes for DAY, THURSDAY, FUTURE-DAY, RAINY-DAY, YEAR, NANOSECOND, and so on. The temporal area "July 4, 1776" (which by convention runs from one midnight to another) is a DAY, a PAST-DAY, a THURSDAY (or whatever), and a FINITE-TIME-PERIOD in the type-hierarchy; in the PART-OF hierarchy, it occurs in the YEAR-1776, the EIGHTEENTH-CENTURY, the AGE-OF-REASON, and so on. It is important to keep in mind that there are three distinct partial orderings or tangled hierarchies at work here: the type-hierarchy, the PART-OF hierarchy linking temporal areas to their sub-areas, and the partial ordering of the instants in time. Though they intersect at various nodes and sometimes follow the same links, these hierarchies are distinct and must not be confused with one another.

An *event* is an individual entity, represented in the knowledge-base by an *INDV node. Each individual event is an instance of some event-type in the type-hierarchy, just as a statement is an instance of some statement-type. The event-types and the individual events are all descended from the EVENT *TYPE-node, which lives near the top of the type-hierarchy, just under the THING node. The hierarchy of event-types is very general at the higher levels and becomes increasingly specialized

and precise as we move down the tree. The
DEATH-BY-DROWNING and DEATH-BY-ELECTROCUTION
event-types, for instance, are below the more general DEATH
event-type in the hierarchy. These event-types inherit all of the
information attached to the general DEATH node, and add
specific information of their own concerning the way in which
the death occurred. (We will see in a moment how to describe
the way in which an event occurs.) Just as in the hierarchy of
statement-types, a new role may be created for an event-type at
one level, restricted or modified at a lower level, and filled by a
specific role-player at a level that is lower still. The restrictions
are represented by *VC links, and are enforced by the
clash-detection mechanism.

This ability to create a hierarchy of event and action
types is critically important in a system that must reason about
real-world situations. It allows us, for instance, to state that
RUN and WALK are both special cases of TRAVEL-BY-FOOT,
which is a special case of TRAVEL, which is a special case of
MOVE. (To travel, as used here, is to move one's own body,
rather than some external object.) As Schank [1973] points out,
MOVE (or as he calls it, PTRANS) has an important
implication that must be captured if the event is to be
understood at all: the object's position in space changes. The
critical roles that structure the event, in this case an OBJECT, a
SOURCE and a DESTINATION, are also created at the MOVE
level. Clearly, any adequate representation of the meaning of
RUN and WALK must include this information from the MOVE
definition, either directly or by inheritance. But what about the
implications that are tied directly to the RUNNING or
WALKING definition? In some situations, this information is
more important than the change in location: running in the
hallway of a school may be a punishable offense; walking in the
hallway is encouraged. If there is no mechanism for the
inheritance of implications from one action-type to another, we
must either copy out all the implications of every action type or
treat the implications tied to lower levels as secondary, available

only upon special request. As we see in Schank's early work, this leads to many difficult decisions about which actions have the most important implications and should therefore be treated as primary. In a system with an effective virtual-copy mechanism, we can get the implications from all levels in the hierarchy at once, and we do not have to select any particular collection of action-types as being special or primitive.

As with statement-types, an event-*type* is just a template, regardless of how specific it has become by the restriction and filling-in of roles; it takes an individual event-*instance* to represent an actual occurrence. There is one key difference between an event and a statement, however: an individual event is represented by an *INDV node, not by an *IST node. This means that an event *exists* or *occurs* somewhere within a specified area of space and time; it does not, like a statement, have an area of validity that encompasses *all* of a specified area. In this respect, an event behaves more like an object than like a statement.

An *action* is a type of event with a special role defined for the ACTOR: the person, animal, robot, deity, or other "animate" entity that has caused the event to occur. (The word "actor", as used here, has no relation to Carl Hewitt's ACTORS.) Figure 41 illustrates the difference between an event and an action: a DEATH is an event-type with one defined role, the VICTIM; a KILLING is an action-type, with an ACTOR (called the KILLER) who *causes* a death-event to occur for some VICTIM. The VICTIM role may be filled by any member of the class of BIOLOGS, which includes all plants and animals. (Actually, this class is named LIVING-THINGS, but in this context the name would be confusing.) The KILLER slot may only be filled by a member of the ANIMATE class -- any attempt to fill this role with a dead animal, a rock, or a cabbage would produce a clash. Note that the causal link between the ACTOR and the event itself is labeled ACAUSE (for "actor cause") to distinguish it from ECAUSE ("event cause"), in which an event is caused by some previous event rather than by the

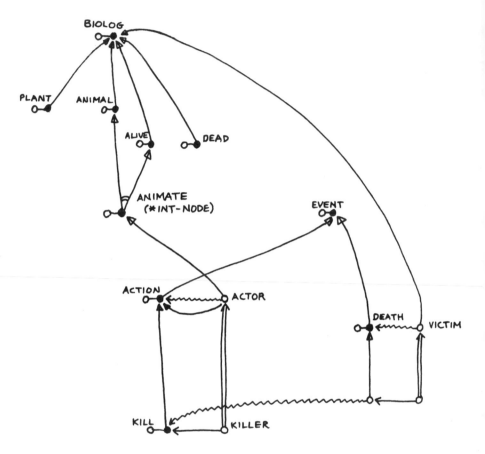

Figure 41: DEATH as an event-type; KILLING as an action-type.

actions of some animate being. If someone is killed by a falling rock, the internal representation would be a DEATH event rather than a KILL action, with the ROCK-FALLING event as the ECAUSE. (This may be wrong: perhaps we should treat the rock and Jack the Ripper in roughly the same way, placing both in the ACTOR slot of their respective killings. This would be closer to the surface structure of English, but would obscure certain aspects of the underlying meaning. More experimentation is needed to resolve this and related questions.) Both flavors of CAUSE are treated as primitive relations by the system: there is no attempt to define them in terms of other, more basic concepts.

(In this attempt to represent causality, we are treading dangerously close to the borders of metaphysics. For thousands of years, philosophers have argued about the nature of ultimate causality. Can an event really be caused by the will of an individual actor, or are events caused only by the prior occurrence of other events? If an action can, in principle, be predicted, can we really say that the individual actor has caused it? Is there perhaps one Big Actor In The Sky who is responsible for all of the things that seem, to us, to be our own free actions? And so on. I have no intention of grappling with these questions here (or anywhere else, for that matter). Whatever the Ultimate Realities may be, our everyday modes of thought and language seem to be tied very strongly to the idea that individual animate beings cause individual actions -- in fact, the basic SUBJECT-VERB structure of English and related languages practically forces this viewpoint upon us, though we can escape this framework by such devices as the use of a passive sentence structure. It seems reasonable to conclude, therefore, that ACTOR and ACTION are pragmatically useful concepts, and that NETL should freely employ these concepts in roughly the same ways that English-speaking people do.)

An event or action has two roles for its temporal boundary points, the EVENT-START and the EVENT-END, both of which are descendants of the INSTANT *TYPE-node.

The DATE, YEAR, and TIME-OF-DAY for these instants might or might not be specified. In any given event, the EVENT-END is LATER-THAN the EVENT-START, but the temporal ordering between these boundary points and other events and instants may not be known. The DURATION of the event is the length of time between the EVENT-START and the EVENT-END; given either of these boundary-points and the DURATION, we can find the other point by simple arithmetic. For many event-types, there is a typical default DURATION. For example, the typical COMMITTEE-MEETING takes about an hour, the typical BROKEN-ARM-RECOVERY takes one or two months, and the typical SNEEZE takes a few seconds.

If a statement is said to be true "before" an event, this means that the statement is scoped in the BEFORE context of the EVENT-START instant; if it is true "after" the event, it is placed in the AFTER context of the EVENT-END instant; if it is true "during" the event, it is placed in the event's DURING context, which lies between the EVENT-START and the EVENT-END. To represent what a particular event-type *does*, we simply place the appropriate statements in the BEFORE and AFTER contexts. In a DEATH event, for instance, the VICTIM is ALIVE in the BEFORE context and DEAD in the AFTER context. This implies, among other things, that the victim is no longer ANIMATE, and therefore can no longer initiate any actions. This event-type is illustrated in figure 42.

In a CREATION event, the *EXIN wire (or link) of the thing being created is tied to the AFTER context: before the CREATION event the thing does not exist; after the CREATION it does exist. In a DESTRUCTION event, the *EXIN wire is placed in the BEFORE context. In a TRANSFER-OWNERSHIP event, there are roles for a DONOR, a RECIPIENT, and an OBJECT. In the BEFORE context, the DONOR owns the OBJECT; in the AFTER context, the RECIPIENT does. The transfer can be either a GIVE-OWNERSHIP or a TAKE-OWNERSHIP, depending on whether the DONOR or the RECIPIENT is the ACTOR. SELL

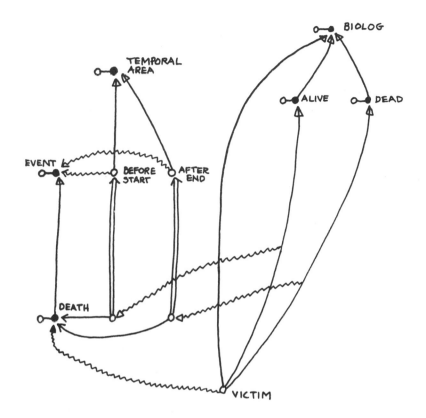

Figure 42: The DEATH event-type, with BEFORE and AFTER contexts.

is an action in which there are two TRANSFER-OWNERSHIP events: a transfer of some object from the ACTOR to the BUYER, and a transfer of MONEY in the opposite direction. And so on.

The statements in the BEFORE and AFTER contexts of an event provide us with a global view of the state-transformation associated with that event. It is perfectly legitimate to view an event in this way and to say nothing more about it. If we want to look more closely, however, we will see that an event is really an envelope containing a collection (usually, but not always, a linear sequence) of sub-events. Each of these, in turn, is a package containing still more sub-events, and so on as far down as we want to pursue the matter. At some level, of course, we will have to terminate this recursion by treating certain events as primitive, described only in terms of the external transformations that they cause, not in terms of any internal structure of sub-events. It is important to note, however, that the decision to stop expanding the steps of a description at some level is an arbitrary decision, made because more detailed information is unavailable or is not needed for task at hand. There are no primitive event-types *per se*, only events for which we have not specified the expansion. Actions, likewise, are really a collection of sub-actions, usually by the same actor, but sometimes by sub-actors who are ordered, hired, asked, or otherwise induced to carry out some of the steps.

This hierarchy of events and sub-events is represented in NETL by giving each EVENT an EXPANSION role. The EXPANSION has a set of STEPS, each of which is a PART of the parent event and also an EVENT in its own right. The EXPANSION may or may not be filled in for a given event, depending on whether we know the details of the event or merely the overall results: we might know only that a thief has stolen the Crown Jewels; we might know, in addition, that among the STEPS in this action were the breaking of a skylight, the lowering of the thief on a rope, the opening of the case with a chainsaw, and so on. Usually, if the STEPS in an event are specified, the time relationships among these steps are specified as well, but again this is not always true: we might know that the thief cut himself on the glass of the skylight during the crime, but we might not know whether this injury occurred during the entry or the exit. It might be useful to distinguish between parts of the jewel-theft *action*, which must be intentional, and parts of the jewel-theft *event*, which would include everything that happened in the course of that event -- the thief cutting himself, for instance.

In the above example, the EXPANSION was for an individual JEWEL-THEFT event. An EXPANSION can also be specified for the generic JEWEL-THEFT *TYPE-node. This would describe the steps and their order of occurrence in a typical JEWEL-THEFT. This expansion, in all its detail, is inherited by each individual JEWEL-THEFT event, unless it is specifically cancelled or modified. The mechanisms responsible for this inheritance are the same mechanisms that we developed for the inheritance of the parts and properties of an object. If there are several stereotypical ways to conduct a JEWEL-THEFT, then we have several sub-types of JEWEL-THEFT, each with its own EXPANSION. The EXPANSION, or some feature of it, can also be used to define a class of events. Just as a JEWEL-THEFT is defined as any THEFT event in which the LOOT role is a member of the JEWELRY class, a DEATH-BY-DROWNING is any death in which the EXPANSION of the event includes the movement of water into the lungs, and in which this particular STEP is the ECAUSE of the DEATH-event itself. Defined event-types are, of course, represented by *EVERY-nodes rather than *TYPE-nodes, and the existence of the critical expansion-step becomes a clause in the specification of this *EVERY-node. In most subject domains the majority of event-types will be created by this process of partly specifying various possible expansions for more general event-types.

Note that the BEFORE, DURING, and AFTER context-areas of these nested events must be woven together into a coherent structure. It must be possible to pick any time-instant within an event and tell which statements are to be considered active at that instant. The finite time-areas are nested in a PART-OF hierarchy: the DURING context of each step in an event is a part of the DURING context of the surrounding event; the time areas between the steps in a sequence are parts of the outer DURING context as well. Any semi-infinite BEFORE context includes as a part any temporal area with an ENDING-TIME earlier than its own; an AFTER context includes any area with a STARTING-TIME later than its own. You will recall from section 3.6 that, in order to activate all of the statements which are supposed to be active within some context X, we must activate X itself and all of the areas of which it is a part. This means that we must activate all of the surrounding DURING contexts, and must propagate markers through the LATER-THAN hierarchy to catch the appropriate BEFORE and AFTER contexts and the statements that reside within them.

The LATER-THAN lattice can become quite deep, but it can be cut down to a reasonable depth by the judicious placement of a few shortcut links; if, for example, we have a direct LATER-THAN link from the Apollo-11 landing to the Fall of Rome, some of the propagating markers can leap ahead while their brothers scan through the points between these events. A hierarchy can provide us with the same effect by declaring, for instance, that Apollo-11 is a part of Modern History, the fall of Rome is a part of Ancient History, and that there is an inherited LATER-THAN between any point in one and any point in the other.

There are still a number of problems to be solved with the details of this scheme for representing actions and events. For one thing, the prerequisites of an action or event should not really be placed in a semi-infinite BEFORE context. In a DEATH event, for example, we really want to require that the victim be alive *at* the STARTING-TIME of the DEATH, but we do not care how long he has been alive. We certainly do not want to require that he has been alive since the dawn of time. When we say that a statement is true "at" a given instant of time, we presumably mean that it is true in some unspecified area surrounding that instant, but there is not at present any machinery to represent this situation. We will probably need a new kind of scope-link for AT-statements. These AT-links should work for spatial points as well as temporal ones.

The semi-infinite nature of an event's AFTER context can also be troublesome, since it implies that the results of an event last forever unless they are explicitly cancelled by a later event. What if we have created a BIRTH event for some citizen of the Roman empire, but we have not created an explicit DEATH event for him? It would appear that if we ask in a modern context whether this Roman is alive or dead, the system would reply that he is alive. We need some way to put a statute of limitations on the results of an event, after which they are assumed to have been obliterated unless we have specific information to the contrary. Perhaps a default DEATH-event should be created along with every BIRTH-event, but this seems a rather clumsy solution.

There may also be some problems in the implementation of the LATER-THAN scan. Some of the LATER-THAN relations must be inherited from higher levels and, as we saw in the PART-OF scan, this can sometimes lead to serious inefficiency. It might be necessary to replace some of the implicit, inherited LATER-THAN links with explicit ones, as we did in the PART-OF hierarchy. These problems do not appear to be particularly serious, but they do indicate that this area needs some more work before it can be successfully implemented.

Given a facility for describing action-types, we can represent procedures as well -- there is no real difference between the description of the steps in a typical successful JEWEL-THEFT and a list of instructions on how to conduct such a theft. The only necessary addition is a statement or two describing which of several possible expansions should be used, and under what conditions this choice might vary. Given an initial state and a goal state, the system can select an appropriate action in a way that is reminiscent of STRIPS [Fikes, Hart, Nilsson, 1973]: an action-type is sought whose AFTER context differs from its BEFORE context in the same way that the goal state differs from the initial state. In NETL, the parallel intersection machinery can aid us in performing this search. We can locate a known action-type with the desired elements in it BEFORE and AFTER contexts in much the same way that we would locate an animal-type or a disease-type by intersecting an observed set of features. Once an action-type is found that can do the job, an expansion is selected (if more than one expansion is known), the steps are expanded out, and the process repeats until the level of directly executable primitive actions is reached. Then the plan is executed. If the steps in an expansion are only partially ordered, we can use some of the techniques developed by Sacerdoti [1975] for his NOAH program to pick an advantageous ordering which does not conflict with other steps in the plan.

Of course, this is only an outline, and considerable work will be required to fill in the details. Eventually, however, it might be possible to put the system's own library of search, digestion, and other procedures into the network with the rest of the knowledge, and to reduce the controller program to a small, fixed interpreter. This would mean that the system could alter and improve its own procedures, and by switching contexts could adopt various styles of thinking: legal, mathematical, metaphorical, etc. The original, basic mode of thought should probably be in a separate, non-alterable context so that the system can recover if it makes a mistake while altering its own processing strategies.

There are several other uses for multiple context areas, besides the ones already described. As Hendrix pointed out [1975a, 1975b, 1976], a context (or, in his system, a *partition*) can be used to represent any conjunction of statements that we want to manipulate as a unit. A *TYPE-node used as a context represents a *class* of situations in which the attached statements happen to be true. An *EVERY-node used as a context for some of its specification clauses represents every situation (real or imaginary) in which that set of statements is true.

We might, for example, have two sets of statements, X and Y, one of which must be true in the real universe. Either Smith is the engineer and he plays cards with the brakeman (this is situation X) or Jones is the engineer and he lives across the street form Smith (situation Y). We can represent these two situations by *EVERY-nodes: X represents every unverse in which Smith is the engineer, etc. We can indicate that REAL-U (or PUZZLE1-U) must be one of the above by placing X and Y into a *complete* exclusive split relationship. The digestion machinery will then see to it that if either X or Y is ever ruled out, REAL-U will be placed into the other class, and the statements in that class will become active in REAL-U.

To indicate that some particular conjunction of statements, taken as a whole, is untrue, we can define (with an *EVERY-node) the set of universes in which these statements are *all* true, and then state that REAL-U is not a member of this set. Once again, the regular digestion machinery will catch any violations. This is NETL's mechanism for handling external negation -- statements of the form "It is not the case that ..."

To represent the concept that someone WANTS a statement to be true, we must be able to represent the desired statement without placing it actively into the knowledge-base. One way to handle this would be to specially mark the target statement as being inoperative. If we have a multi-statement desire, however, we might want to enter and explore this fantasy-world. To achieve this, the WANTS statement should point at a context full of statements rather than at a single fact in isolation. This allows us to quarantine the desired situation in its own separate compartment; normally this compartment is inactive, but it can be deliberately turned on for exploratory purposes. Of course, an individual can have several distinct and inconsistent fantasy-worlds, stored in separate contexts. States of belief and knowledge are handled in essentially the same way.

Note that we can start a fantasy-world or belief-world as a copy of REAL-U, and then simply note any changes.

3.10 Abstraction and Learning

Much of the representational power of NETL depends on the existence of a rich, multi-leveled structure of *TYPE-nodes and *EVERY-nodes, each with its own contribution to make to the structure and properties of the individuals below it. In this final section of Chapter 3, we will take a quick look at the question of how all of these intermediate-level nodes come into being. Few of the ideas in this section are original -- some, in fact, have become so commonplace that I am unable to determine their origin -- but I discuss them here because they fit so well into a system in which inheritance through a tangled hierarchy of types is a central feature.

As Winston [1977] points out, there is a spectrum of methods by which people learn new concepts, ranging from those in which the learner does very little work to those in which he creates the new concept entirely on his own. At the low end of the scale is rote-learning, in which a body of information is put away in a form which can be retrieved later, but in which very little actual processing or digestion is done by the learner. One would expect that in learning of this type, many implications of the learned material would be missed and many absurdities -- even obvious ones -- would slip by. In people, that is exactly what we find, and this is why rote learning is currently held in rather low esteem. In NETL, rote learning would correspond to simply accepting and storing input, with no checking for relevant *EVERY-nodes, **NOT statements, and so on. This saves time and allows input to be accepted at a very high rate, but the disadvantages are so great that the system should only operate in this mode when there is no other choice.

Winston's second level is learning by being told, where the learner takes the role of an active listener, drawing inferences and integrating the new knowledge into his existing memory structure. This would correspond in NETL to accepting external inputs and digesting each fully before going on to the next item. Actually, since digestion is an open-ended process, we can never say that an item has been totally digested, but in active-listener mode we would expend a considerable amount of effort on each item. The teacher might tell us, for instance, that there exists a sub-class of animals named "elephant", whose members share some specified list of properties. If this list of properties includes the statement that an elephant weighs several tons, and if we have an *EVERY-node for LARGE-ANIMAL that has some associated properties, we could hardly claim to have assimilated the new information if the ELEPHANT *TYPE-node does not end up with a *VC connection to this LARGE-ANIMAL node. In addition to trying to match and clash the central concept being learned, the learner should examine the roles and sub-roles, trying to digest them as well. Actions should be expanded out a level or two (just as they would be in generating a plan) to see if the sub-actions clash or qualify the action for membership in some defined class. Such efforts can pay off handsomely in the availability of additional inherited facts that would be unavailable to the rote-learner, and in the detection of subtle inconsistencies.

  As an example of the perils of incomplete digestion, consider the case of a friend of mine who was told, during a class in high shcool, that the painter Van Gogh had bitten off his own ear and sent it to his girlfriend. Though his mind was on something else at the time, my friend dutifully filed this fact away. Years later, in another art class, he retrieved this fact, realized the absurdity, and started laughing. Note that there is no surface-level clash here: an ear is a reasonable, if painful, thing to bite, and there is no absolute restriction against a person biting off some part of his own body if he is sufficiently disturbed. It is only when one attempts to expand out the action in terms of the necessary movements of hand, ear, jaw, and tongue that the difficulty becomes apparent. If the teacher had said that Van Gogh had bitten off the end of a steel I-beam, the conflict might have been caught by shallow surface-level clash-detection.

  It may seem, at first glance, that learning by being told is the principal mechanism by which our heads are filled with categories, but upon closer examination we find that Winston's third level, learning by analyzing samples, is of equal, or perhaps greater, importance. By this, Winston means that someone (or something) tells the learner that a new class exists and points out or describes some sample members of that class. The learner must then decide for himself which are the class's typical or defining features. This is the paradigm analyzed in Winston's original [1975] thesis.

Winston's emphasis is on clearly defined classes -- in NETL they would be *EVERY-nodes -- and he therefore requires rather strong proof that a particular feature is a defining one. It is not sufficient that all known examples of ARCH have a hole; Winston's system must also see some non-arch whose only obvious fault is the lack of a hole. This is the reason for Winston's stress on the near-miss concept and the idea that examples should be presented in an optimal order. But suppose we are looking not for *defining* features, but for *typical* ones -- that is, suppose we are trying to characterize the class not by a formal definition but by an exemplar. (Again, recall the findings of Rosch [1975], showing that people make extensive use of such exemplar-based classes.) In this case we can loosen up Winston's rules somewhat. If we are trying to understand what an ELEPHANT is, and someone shows us a dozen gray examples, we simply add the GRAY property to the generic description. We do not need to determine that an elephant *must* be gray; in fact, if eleven of our samples are gray and one is white, we can still abstract the GRAY property and treat the odd elephant as an exception in this respect. The same holds for big ears, long noses, eating vegetation, and so on.

Note that by moving properties, roles, and other structural relationships up into the generic ELEPHANT-description, we are reducing the total number of nodes used: one GRAY property is now doing the work of twelve. Note also that all twelve of the elephants (including the exceptional white one) still have the same effective description that they had before; the restructuring of the description is transparent. This seems like a good criterion to use in deciding whether to make a given abstraction: *if the total number of elements used (including cancellation links for non-conforming individuals) is decreased by a change which does not alter the effective description of any individual, the change should be made.* In a system in which inheritance is expensive or cancellations are not allowed, we must be very careful when considering a feature-abstraction of this sort, but in NETL such changes can be made liberally. In a system in which tangles are not allowed in the type-hierarchy, we must carefully consider what is the optimal way in which to carve up a class into sub-classes; again, NETL has no such problem. Abstraction of features, then, becomes a powerful tool, and one that is not very complicated to apply.

While a human teacher only teaches by example on occasion, we all have a much more powerful teacher in the language in which we are immersed. If there is a word for some class, that means that the culture has decided, by some subtle form of natural selection, that the class to which this name applies is worthy of having a name, either because it captures some interesting correlation between certain features or because it adds to the overall efficiency of the description. When we first hear a new class name, we begin to observe the set of objects to which this name is applied, and eventually we formulate a class-description by abstracting the common features of these examples. I suspect that a substantial majority of the class-descriptions that we carry in our minds are formed by this sort of process, and it seems likely that a majority of NETL's intermediate-level nodes could be formed in this way as well. This is an exciting prospect: a system that can learn new concepts without being reprogrammed, or even told in so many words what the concept represents. Of course, the idea is a long way from being implemented, but it should be considerably less difficult given NETL as a substrate.

Winston's final level of learner-involvement is learning by discovery, with no teacher at all, and presumably not even a class-name to alert us to the presence of a useful grouping. This sort of discovery may happen relatively infrequently, but it is an essential process: someone, after all, must identify and name a class in the first place, so that the rest of us can learn it by the easier process described above. Here we have only the samples themselves to work from, but the process is similar: we look around for descriptions that have features in common; when we find some, we decide whether it would, indeed, be profitable to create a *TYPE-node over these descriptions and, if so, which features should be abstracted up to that *TYPE-node's level. This decision is made according to the same criterion of overall parsimony that we used earlier. The principal difference between this type of learning and learning by analyzing samples is that here, without external guidance telling us which nodes to consider grouping, we must search for such groupings by ourselves. There are probably some heuristics that can be used to increase our chances of finding a useful classification to make. It might, for example, be a good idea to compare the members of any particularly large set, looking for subsets that can capture more than one property at once. The arrival of new individuals might be used to trigger a search for other individuals that have properties in common; the parallel network could help with this search, but it would still be non-trivial. Certain classifications are probably obvious to everyone and are made even before we happen to hear a name for the class. Other, more subtle groupings may take a generation or more before anyone stumbles across them.

None of this has yet been implemented, though some of the simpler strategies may be installed soon. In order to properly study which generalization techniques and search strategies are useful, we will need a rather large knowledge base, embedded in a system which is not changing very rapidly. Only in such a test system will we be able to see the global results of our local reorganization strategies. Such size and stability does not yet exist in the simulated NETL, which at the moment is evolving very quickly just to deal with the steady-state problems that we want it to handle. When the situation has stabilized a bit, however, I believe that this general area of abstraction and learning will be an exciting area for further research.

4. Simulation Results

4.1 Description of the LORIS Simulator

As stated earlier, a simulator for the parallel network system is now running in MACLISP on the PDP-10. This program is named LORIS, after a type of animal (a prosimian primate) that climbs around on trees, but *very* slowly. The simulator does indeed run slowly compared to the hardware network, but it runs fast enough to handle our current experimental needs in systems up to a few thousand elements, with reasonable response times. A certain amount of effort was devoted, on the one hand, to making the system's inner loops run as fast as possible in compiled form and, on the other hand, to making the user interfaces of the system reasonably flexible and convenient to work with. Note that the term LORIS refers only to the programs that simulate the hardware network itself; the current implementation of the NETL semantics is built on top of this. LORIS provides the following set of facilities:

Functions for creating and destroying element-units, and for connecting and disconnecting their link-wires.

All elements have the same number of link-wires, currently 6, but easily converted to any other number. Some elements use fewer wires than are available, and simply leave the extra ones unconnected. The link-wires are represented by pointers to the appropriate destination-element, or to NIL if the wire is not connected; reverse pointers are also used so that the link-wires may be traversed in either direction. Every element has a unique name, either supplied by the user or generated by the system; this name will play no part in any ultimate natural-language interface, but it is essential for the debugging and development of the sytem in the meantime. And, of course, each element has storage for its marker-bits and type-flag bits.

Each element is stored as a HUNK (like a CONS-cell, but with an arbitrary number of pointers) in the current implementation, though arrays could be used equally well. Including external structures, such as the atom-header for the name and a FIXNUM cell for the flag and marker bits, each element requires about 10 to 15 36-bit words of memory. By converting to machine language and squeezing hard, we could save about half of this space.

Functions for adding or removing any of the 15 available marker-bits from a given element. Functions for visiting every node that has a given marker or combination of markers. Functions for viewing the marks in a node, and for erasing a given mark from every element in the system.

Each marker is assigned to a particular bit in an element's flag-word. When the word is marked, this bit is set. In addition, a list is kept for each marker of the elements in which that marker-bit is set. This is necessary so that the set of marked nodes can be scanned without examining the whole memory. Each marker also has a count of how many elements it currently marks; during marker-intersections, this allows the system to scan down the shortest marker-list, looking for nodes in which the other markers are set. As markers are propagated and cleared, a large number of CONS-cells are incorporated into the marker-lists and then discarded. An option exists for returning such a list directly to the FREE-STORAGE list, easing the load on the garbage-collector. This is only worthwhile in very large systems, since the overhead of such an operation is very high in MACLISP.

Functions for naming any of the 20 available type-flag bits, for setting, clearing, and viewing the flags in a given element, and for testing an element for any desired combination of type-flags and markers.

Both the flag-bits and the marker-bits for a given element are stored within a single 36-bit machine-word. This means that a single boolean PDP-10 instruction can check both markers and flags simultaneously, which speeds up the propagation-scans. It also means that the total of marker and flag bits cannot exceed 36 (unless we are prepared to change this part of the implementation).

Assorted utility functions for recording and printing real and simulated run-times, performing boolean operations, defining macros, dumping the data-base, and so on.

That is all there is to the LORIS program itself. It has been complete and stable for some time, and there is very little that could be added to it. The rest of this section will be devoted to a description of the NETL program that runs on this simulator. This program is intended to implement the current version of NETL, as described in chapter 3 of this report. This program is still under development, and at present implements only a subset of the mechanisms that were described in section 3. Of the digestion routines, only the simpler forms of clash-detection are currently implemented; the matcher, which handles *EVERY-node digestion, clashes involving **NOT statements, and which is the entry point for recognition problems is not yet programmed. Most of the accessing machinery has been installed: the system currently handles inheritance, all but the most complex kinds of role mapping, cancellation, *INT-nodes, and simple context-switching. Some of the heuristic scans described in section 3.7 are not yet installed, nor is the machinery for the proper handling of *OTHER-nodes.

The NETL program can be divided into an inner core of basic machinery and an outer layer which contains user-interfaces and other functions that drive the core machinery. Included in the inner core are the following:

Definitions for the element-type and option flags currently in use.

The element-type flag-bits specify what kind of node or link a given element represents: *INDV, *VC, or whatever. The full list of defined element-types is given in appendix B. The option flags are also listed there. These definitions make it possible to call these flags by name rather than having to remember and specify individual bits.

Primitive routines for creating each type of node and link, and for connecting up the appropriate link-wires.

These element-creation routines do no checking or digestion; they simply create the element, set the appropriate type-flags, and connect the wires as specified by the user. Their principal purpose is to isolate the layers of the system and to serve as living definitions for the various element-types. More powerful structure-creating functions, intended for external use, reside in the outer layer of the system; these do the checking and digestion, but call the inner functions to actually create the appropriate elements.

Marker-allocation routines.

When any function in NETL wants a marker to use, it must send a request to the GETMARK function, stating what the marker is needed for. GETMARK assigns a marker from the free-marker list, or tries to free a marker if none are currently free. At present, the attempt to free a marker consists of asking the user, but eventually it will be automated. The marker-number is then passed to the requesting function, which will return it when it is no longer needed. At present, I am experimenting with a scheme which does not clear a returned marker until it is actually needed for some other use. If one function performs a certain scan -- marking the ancestors of Clyde, for instance -- a later function might be able to use the same set of markers instead of having to repeat the scan. The later function must determine whether anything relevant to the outcome of the scan may have changed in the meantime.

Programs to perform each type of marker-propagation scan.

Once a marker has been selected and placed on a starting node, these functions are called to propagate it through the network. Since the *CANVC links must function during the various scans, most of the scanning routines require the use of a second marker to represent these cancellations. Each of the scans supplies a different set of instructions to a LORIS macro that expands into the desired marker-propagation program. The L-UPSCAN ("L" for "legitimate") call, for instance, is the basic scan for activating a description. It propagates markers *up* *VC-links and parent-wires, across *EQ links in either direction, and across those map-wires that are activated by some specified activation marker. (Several activation markers may be specified at once.) It also sends a cancellation marker up any *CANVC link that the scan encounters, and respects this and other cancellation markers during the scan. The *INT node is handled appropriately: if a marker arrives at this node's PARENT-1 wire, it enters the node if and only if the same maker is present on the PARENT-2 wire, and vice-versa. As each level of scanning is completed, the cost is recorded: at present, L-UPSCAN costs 5 simulated bus-cycles for setup, and 23 cycles for every level that the markers travel. The scan continues until, at some level, no new markers are placed.

In addition to L-UPSCAN, there is L-DOWNSCAN which is identical except for going *down* *VC links and parent-wires. This is used to mark all the members of a class. L-EQSCAN crosses only *EQ links and activated map-wires; it is used to mark a node's equivalents in the network, as opposed to its ancestors or descendants. There is also an H-UPSCAN ("H" for "heuristic") which is like L-UPSCAN, except that it travels up non-activated map-wires; this is used to implement the heuristic scans described in section 3.7. An H-DOWNSCAN exists as well; it is used for quick and dirty set-membership checking. ECHO-DOWNSCAN is used to follow a path of markers back down to its source from a selected target-node; it is used after various heuristic scans to find the *MAP-node which should be activated legitimately. ACT-SCAN is used to activate a context for data-access; it sends markers up both the type-hierarchy and the PART-OF hierarchy. All of the scans follow the same general pattern, so it is relatively easy to implement new ones.

In addition to the scans, there are a number of "steps" or single-level marker-passing routines. CANCEL-STEP is used to send cancellation markers across all *CANCEL-links whose A-end has a specified activation marker. SPLIT-STEP is used to mark the B-end of any *SPLIT link with a specified mark on its A-end. ACT-STEP is used to place an activation marker on any statement whose scope-node is marked as active. And so on. All of the scans mentioned are currently running, though some of them are unused in the current system.

The outer layer of the NETL simulator contains the routines that initiate these scans and other primitive operations in response to commands from the user. These are the routines that one actually deals with in building up and interrogating a knowledge-base. Most of the user-accessible functions in this area have prefixes, indicating what they do: "C" means *create* some sort of object; "S" means *state* some assertion; "F" means find some item; "FM" means *find* an item, or *make* it if it does not already exist; "YN" means *yes-no* question, which will test whether some condition is definitely true, definitely false, or unknown; and "Y" means *yes-question*, which checks only for the definitely true case. Thus, C-INDV means "create an individual", and so on. The above list is not meant to be exhaustive: eventually we will need existence questions, where, when, why, and how questions, modal and conditional statements, and many other things. I will briefly describe the facilities that are currently available, but will not try to make this a user's manual; the system is changing too rapidly in this area for such a manual to be useful.

The prototypical structure-creation call is C-INDV, which creates an individual with a given name and type. Thus, one might say (C-INDV 'CLYDE 'ELEPHANT). The new individual is placed within the current addition-context or ADDCON. The ADDCON can be pushed, popped, completely reset, and manipulated in other ways. If no name is specified for the new individual, the system makes up a name, in this case ELEPHANT-1. In addition to C-INDV, there are calls for creating new *TYPE-nodes, new pseudo-individuals, new *OTHER nodes, new *INT nodes, new *EVERY-nodes, new complete and incomplete split-sets, and new *IST-nodes. In each of these calls, the system tries to supply reasonable defaults for whatever the user fails to specify. The calls (IN-ROLE owner x1 x2 ...) and (OF-ROLE owner x1 x2 ...) evaluate the Xn and place any structure that they create inside the owner's type-description, with flags to indicate the type of role. In a similar way, structure created within a C-EVERY call is tied to that *EVERY-node as part of the specification.

The prototypical statement-creation call is S-VC, which creates a *VC link between its arguments, scoped in the current ADDCON. Thus we might have (S-VC 'CLYDE 'CABBAGE). Before anything is created, however, S-VC checks whether Clyde is *allowed* to be a CABBAGE by calling (YN-VC 'CLYDE 'CABBAGE), which runs the clash-detection machinery. In this case, the system finds the clash between PLANT and ANIMAL and reports the problem to the user. The operation may then be aborted, altered, or forced to completion despite the system's objections. S-VC also complains if the new link would be redundant -- CLYDE is already a CABBAGE -- or if placing the link would form a directed loop of *VC-links. S-EQ is almost identical, except that it forms an *EQ-link between its arguments and uses YN-EQ for checking. Among the other S-calls are S-DISTINCT, S-CANCEL, S-LIKE (creates a **LIKE *VC link),

S-EXFÓR, S-EXIN, S-SCOPE, and S-SPLIT. At present, only S-VC and S-EQ do any checking or digestion, but this will change in the near future.

At present, only a few query-commands have been implemented. Y-VC determines whether A is a B; YN-VC determines not only whether A is already a B, but also whether it is allowed to be. Y-EQ determines whether A and B refer to the same entity; YN-EQ determines whether the descriptions *could* refer to the same entity. Y-HAS checks whether A, in any of its currently-active descriptions, has B as a role. Y-HAS-ANY checks whether A has any role that is a member of class B.

As we saw in section 3.7, the process of tracing through chains of roles can be exceedingly complex. It is planned that the simulator will have three functions for tracing out chains of OF-relations: (F-OFLIST '(a b c ...)) will find and mark any nodes equivalent to "the A of the B of C", but will not create any new nodes to represent this entity; it is strictly for looking up values and equivalents. In addition to marking all of the nodes that fit our query, F-OFLIST returns one of them as its value. In making this selection, it favors first any node with the *EXTERN flag; second, any free-standing individual node; and third, the least-deeply nested role or *MAP node.

FM-OFLIST does the same thing, but it makes sure that there is at least one node that uniquely represents whatever entity is requested, creating new *MAP-nodes if necessary. This is used when we plan to state something about the entity being sought. FM-OFLIST only requires that there be *some* unique node upon which the information can be hung: we might ask it for the ASSASSIN of LINCOLN and get back a node for JOHN-WILKES-BOOTH.

FML-OFLIST (the "L" is for "literal") is like FM-OFLIST, but it insists upon returning the exact node specified -- the ASSASSIN of LINCOLN -- even if it has to create this node. This is useful if we have some property that ought to stay with the "Lincoln's assassin" node should we later decide (or hypothesize) that Booth was innocent. These OFLIST functions are currently under development: they are not yet as thorough as they must eventually be to handle all possible cases, to whatever level of heuristic depth and effort the user has specified (see section 3.7). They *are* working well enough to handle some interesting and intricate mapping problems in the electronics-world.

Not really a part of the simulated NETL system, but essential to it, is a file of special nodes and links that are common to all domains. This file, called the *base-load*, must always be the first file loaded into a vacant knowledge-base, since many of the routines which create new structure refer to these basic nodes and links. The base-load is thus a sort of bootstrap for the system. Among the items defined in the base-load are the THING node and its set; the UNIVERSE type-node and its charter members REAL-U and META-U; the SET node with its COUNT, COUNT-UPPER-BOUND, and COUNT-LOWER-BOUND roles; the *TYPE-node for each defined species of link; and a variety of high-level type nodes: PHYSOB, AREA, STATEMENT, NUMBER, VALUE, SUBSTANCE, and so on. At present, the base-load consists of about 100 elements, but I would expect it to reach about 1000 in a mature system. Once the problem-solving and abstraction machinery are in place, it will be interesting to see how small an initial base-load we can get away with, but in the system's current state this would be a needless distraction.

The "outer layer" portion of NETL is far from complete, and I would expect considerable growth and change in this area for some time to come, especially as full-scale problem-domains are implemented. The major parts of the system that are missing entirely at present are the matcher for every-nodes, **NOT-statements, and recognition requests; the spare-time routines for housekeeping and abstraction; the machinery for many-to-many mapping between names and concepts (with the disambiguation machinery that this would entail); the more complex types of context manipulation that are needed for actions and events; and many smaller items. I would estimate that with another year's work, the simulated NETL system can become a genuinely useful tool for creating experimental knowledge-base systems of moderate size, in much the same way that MICRO-PLANNER and CONNIVER served as tools for experimenting with problem-solving ideas. In order for the simulator to be generally useful in this way, it must be possible to create and use a knowledge-base without knowing very much about the inner workings of the system.

In compiled form, the LORIS system requires about 4K words of core, and the current NETL simulator takes about 12K. The figure for NETL might be expected to double within the next year or so. This figure includes only the programs and internal data-structures of the system; to this must be added storage space for the elements at about 10-15 words apiece, several thousand words of working space, and the LISP system itself. MACLISP, at present, weighs in at around 40K words, much of which is devoted to arithmetic functions and complex I/O that LORIS and NETL do not use; the system could be implemented in a smaller LISP or some other language without much difficulty.

4.2 Animal-World Test Results

To date, examples from two problem-domains have been implemented and run. The first of these is a portion of the hierarchy of animal-types, with their various parts, distinguishing features, habitats, and so on. A few token plants have been added for the sake of variety. This is a good world for debugging the basic parts of the system and for obtaining timing information, since there are many sub-hierarchies and branches that tangle together in interesting ways, many facts and properties to add at each level, and many exceptions and special cases. There are parts of the NETL system that the animal domain (as presently constituted) does not exercise, but we will catch at least some of these in our other test-domain, electronics.

Probably the best way to explain such a straightforward domain is to display a chunk of the actual input, followed by some statistics and examples of interaction with the system. The code is in MACLISP syntax, but it should be self-explanatory to readers who do not use LISP. Everything between one or more semi-colons and the end of that line is a comment, which has no effect on the system's operation. The information in this example is meant to be illustrative only: it is an amalgam of half-remembered high-school biology and old episodes of Wild Kingdom. I do not vouch for its accuracy.

All runtimes given in this and the following section are for compiled MACLISP code on the MIT-AI KA-10 system. A KL-10 system would be 3-5 times faster. Actual waiting times are several times longer than this, due to time-sharing. The simulated cycle times are the number of bus-settling cycles that would be required using very simple hardware elements of the type described in Appendix A.1. To propagate a mark across a *VC link takes 4 cycles; to propagate markers one level in an activation scan, in which a variety of link-types must be checked for, takes about 25 cycles. More complex element-unit hardware could cut this per-level cost down to 3 or 4 cycles, but the expense would probably outweigh the added speed. A very conservative figure for the cycle-time would be one microsecond, though much higher speeds could be achieved if necessary by careful design.

```
;;; Here begins the actual computer input.
;;; A line that looks like this is a comment or section heading.

;;; This is a file of assorted information about animals, plants,
;;; and other living things.  It is fed into a LISP in which LORIS,
;;; NETL, and the base-load have already been loaded.

(pop-c-to nil)                ;Clear out old context, if any.

(push-c 'real-u)              ;This is claimed to be true in real-U.

(c-alltypes 'physob           ;A physob can be living or non-living.
            '(living-thing    ; PHYSOB is defined in the base-load.
              non-living-thing))

(c-alltypes 'living-thing     ;A living thing must be one of these.
            '(plant           ; C-ALLTYPES makes a complete
              animal          ; exclusive split.
              virus
              bacterium))

(c-alltypes 'living-thing     ;A living thing must also be one of
            '(multi-celled    ; these.  This partition is orthogonal
              single-celled   ; to the one defined above.
              sub-cellular))

(c-type 'cell 'physob)        ;There is a thing called a cell ...

(inrole 'cell                 ;It has an individual nucleus.
  (c-indv 'nucleus 'physob))  ; The nucleus is an IN-role in cell.

(s-vc 'single-celled 'cell)   ;A single-celled thing IS a cell.

(inrole 'multi-celled         ;A multi-celled thing has a set of
  (c-type 'body-cell 'cell))  ; body-cells.  This creates an IN-role
                              ; that is a set-type pair.
```

```
;;; Now for some information about habitats.

(c-alltypes 'living-thing         ;A living thing must be one of these.
            '(water-dwelling      ; A water dweller.
              land-dwelling       ; A land-dweller.
              amphibious))        ; Happy in either.

(c-types 'water-dwelling          ;A water dweller may be one of these.
         '(aquatic                ; Lives in fresh-water.
           marine))               ; Lives in salt-water.

(c-type 'flyer 'living-thing)     ;Some living things are flyers.

(ofrole 'living-thing             ;Every living thing has a habitat
        (c-indv 'habitat          ; which is a spatial area.
                'spatial-area))

(s-exin 'living-thing             ;Every living thing exists within
        'habitat)                 ; its habitat.


(c-types 'spatial-area            ;Some types of spatial area.
         '(land-area
           water-area
           coastal-area
           air-area
           vacuum-area))

(c-types 'water-area              ;Make two flavors of water area.
         '(fresh-water-area       ;C-TYPES implies there may be others.
           ocean-area))
```

```
(s-vc (fm-oflist            ;The habitat of a land-dwelling thing
        '(habitat          ; is a land-area.  FM-OFLIST finds
          land-dwelling))  ; or makes a unique role-node, which
        'land-area)        ; is given a *VC-link to LAND-AREA.

(s-vc (fm-oflist            ;The habitat of a water-dwelling thing
        '(habitat          ; is a water-area.
          water-dwelling))
        'water-area)

(s-vc (fm-oflist            ;The habitat of a marine thing is an
        '(habitat          ; ocean-area.
          marine))
        'ocean-area)

(s-vc (fm-oflist            ;The habitat of an aquatic thing is a
        '(habitat          ; fresh-water-area.
          aquatic))
        'fresh-water-area)
```

```
;;; Note: the machinery is not yet implemented to say that amphibious
;;; organisms sometimes inhabit water and sometimes land.  Or that
;;; flyers sometimes inhabit the air and sometimes land or water.
```

```
;;; Information about non-animals: PLANTS, BACTERIA, VIRUSES.

(s-vc 'virus 'sub-cellular)        ;A virus is sub-cellular.

(c-type 'herpes 'virus)           ;A random virus to play with.

(s-vc 'bacterium 'sub-cellular)   ;So is a bacterium.

(c-type 'E-coli 'bacterium)       ;A random bacterium to play with.

(c-alltypes 'plant               ;A plant must be one of these.
            '(green-plant
               fungus))

(c-type 'slime-mold 'fungus)      ;A random fungus to play with.

(inrole 'green-plant              ;Green-plants have chloroplasts.
  (c-type 'chloroplast 'physob))

(c-type 'cabbage 'green-plant)    ;Create a plant-type for testing.

(s-vc 'cabbage 'multi-celled)     ;A cabbage is multi-celled.
```

```
;;; Information about animals.

(c-int 'protozoan              ;A single-celled animal is a
       'single-celled          ; protozoan.  This creates an
       'animal)                ; *INT-node for protozoan.


(c-type 'amoeba 'protozoan)     ;We can now connect under the *INT ...

(c-type 'paramecium 'animal)    ;Or directly under both parents.
(s-vc 'paramecium
      'single-celled)

(s-distinct '(amoeba            ;This will make a DISTINCT statement.
              paramecium))


(c-int 'metazoan                ;A multi-celled animal is a metazoan.
       'multi-celled
       'animal)

(c-types 'metazoan              ;Make some phyla of metazoans.
         '(coelenterate         ;Jellyfish.
           platyhelminth        ;Flatworms.
           nematode             ;Roundworms.
           annelid              ;Segmented worms.
           mollusc              ;Clams, octopuses, snails.
           arthropod            ;Insects and their relatives.
           echinoderm           ;Starfish.
           chordate))           ;Vertebrates and sharks.

(c-type 'worm 'animal)          ;Make a group of all worms.

(c-alltypes 'worm
            '(platyhelminth
              nematode
              annelid))
```

```
(c-types 'mollusc              ;Make some molluscs.
         '(univalve            ;Snails, etc.
           bivalve             ;Clams, etc.
           cephalopod))        ;Octopuses, etc.


(c-type 'snail 'univalve)      ;Some univalves are snails.


(c-types 'snail                ;Snails come in land ...
         '(land-snail
           water-snail))       ;and water varieties.


(s-vc 'mollusc                 ;Molluscs live in water.
      'water-dwelling)


(s-canvc 'land-snail           ;Except for land-snails ...
         'water-dwelling)


(s-vc 'land-snail              ;Which are land-dwelling.
      'land-dwelling)


(c-types 'bivalve              ;Create some bivalve types.
         '(clam
           oyster
           scallop
           mussel))


(c-types 'cephalopod           ;Create some cephalopods.
         '(octopus
           squid
           nautilus))
```

```
(c-type 'shell-bearer              ;Some metazoans are shell-bearers.
        'metazoan)

(ofrole 'shell-bearer              ;A shell-bearer has a shell.
        (c-indv 'shell
                'physob))

(s-vc 'mollusc                     ;A mollusc is a shell-bearer ...
      'shell-bearer)

(s-canvc 'cephalopod               ;Except for cephalopods ...
         'shell-bearer)

(s-vc 'nautilus                    ;But nautilus IS a shell-bearer.
      'shell-bearer)


(c-types 'arthropod                ;Insects and their relatives.
         '(insect                  ;Bugs.
           crustacean              ;Crabs, shrimp, lobsters
           arachnid                ;Spiders and scorpions.
           myriopod))              ;Centipedes and millipedes.

(ofrole 'arthropod                 ;An arthropod has an exoskeleton.
  (c-indv 'exoskeleton
          'physob))
```

```
(c-types 'echinoderm            ;Starfish and their relatives.
          '(starfish
            sea-cucumber
            sea-urchin))


(c-types 'chordate              ;Vertebrates and relatives.
          '(vertebrate          ;These have real backbones.
            cartilaginous-fish)) ;These do not.  Sharks, rays, etc.

(inrole 'chordate               ;Chordates have an endoskeleton.
   (c-indv 'endoskeleton
           'physob))

(c-type 'skeleton 'physob)      ;The term skeleton covers both
(s-vc 'endoskeleton 'skeleton)  ; endo and exo.
(s-vc 'exoskeleton 'skeleton)

(c-alltypes 'vertebrate         ;The classes of vertebrates.
             '(fish
               amphibian
               reptile
               bird
               mammal))

(c-types 'mammal                ;Create some assorted mammals.
          '(elephant
            aardvark
            pangolin
            numbat))


;;; Here ends the sample input from the animal world.
```

Obviously, this could go on for many pages in much the same way. Once this file is loaded, we can begin adding to it and querying it. Here are some sample interactions, just to give some idea of how the system might be used. Again, comments have been added after the semicolons.

```
(c-indv 'clyde 'elephant)       ;Creates the *INDV node for CLYDE.
(NODE CLYDE)                     ;The reply from LISP.


(s-vc 'clyde 'cabbage)          ;We tell it that Clyde is a cabbage.


(COMP-SPLIT-ST-4 SAYS A ANIMAL CANNOT BE A PLANT)
RETURN 'FORCE TO MAKE AN EXCEPTION.


;The system objects to this, but can be overridden.


(yn-vc 'clyde 'octopus)         ;Can Clyde also be an octopus?
NO -- (CHORDATE MOLLUSC)        ;No, because chordate and mollusc
                                ; are in a common split-set.


(y-has 'clyde 'shell)           ;Does Clyde have a shell?
NIL                             ;NETL does not know of one.


(y-has 'snail 'shell)           ;Does a snail have a shell?
YES                             ;Yes.


(y-has 'octopus 'shell)         ;Does an octopus have a shell?
NIL                             ;No.  The cancellation worked.


(y-has 'nautilus 'shell)        ;Does a nautilus have a shell?
YES                             ;Yes.  The reassertion worked.


(yn-vc 'paramecium 'protozoan)  ;Is a paramecium a protozoan?
YES                             ;Yes.  The *INT-node worked.
```

The system still does not have much of the machinery that it will eventually need. As noted in the code, for example, there is not yet support for the concept of "sometimes". An irritating feature of the system, when it is used directly by people, is the need to assign a unique name to each node. Thus, we were prevented from assigning the name "cell" to both the cell class and to the typical cell in a multicelled animal (which we named BODY-CELL instead). Still, a lot of information can be stuffed into the system quickly, and in a way that seems reasonably intuitive.

This small knowledge-base contains 433 elements, 100 of which are part of the base-load. CLYDE has 11 superiors in the network. The questions answered above typically took 200-400 simulated bus cycles, and 0.3 to 0.6 seconds of CPU-time. To mark every node in the network by sweeping down from the THING node takes 221 simulated cycles and 1.9 seconds of CPU-time.

A test-system of this size is still rather small to extrapolate run-times from, but we can make some crude estimates. A 10,000-element system is thirty times as large as the one shown here; it should take, at worst, 60 seconds to mark all of its nodes in a full downward scan. In a recognition system, such scans would be common; in property-finding scans, which move upward, it would be uncommon to find more than a small fraction of the nodes marked. We might estimate 10-20 seconds for the worst of these.

Time sharing costs us a factor of perhaps 3-5 in speed; moving to a KL-10 system would increase the speed by a comparable factor. In any event, it seems clear that for experimental purposes, at least, a knowledge base of 10,000 to 20,000 elements could be handled, with response times under a minute for simple questions and somewhat longer for recognitions and multiple-scan questions. A system of 20,000 elements or so would exhaust the 256K address space of the PDP-10, so response-times become irrelevant after that point. On a faster, dedicated machine with sufficient main memory, we might reach 100,000 elements. It is not clear whether the system will page well in a virtual memory system; unless a deliberate effort is made to pack related material together on pages, the network might sprawl randomly through the available memory space.

What could we fit into 10,000 to 20,000 nodes? This is certainly enough space for most developmental systems. It could handle a rather sizable blocks-world, restaurant-script, electronic network, travel advisor, or collection of animal trivia. On the other hand, it is probably too small to contain a practical consultant system in any but the most tightly bounded domains. We might be able to fit a small kidney-disease consultant into the knowledge-base, but not a whole medical-diagnosis system. We might be able to keep track of the Navy's ships, but not all of its people. We might be able to handle some particular area of chemical analysis, but not any sizable part of chemistry as a whole. Within these boundaries, however, there is plenty of room for interesting research to be done.

4.3 Electronics-World Test Results

The analog electronics world has been a constant source of good examples for the development of various parts of NETL. In fact, the whole idea of using a parallel network for inheritance (in those days I was calling it "symbol mapping") of structure and properties alike was spawned while I was considering some difficulties that Sussman, McDermott, and Allen Brown were having in representing electronic circuits. Part of the value of this domain is that it presents in a concentrated way some effects that are seen only in diluted forms in everyday domains: complex hierarchies of parts and sub-parts, teleological as well as structural descriptions, recursive descriptions (two-terminal devices built out of smaller two-terminal devices), the need to interface the knowledge-base system to a problem-solver, and so on. By itself, this domain might have too many idiosyncrasies for use in developing a real-world knowledge handling ability, but it nicely complements other, more mundane domains like animals, stories, or family relationships.

The demonstration system that has been implemented is intended to serve as the knowledge-base component for an electronics-world problem solver being developed at M.I.T. by Sussman, Doyle, de Kleer, Stallman, and others. A knowledge-base might serve many purposes in such a system, but the current implementation concentrates on one task: allowing the user to describe a network in terms of an interconnection of components, each of which is itself a virtual copy of some existing network-description. An ability to deal with virtual copies is critical to such a system: the electronic network's behavior must ultimately be understood in terms of the interaction of elements on the most primitive level of description, but to actually represent the network in such a fully-expanded form would be too slow and would use too much space in memory. (This unacceptable slowness is not a mere hypothesis: it has been demonstrated in practice by versions of the problem-solver that expand everything out to the level of primitive operators such as adders and multipliers.)

In the NETL representation of such networks, we use structures called "information boxes" or IBOXES. These do not deal with currents or voltages as such, but rather with *values* in the form of numbers or algebraic expressions. Thus, the approach is more general than electronics and could be used in many kinds of analog simulation problems. Some of the IBOXES are primitive ones, called PIBOXES; others are compound IBOXES (or CIBOXES) made up from some interconnection of other IBOXES, either primitive or compound. Each IBOX has a set of terminal values, called its *value-wires*, which can be equated (by an *EQ-link) to the value-wires of other IBOXES or to externally-meaningful values like "37" or "(X + 1)". A MULTIPLIER PIBOX, for instance, has two input value-wires and one output value-wire. The assignment of an external value to a wire is done by a function called SET-VALUE that creates an *INDV node of type VALUE, places the desired expression in the name-slot of this node, sets the node's **EXTERN flag, and creates an *EQ-link between the external value-node and the wire-node.

Each primitive IBOX has an associated demon program which implements the constraints between its inputs and outputs. If any two values of a given MULTIPLIER are known, for instance, its demon can be run to find the third value. The NETL system stores a pointer to the demon in the DEMON role of each PIBOX or PIBOX-type. It retrieves the demon-pointer for any PIBOX on command, but it has no responsibility for actually running the demon or asserting new values -- that is the problem-solver's job.

To describe a new type of compound IBOX, we specify a list of terminal value-wires, an optional list of internal value-wires, and a list of components. The components are *INDV nodes under some already-existing IBOX type. We then list the set of interconnections that we want among all of these value-wires. We may also specify particular permanent values for certain wires. In figure 43 we see how a compound IBOX-type

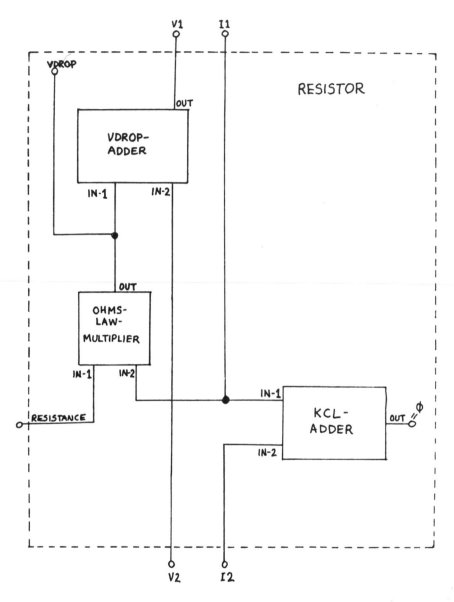

Figure 43: The compound IBOX-type RESISTOR, built from primitive ADDER and MULTIPLIER IBOXES.

for RESISTOR can be built up from primitive IBOXES: a multiplier, named OHMS-LAW-MULTIPLIER, and two adders, KCL-ADDER and VDROP-ADDER. The RESISTOR has five terminal value-wires: I1, I2, V1, V2, and RESISTANCE. In addition, it has an internal value-wire, VDROP, where OHMS-LAW-MULT feeds into VDROP-ADDER. This internal wire allows us to talk about the VDROP of a given adder, rather than the OUT-wire of the OHMS-LAW-MULTIPLIER of that resistor -- in other words, it reduces the depth of nesting. Note that the value at the output of the KCL-ADDER is 0 for all members of the RESISTOR set. A function called NEW-CIBOX exists which will build up the proper NETL-description of a device-type from a list of the device's wires, components, interconnections, and internally-set values. Once the type-description for RESISTOR has been created, we can create individual resistors at will, mapping only those wires that we want to set or connect; the user can forget about the internal structure of the device.

Resistors can now be used as elements in creating other, more complex devices. In figure 44, then, we see a two-resistor voltage-divider (or VD) built up from two instances of RESISTOR, named RTOP and RBOT, and a three-input KCL-ADDER. This device has eight terminal value-wires: ITOP, IMID, IBOT, VTOP, VMID, VBOT, TOP-RESISTANCE, and BOTTOM-RESISTANCE. The output of the KCL-ADDER is set to 0. Note that nothing is said here about the internal adders and multipliers of the resistors.

Now, suppose that the problem-solver applies a value of 37 to VMID of an individual voltage divider, VD-1. As noted above, this act requires the creation of an **EXTERN *INDV node for the value 37, which is then equated to the *MAP-node of VMID in the VD-1 description. In applying this voltage, however, SET-VALUE must check two things. First, there might already be a value, "(X + 1)" perhaps, on this node or one of its equivalents. This value should be located and passed back to the problem-solver, which can then perform the proper algebraic

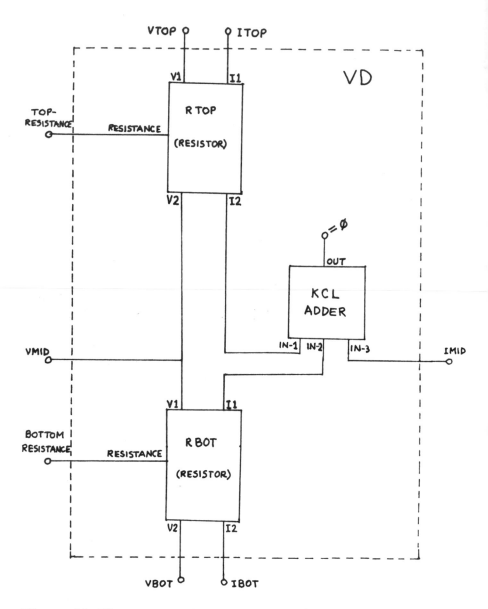

Figure 44: The compound IBOX-type VD (voltage divider), built from two RESISTORS and an ADDER.

substitutions for all appearances of X. Second, in the nest of expansions of the VD description, the VMID wire is probably attached to one or more wires of primitive IBOXES. These primitive IBOXES must be identified so that their demons can be run and any new values found can be attached to their other wires. As the problem-solver is currently set up, any single equivalent value is sufficient, and the demons need to be run only if an equivalent value is not found. SET-VALUE, then, in addition to adding the new value, returns with either an older value for the same wire (or an equivalent wire), or with a list of the wires of primitive IBOXES that, in the fully expanded network, would be tied to the wire whose value was set. Since these primitive IBOXES do not really exist in the representation, and we do not want to create them, they cannot have individual names; instead we identify them by a list, (A B C D), which is read as "the A of the B of the C of D". Such lists may be of any length greater than two, though if the list is too long to be handled with the available number of marker-pairs, special techniques (not yet implemented) will have to be used.

In setting VMID of VD-1 to 37, SET-VALUE finds no equivalent values, so it returns a list of equivalent PIBOX wires. This list has two members: (IN-2 VDROP-ADDER RTOP VD-1) and (OUT VD-ADDER VBOT VD-1). To find the demon associated with the first wire on this list, the problem solver calls F-OFLIST with the argument (DEMON VDROP-ADDER RTOP VD-1). Note that this is just the list returned by SET-VALUE, with DEMON substituted for the wire-name. To find the values, if any, attached to the IN-1 and OUT wires of this adder, we call F-OFLIST with these wire-names substituted at the head of the list. The demon may then want to set one of these wires to some value it has computed. It calls FM-OFLIST to obtain a unique node for the wire it wants to set, then does a new SET-VALUE for this node.

F-OFLIST is essentially the algorithm that we saw in section 3.7, in finding the WEIGHT of the TRUNK of CLYDE. It activates the outermost description first, then the next one in, and so on, using a pair of markers to handle the activation and cancellation for each term in the list. When it gets to the term that it wants, it begins backing out, level by level, erasing any answer-marks in recursively shared descriptions as it goes. FM-OFLIST is almost identical, except that as it is backing out, it makes sure that at least one answer-mark is on a node whose owner-wire or existence wire is tied to some node that actually appears in the argument-list or to the current context-node, and not just to an ancestor of such a term; if necessary, it makes a *MAP node to enforce this rule. This produces the minimum necessary extra structure to uniquely specify the entity in question. These functions are both limited in the depth to which they can follow an OFLIST by the number of marker-pairs available, though if there are no cancellations within an activation, no marker is assigned. With the current fifteen markers, the system can get five or six levels deep, or more if there are no cancellations in some of the activated descriptions.

The primitive-wire finder, GETPRIMS, which is called by SET-VALUE, is passed a wire-name and a component-name. It activates the component-description, then marks the equivalents of the specified wire within the component-activation. The marked wire-nodes are then examined. This examination is serial in the simulation, though the hardware NETL would do it in parallel. If an **EXTERN node is encountered, signifying an equivalent value, then GETPRIMS returns with this value immediately. If a PIBOX wire is encountered (all of these carry a special flag-bit, defined for this electronics system only), it is placed on an answer-list and the search continues. If a regular *MAP-node is encountered, it is put on a list for later investigation. When all of the nodes found by one activation have been checked out, the markers are released and GETPRIMS is called recursively for each of the *MAP-nodes. This, in effect, expands out each of the component-boxes to which the original value-wire is attached. When the list of *MAP-nodes has been exhausted, GETPRIMS returns with its list of primitives; as these lists are being passed back through the levels of recursion, each level splices on the name of the box it was investigating, to produce the OFLISTS in the format described above. Note that since each level releases its markers before making a recursive call, this function can go to any depth. It requires a two scans -- activation and wire-marking -- and two (simulated) parallel tests for each virtual IBOX that it investigates. Even in the serial simulator, this is much less work than actually expanding everything out.

In the demo that is currently running, the ADDER, MULTIPLIER, RESISTOR, and VD IBOXES are defined as described above. To create a new VD requires only 1 new element, the *INDV node for this VD. The checking associated with this creation takes 82 simulated cycles, and the real CPU-time required is about .3 seconds. To set the value of one of the value-wires of this individual VD takes 500-1200 simulated cycles, and between .7 and 1.3 seconds of CPU-time, depending on how many component IBOXES are actually investigated. To retrieve whatever value may be on some wire using F-OFLIST takes about 600 simulated cycles and from .5 to .8 seconds. These times suggest that moderate-sized circuit diagrams can be explored using the simulator with the response time for a typical knowledge-base call staying well under one minute. The CPU-time for such a call depends only weakly on the total size of the network-description, but it varies directly with the depth and complexity of the structure that is attached to the wire being checked or altered.

5. Conclusions

In this final chapter, I will try to answer a few global questions about this work: What lessons have been learned from it? What should be done next? How might it relate to neighboring fields, particularly psychology and computer science?

Looking first at the parallel network system, I would draw the following overall conclusions:

First, that the intersection of large explicit and semi-explicit sets is a ubiquitous and important problem in that part of AI that deals with knowledge. So far, we have found ways to avoid and limit these intersections on a case-by-case basis, but it is easier just to do them.

Second, that much of the fog and confusion in this area of AI is the result of our mixing together deep, poorly defined problems of representation with the difficult but clear-cut technical problem of getting the intersections done. This is especially dangerous because, at present, neither problem is understood very well. The time may come to integrate our solutions to these problems, but for now they should be separated. Without such a separation, NETL could not have been developed to its present level.

Third, that an externally controlled parallel network, of the type described here, is at worst a good metaphor for enforcing this separation of problems in our minds; at best it may be a practical solution to the intersection problem.

Fourth, that for building a knowledge-base, the type of parallelism described here is better in several respects than the more familiar system of co-operating but autonomous processors. The network elements are very simple, so many more of them can be bought for a given sum of money. For performing the tasks we have described here, little advantage would be gained by having a more complex processor at each node. In fact, it can be viewed as a positive advantage that the elements of this network are too simple to fight over control or access to data, or to require complex signaling conventions and internal languages. All power is in one place: the central controller. If nothing else, this makes the system understandable -- a rare feature in parallel systems.

The parallel network system is easy to generalize about; the notational system, NETL, is a much less unified concept. It is the result of three years of intensive work, seven or eight cycles of throwing everything away and starting over, and perhaps fifty smaller reorganizations. Readers who are familiar with my progress report of two years ago [Fahlman, 1975] will notice that, in its external appearance, the notational system I had in mind at that time differs only in small details from the current one. These small, subtle differences make a big difference in the ease with which the notational system can be implemented and used. They are the difference between a system that can be *made* to work on certain simple cases, and a system that handles most cases in a way that seems natural and unforced. Since the system assumed its current form in January of 1977, it has seemed quite solid, a condition that was never achieved during the previous two and a half years. For the first time, I can think of potentially troublesome examples like "Every elephant believes that every other elephant hates himself," can try the obvious representation in NETL, and more often than not find that it works without any changes.

Like any system of notation, NETL is essentially a bag of tricks, some elegant, some ugly. It was the clear enunciation of the virtual copy idea, and the decision to keep this idea before me at all times, that first gave me a way to determine whether these techniques were working together properly. The words "virtual copy" stated clearly, for the first time, exactly what the system was trying to do. And this was the weapon with which I was finally able to isolate and deal with the copy-confusion problem. Perhaps I have over-emphasized this idea -- it has, after all, been lurking in the background of every knowledge-base system developed in recent years, and perhaps has been obvious to everyone else -- but its arrival marked a turning point in the development of NETL.

The copy-confusion problem was the one potentially fatal bug that persisted until very recently. If no way had been found of dealing with this problem, the role-mapping scheme of section 3.5 would have been doomed. By itself and masked by the less-serious binding-ambiguity bug and a generally high level of overall confusion, copy-confusion caused most of the difficulties during the middle year of NETL's development. I believe that this bug can cause no further trouble, now that it has been recognized and understood. By resorting to heuristic and depth-limited searches, we have limited NETL's ability to make deductions, but it is a human-like limitation and I believe we can live with it. Note that the serial problem-solving processes residing in the central control computer are still as general as any computer-based system, and can read the information stored in the network at any depth; it is only the component of reasoning done by fast parallel scanning through the network that is limited in certain ways.

There are still many problem areas in NETL, but I believe that the visible problems, at least, are minor ones. The representation of actions and events needs more work. The interaction between the PART-OF and IS-A hierarchies is not yet really satisfactory. The "in" and "of" distinction among roles still looks rather arbirtrary, and "at" is not handled at all. There is too much difference between the base-node of a description and a role; role-reversal should be a smoother process than it currently is. Location is handled awkwardly ("at" again), and so is movement and the representation of space. Continuous quantities, measurements, and substances have not yet been added to the system. There are many more complaints like this -- enough to keep us busy for several years, and we will have discovered many new problems by then. Still, if there is a system-killer in this group of problems, it has yet to make its identity known.

As I said earlier, I believe that the simulated version of NETL is about a year away from being a generally useful experimental tool, possibly with some practical uses as well. At present, however, the simulation is incomplete and it has been exercised very little by the existing example systems. I believe that the ideas presented in this report stand on their own merit, but they will be far more convincing when they are given a more tangible form, embedded in a large, working system, performing some task that is known to be very difficult for other systems. A large simulation could have been started earlier, while NETL was still plagued with internal problems and inconsistencies, but I felt that it would be more valuable, given the limited time available, to try to solidify the semantic foundation of the work. In light of the last-minute insights and clarifications provided by the virtual-copy concept, I believe that this decision was the right one. NETL is now a tool rather than a problem.

The next step, then, is obvious: to use the simulator to attack large, real problem-domains. Each of these domains will require some new and interesting machinery, and will raise new questions. Let me suggest some possible areas of implementation, and the unique problems that each will raise. Many of these problems have already been attacked by other methods, and a comparison of the difficulties encountered should be informative.

The world of animals has already been started. It contains a very large and tangled type hierarchy, with many odd cases and exceptions. Eventually, an animal-world system would have to include descriptions of actions and habits, and the structural descriptions of animals would lead naturally into recognition, shape-description, and an interface with vision research.

The world of analog electronics has also been started. It would thoroughly exercise the system's representation for parts and sub-parts, and would also require a strong ability to handle multiple representations. This world overlaps considerably with problem-solving. See McDermott [1977], Sussman [1977], Brown [1977].

The closely related worlds of digital hardware and computer programming would require a strong ability to represent states and transitions, the abstract concepts of information and representation, and the ideas of plan expansion and modification. See Rich and Shrobe [1976].

The world of cooking is an ideal one for studying the representation of actions and the formation of simple but flexible plans. Initially, these would be strictly serial, but parallel plan-execution is also possible, and sometimes essential. This world would also throughly exercise the representation for measurements, substances, and continuous quantities. Scragg [1975] has done considerable work in this domain.

A history knowledge-base would exercise the machinery for representing actions, time, causality, and perhaps human motivations. Geography would exercise the ability to represent space and changing boundaries. As Collins and his group have shown [1975], geography can also be an excellent test-bed for developing inductive reasoning and abstraction.

Medicine introduces some very complex recognition problems dealing with varying weights and confidence factors, masking, explaining discrepancies, the interaction of multiple diseases in the same patient, and so on. I believe that a medical dignosis system would help to develop the flexible kind of recognition strategies that will eventually be needed in high-level visual recognition.

The world of legal reasoning introduces the problems of conflicting sources and authorities, conflicting versions of an event, human motivation, and reasoning by analogy. In some areas of law, it is specified how certain evidence is to be weighed and interpreted; in other words, a legal reasoning system must be prepared to accept instructions about how to think. Meldman [1975] has made a start in this area.

And story understanding, as we all know, exercises almost everything. Each of these projects would require significant additions to the currently-existing NETL system, but I believe that each would be made significantly more manageable by building on the existing foundation of NETL. After a few of these projects have been attempted, it will be time to reassess the basic ideas of NETL in light of what has happened.

What, if anything, do the ideas in this report have to do with psychology and the study of brains? Is it really possible that the human mind might be constructed using the same kind of network that has been described here? On a detailed level, there are clearly some differences: it seems very unlikely that the brain has an address bus and a set of elements with unique serial numbers, or that it operates on precise clock-pulses. A more interesting question, however, is whether the brain could be making use of the same general kind of parallelism, controlled from some specialized central region. Small groups of neurons could probably be set up to function as link and node units, and the system of interconnections and synapses form an excellent switching network to connect these elements to one another. I have no direct evidence that the brain does work in this way, but I think that this type of parallelism is worthy of investigation as a model. It is one of the very few precisely-stated models in existence that can capture all three of the following: a huge storage capacity, an ability to obtain direct, precise answers to queries, and an ability to produce human-like response times with processing elements that themselves are not particularly fast in comparison with electronic switching devices. If other models do not meet these basic criteria, then any human-like properties that they do have seem irrelevant.

What, if anything, might these ideas contribute to computer science? Perhaps a new class of devices to study. What we have here is, to the best of my knowledge, a new kind of parallelism, rather different from the parallelism that is usually studied in that its control is centralized. It is also different from the cellular automata, since each element is free to connect its wires to any other element in the system. This new kind of parallelism is very limited in some directions and very powerful in others, and may have important properties that I have missed entirely. On the practical side, I would suspect that other domains besides AI have trouble computing the intersections of semi-explicit sets; if so, networks such as this might help. Finally, the problem of interconnecting many single elements, or microprocessors representing many elements (see appendix A), is really a problem in computer science, not in AI. Any really good solution to this problem will almost certainly have other important applications as well.

The virtual-copy idea may have some relevance to the theory and practice of designing programming languages. A subroutine or function call, after all, is a way to make a virtual copy of a piece of code. In fact, in computer graphics, a field in which virtual copies of pictures are needed constantly, the standard technique has been to represent a picture as a piece of code and "call" it from several locations. But virtual copies, as NETL uses them, are more general in some ways than subroutine calls. A subroutine instance (or execution frame) cannot usually have multiple parents, though spaghetti stacks come close to this. In a subroutine, only certain pre-defined roles, the arguments, can be mapped and altered, and exceptions (local modification of the parent program from within one of its executions) are usually not allowed. Programs (unlike data-types) seldom have a hierarchy of types: there is just the parent code and a single layer of execution-instances. And so on. I am not saying that NETL, in any direct way, will spawn the computer language of the future, but it may provide food for thought.

NETL would appear to have some usefulness to the philosophers who worry about things like reference and meaning, if only to serve as a stationary target, devoid of the customary fog. Though I believe that NETL would serve as a good substrate for a natural-language understanding system, I do not think that NETL has anything to contribute to linguistics, if we define linguistics as the study of language itself, rather than how it is processed.

The ultimate goal of this and related work is to develop a system that, in any reasonable sense of the word, *understands* what we tell it. I believe that the ideas presented here are a step in that direction, but only time and more experience can tell us how big a step it is and how far we still have to go.

Appendix A: Implementing the Parallel Network in Hardware

A.1 Design of a Typical Element-Unit

As we saw in section 4, the current simulation of NETL can produce reasonably fast responses for knowledge bases up to ten or twenty thousand elements. With a faster, dedicated machine and enough main memory, we might be able to reach a hundred thousand elements or more. Such a system would be more than sufficient for our present and near-future experimental needs. Sooner or later, however, we are going to want a better combination of memory size and speed than a serial simulation can provide; at that point, it will be time to think seriously about implementing the network in hardware. In this appendix, we will take a preliminary look at the problems that such an implementation will face, and will see a few possible approaches to solving these problems.

The discussion will cover three topics. First, in section A.1 of this appendix, we will explore the question of what a typical element-unit (a combined node and link) might look like. A sample circuit-design will be presented for such an element. Next, in section A.2, we will consider ways of forming new link-to-node interconnections as the system acquires new knowledge. This is the key obstacle that must be overcome if we are to realize the network system in hardware, and several distinct approaches will be explored. Finally, in section A.3, we will look at the prospects for using more conventional technology -- a network of microprocessors -- to achieve a smaller, but still significant, amount of parallel speed-up. Such a system might fill the gap between a slow serial simulation of the network and a full-scale parallel implementation.

Figures A1 through A4 illustrate what the circuit for a typical element unit might look like. This design is for illustrative purposes only; it is not intended to be practical or optimal. TTL NAND-gates and flip-flops are used, since TTL is the logic family that is understood by the largest number of this report's potential readers; a practical design would almost certainly use some other family of logic, since speed is not especially critical, while density and price are.

Each element-unit is connected to a party-line bus from the control computer (or "CPU") on one side; on the other side it has a single node-terminal and a number, W, of link-wires. In the current simulated system, W is 6. Initially, these link-wires are not connected to anything; when an element unit is selected to represent some fact or concept, the link-wires must be connected to the approprite node-terminals of elements already in use. Each node-terminal may have any number of incoming link-wires connected to it; each link-wire is connected to only one node-terminal. These connections are semi-permanent: one seldom wants to *remove* a concept once it is represented, though concepts are often *cancelled* in later contexts. In the design given here, it is assumed that the link-to-node connections are created by some mechanism completely external to the element-unit itself.

The link-to-node connection must allow two-way communication between the node and the attached links: during certain operations, the node part of the element is allowed to pull down the node-terminal line; during other operations, any of the attached link-wires can pull the terminal down. If no one pulls it down, the line floats high (+5 volts). This sort of operation is achieved by the use of open-collector bus-driver gates at the node and link-wire terminals. Of course, open collector drivers are also used to drive the two-way lines of the CPU bus.

Each element-unit has a unique serial number or *address* of N bits; for a million-element system, N would be 20. Each element also has M internal JK-type flip-flops to hold its marker-bits; in the current simulated version of NETL, M is 15. Each bit of the address and each marker-bit has two *select lines* on the CPU bus. The CPU sends commands to some subset of the elements in the system by placing a set of address-bits and marker-bits on these lines. If a given bit must be a 0 for an element to be selected, the CPU pulls down the A line for that bit, letting the complement-line, XA, float high. If the bit must be a 1 for the element to be selected, the CPU pulls down the XA line and lets the A line float high. If the CPU doesn't care what an element has in a given bit position, it pulls down neither line. Marker-bits are specified in the same way, but using M and XM lines instead of A and XA. Using this mechanism, any element can be selected on the basis of its serial number alone, its marker bits alone, or some combination of the two. The assembly in figure A1 decodes this address and determines whether the element-unit is among those selected at any given time.

The circuit, as presented, makes no special provision for flag-bits. These could be handled in two ways. First, the flags could be preassigned to the element units, creating separate pools of *INDV-nodes, *VC-links, and so on. In this case, they would be handled exactly as address-lines are. Alternatively, the flag bits could be set in a node when it is called up for duty. In this case, the flags would be handled as additional marker-bits, though we would probably want to put them in special non-volatile, write-once memory cells so that they would not disappear in a power failure, and could not accidentally be erased by a programming error.

In addition to its marker-bits, each element-unit has two type-D control flip-flops. One of these, the NSEL flip-flop (for "node select"), is used to remember whether its element was among those selected during the previous selection cycle. To read the marker-bits of a particular element, for instance, the CPU would place that element's address on the selection lines and then send out the NPULSE to save each node's SELECT level in its NSEL flip-flop; in this case, only the node with the specified serial number would have its NSEL bit set. Then, the CPU stops driving the select lines from its end and sets the READ level high. This causes each element with the NSEL bit set to place its serial number and marker-bit contents on the select-lines by pulling down the appropriate combination of complemented and uncomplemented lines. The marker-bit contents of the single selected element can then be read from the bus.

If marker-bit contents are used in the initial selection, it may not be true that exactly one element will have its NSEL bit set: there might be many elements with a given set of marker bits, or there might be none. If no elements meet the selection criteria that are currently on the bus, the CPU will sense this immediately: the -SENSE line of the bus will be floating high. If a READ attempt is made while more than element has its NSEL bit set, at least one of the address bits will have both its A and its XA bus-lines pulled down at once. This causes no damage, but it does signal to the CPU that more than one node is trying to respond to the READ command. This means that the selected set must either be reduced by further processing, or it must be polled. The polling procedure finds the highest-order address-line that is conflicted (both A and XA are being pulled down), and repeats the selection process twice: first the conflicted line is set to 0, then to 1. If the new selection resolves the conflict, the selected node's contents are read out. If either or both of the new selections still has a conflict, the next most significant bit must be forced to 0 and 1, and so on until all branches of the search end in single elements. The selected elements will be read out by this process in the order of increasing serial-numbers. If you prefer decreasing serial numbers (that is, the most recently-created element comes out first), force the 1 before the 0.

An alternative polling scheme (not included in the circuit diagrams) would use a daisy-chain system: a single POLL line would run through all of the elements, passing through a gate in each. If the NSEL flip-flop of an element is off, it passes the POLL level on to the next element in line. If NSEL is set, the element breaks the POLL line. Thus, only the first NSEL-selected element along the POLL line can see the POLL level as it comes from the CPU, and this element is the one that places its contents on the select lines. Once an element has been harvested, the CPU can clear that element's LSEL level and go on to read the next selected element in the chain. This scheme makes less work for the CPU, and for harvesting large sets it is faster, but it can cause a reliability problem: a single bad element unit can swallow the POLL level permanently, bringing down the entire system. There is also a timing problem: the POLL signal must pass through as many gate delays as there are elements in the system. This latter problem can be avoided by cutting the POLL line into short, independently polled sections.

(Note that people do a terrible job of polling: we might know the set of states in the United States very well in the sense that we can recognize any member of that set or intersect the set with other sets, but if asked to list all of the states, we boggle. This has been taken as evidence that, in people, markers (or whatever) can only move in one direction through the type-hierarchy. If, indeed, we can mark and intersect stored sets, however, the "States" problem must be due to polling inadequacies.)

To alter the marker bits present in some set of elements, the CPU proceeds as follows: First, the address and marker-bits that characterize the desired set are placed on the select-lines. The NPULSE is then sent out to set the NSEL flip-flop in the selected elements. The control signals for the JK marker-bit flip-flops are then placed on the M and XM lines, and the MPULSE is sent. This pulse reaches only those flip-flops in NSEL-selected elements, triggering them: if only the M line is high, the marker-bit is set; if only the XM line is high, the marker-bit is cleared; if both lines are low, the bit remains in its previous state. Thus, only the markers which the CPU wants to change are altered. A JK flip-flop will toggle if it is clocked while both inputs are high; at present I see no good use for this feature, but we do need the "no change" state that the JK provides.

So far, we have dealt only with the node portion of the element-unit. The link operations are controlled by the LSEL (for "link select") flip-flop. To see how this part of the element works, we will follow the steps involved in propagating an M1 marker upward through a *VC link. First, the CPU must call all active *VC links in the system to attention. Each link-type or node-type has its own special pattern of flag bits, so the flag-pattern specifying a *VC-link is placed on the select-lines. The CPU may also specify that certain context-activation markers must be set for selection to occur, and that certain cancellation markers must not be set. The ATTN ("attention") level is raised and the LPULSE is sent out. This sets the LSEL bit in every element that has the desired set of flags and markers.

Next, the CPU must determine which of the selected links has an M1 mark at the end of its A-wire. Only these links will participate in the propagation; the rest will have their LSEL-bits turned off. The CPU places the "M1 on" requirement on the select lines, raises the WSELA ("wire-select A") level, and sends out the LPULSE. Note that this pulse does not alter the NSEL or LSEL bits of the M1-marked node; rather, it preserves from destruction the LSEL bit in any element tied by its A-wire to an M1-marked node. All LSEL bits that are not so preserved are cleared by the LPULSE.

Finally, the node connected to any selected link's B-wire must have its M1 marker-bit set, unless it has M1 set already. This is done in two phases. First, the CPU raises the LN ("link to node transfer") line and the WSELB ("wire-select B") line, and pulls down the select-line for the M1 bit. Then the NPULSE is sent out. This causes the NSEL flip-flop to be set in all nodes that are attached to the B-wire of an LSEL-selected link, but only if M1 is not already set in this node. The CPU can look at the -SENSE line to determine whether any such nodes exist; if not, the scan can be terminated at this level, since no new nodes have been marked. Once NSEL is set in the desired nodes, the CPU pulls down the XM1 line (plus both lines for all other marker-bits, to preserve them in their current states) and sends out the MPULSE. This sets the M1 marker in the selected nodes. One level of propagation is now complete, after four bus-cycles; to complete the propagation-scan, the CPU

repeats the above sequence until it no longer senses any activity
on the -SENSE line. Of course, in a real activation scan, the
CPU would also have to send M1 marks across *EQ links, active
*MAP-wires, parent-wires, and so on, so a single level of
propagation might take 20 or 25 bus-cycles in all.

The only control signals that we have not yet seen in
action are the HANDLE signal and the -CLEAR signal. The
HANDLE signal is used when we have selected some link, as
described above, but instead of marking a node attached to one
of the link-wires, we want to mark that link's own handle-node.
The CPU, by raising the HANDLE line and sending out
NPULSE, can set the NSEL bit in every element that currently
has the LSEL bit set. The -CLEAR line is pulled low to reset
all of the flip-flops in the network.

Adding up all of the logic for an element with 6
link-wires, 20 bits of address, and 15 marker bits, we find that
we need 17 flip-flops, one 37-input selection gate, one 7-input
gate at the input of the LSET flip-flop, 58 assorted bus driver
gates of three or fewer inputs, and 62 regular gates, most of
which have two inputs. The bus has 70 select-lines, 14 control
lines, 1 sense line, and one clock line, for a total of 86. This
seems like a lot of logic, but it is considerably less than would
be required in a conventional system just to store an assertion of
three 20-bit fields in flip-flops. The reason for this economy is
that the information represented by an element is not stored
within it, but rather in the pattern of interconnections. It is
probable that with current technology we could pack a hundred
of these elements on a chip and perhaps even a thousand -- if
not now, then soon. The real problem is in packaging: 86 bus
lines is a lot to get into a DIP package, and when you add 700
or 7000 link-wire and node-terminal lines, the problem becomes
hopeless. I have no idea what to do about this problem, except
to build a bigger package with more wires.

One final comment: We can reduce the number of
bus-lines coming into an element (and the number of bus-driver
gates per element) by 20 by decoding the ten high-order address

lines once for an entire group of nodes. These twenty lines would be boiled down to a single "group-select" level which would go to all 1024 elements in the group. Similarly, by pulling down a special "group-reply" line, any node in the group could cause the decoder to place the group's serial number on the address lines that it intercepts.

(Appendix sections A.2 and A.3 appear after the following diagrams.)

Table of CPU-Bus Signals

An   Address select lines, one per bit of serial number, 2-way level.

XAn   Complement address select lines, one per address bit, 2-way level.

Mm   Marker-bit select lines, one per marker-bit, 2-way level.

XMm   Complement marker-bit select lines, one per marker-bit, 2-way level.

READ   Level, from CPU. When high, all elements with NSEL set put their address and marker contents on the select lines.

ATTN   Attention, level, from CPU. When high, LPULSE sets LSEL flip-flop if element address and markers match select-lines.

LN   Link-to-node transfer, level, from CPU. Used in conjunction with one of the wire-select levels. When high, NPULSE sets NSEL in any node attached to an LSEL link with the specified wire.

WSELw   Wire-select A, B, C, etc., one for each wire. Level, from CPU. Specifies which link-wire to use in node-to-link and link-to-node transfers.

HANDLE   Level, from CPU. If high, NPULSE stuffs LSEL level into NSEL flip-flop.

-CLEAR   Level, from CPU, normally high. When low, resets all marker, LSEL, and NSEL flip-flops in the network.

-SENSE   Level, to CPU, normally high. When low, at least one element is selected.

-CLOCK   Low-going pulse, from CPU. Used to create NPULSE, LPULSE, and
         .MPULSE within each element.

NSTROBE Level, from CPU. When high, -CLOCK produces NPULSE, triggering
         NSEL flip-flop.

LSTROBE Level, from CPU. When high, -CLOCK produces LPULSE, triggering
         LSEL flip-flop.

MSTROBE Level, from CPU. When high, -CLOCK produces MPULSE if NSEL is
         set, triggering the marker-bit flip-flops.

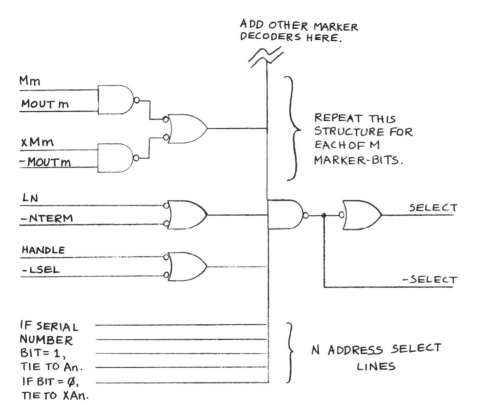

Figure A1: Sample Element-Unit Circuit, Selection Logic.

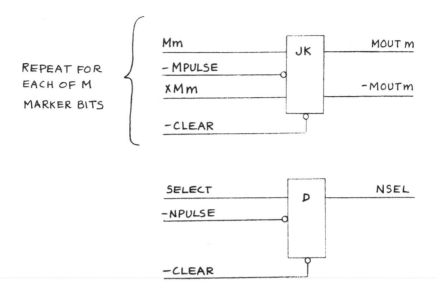

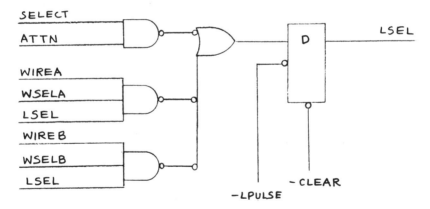

Figure A2: Sample Element-Unit Circuit, Flip-Flop Logic.

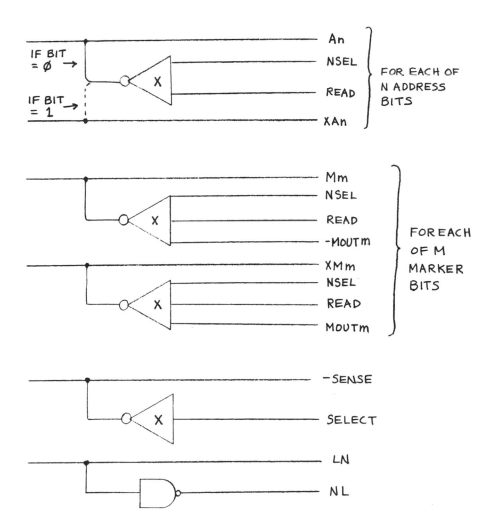

Figure A3: Sample Element-Unit Circuit, CPU-Bus Interface Logic.

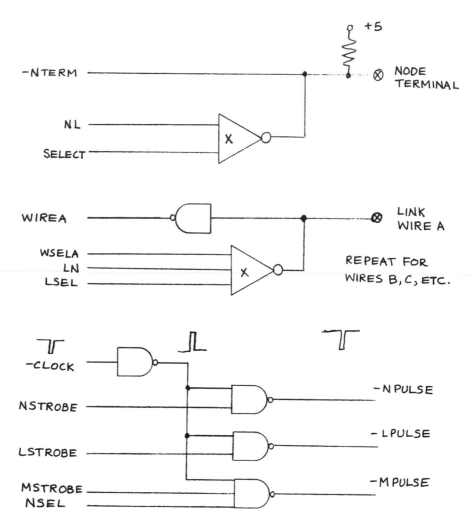

Figure A4: Sample Element-Unit Circuit, Node-Link Interface and Clock Decoder.

A.2 Connecting Link-Wires to Nodes

If we leave aside the problem of connecting the link-wires to the proper nodes, the parallel hardware system looks quite practical, even using current technology. Unfortunately, we cannot leave the interconnection problem aside. In a million-element system, we must somehow be able to connect any of six-million link-wires to any of a million possible destinations. The connections should not be volatile, so that the system does not lose all of its knowledge every time the power is turned off. The process of making a connection does not have to be especially fast, at least for human-like performance: something on the order of ten link-wire connections per second ought to suffice. If many facts arrive in a burst, the CPU can store some of them for later assimilation. Another small factor in our favor is the fact that, while a node may be tied to many link-wires, each wire is tied to only one node. This means that there is no possibility of "sneak paths" forming through multiple connections, tying together elements that are not intended to be. In many memory sytems, such sneak paths can be eliminated only by the use of a diode at each connection-point.

In a mass-produced consultant system with a large body of unchanging expert knowledge, the necessary connections could be added at the factory using some sort of printed circuit. Such a system would be useless for experimentation and for development of the original expert knowledge-base, but it might be a practical and relatively inexpensive way to disseminate a large body of knowledge once that knowledge-base has been assembled. Even in a knowledge-intensive consultant, however, there will still have to be a large section of modifiable network for representing the purely local or exceptional aspects of the local situation that the system is dealing with. Though the link-wires originating in the fixed portion of the network will all be tied up neatly, the node terminals must still be made accessible to link-wires originating in the modifiable area.

There are two basic approaches to connecting link-wires to nodes: first, we can actually create new wires as we need them. We might, for instance, envision a computer-driven wire-wrap machine installing new connections as they are called for. Of course, for a wire-wrap panel on the familiar scale, with spaces of at least a centimeter between adjacent posts, a field of seven million posts would occupy a square about twenty-five meters on a side. A miniaturized version with one-millimeter spacing between posts, would be only 2.5 meters on a side; at this sort of scale, however, we would probably have to use some sort of spot-welding technique to make the connection, since mechanical connections would be too fragile. Even smaller micro-manipulators are not unimaginable, but the technology does not exist at present. The advantage of such a machine is that only 7N connection points are needed for N elements, and that the third dimension is being exploited to eliminate interference when one wire must cross another. The disadvantage is that such a machine would be expensive, unreliable, and would probably not be able to acheive even our limited goal of ten connections per second.

Two more-exotic wire creation techniques might be worthy of some investigation, though neither seems likely to succeed. One is to create a "wire" by finding a path through a large three-dimensional array of cellular automata, each of which can establish a connection with any two of its six neighbors. If these are just tiny switches, and the route is selected externally, the question is how to make the selection and how to get the orders into the network. If the automata themselves are computing the route, the question is how complex they must be to do this, and how many are needed. I do not know the answers to these questions.

A more bizarre possibility is to grow the wires out of some sort of electrolytic solution by establishing a current between the two terminals to be connected. Under the proper conditions, a long, thin "whisker" will grow along the path of least resistance, but I am not confident that this process would work in the presence of thousands of other whiskers. In any event, unless the wires could be made to insulate themselves as they grew, the system would have to be drained of electrolyte before it could be used, and there would be many short-circuits. It seems unlikely that this sort of technology could be made reliable and controllable enough for use in a network system in the forseeable future.

The second general class of solutions is to use some sort of switching network to achieve the desired pattern of interconnections. Of the possible candidates for such a network, the simplest is the crosspoint switch. Imagine that the link-wires, six from each element in the network, are stretched out side-by-side, horizontally, in a north-south direction. Above them is a layer of insulating substance, and above that are wires from the node-terminals, stretched out in an east-west direction. Wherever an east-west wire crosses a north-south one, that is a potential connection point.

We could imagine that an actual switch is present at the cross-point, but that would be expensive: in a million-element system, we would have $6x10^{12}$ potential connection-points, only six million of which -- one per link-wire -- would ever be used. A more attractive solution is to create nothing at *potential* connection-points; where a connection is actually wanted, the insulating material between the wires would be replaced by, or converted to, conducting material. Performing this replacement mechanically -- drilling a hole through the insulator and filling it with metal, would entail all of the problems of our wire-wrap machine and many others. The only hope, then, is to find some material which can be converted from an insulating state to a conducting one at a the desired spot. This conversion might be triggered by some external stimulus, like a beam of light or electrons; it might also be made in response to an applied electric field between the two wires that are to be connected. Other things being equal, the electrical triggering would be preferable, since it requires no critical alignment of optics and no access to the connection-plane from the third dimension.

This means that the plane could be folded into a compact volume.

It appears that certain chalcogenide glasses, members of the family of amorphous semiconductors, would be ideal for this task. These glasses can exist in either of two stable states: a glassy state of high resistivity, and a crystalline state with a much lower resistivity. The state of any given sample of the material depends on the way in which it was cooled: fast for glass, slow for crystals. By applying a voltage across the glassy form -- anywhere from two volts to hundreds, depending on the thickness of the layer -- one can cause a breakdown to occur and a small conducting filament of plasma (or some plasma-like phase -- this is a subject of current investigation [Adler, 1977]) to appear between the electrodes. The voltage is removed after a few milliseconds, and the material in the affected area cools slowly into the conducting state. It will remain in that state indefinitely, but it can be returned to the glassy state by applying a quick pulse of current -- enough to partially melt the material in the gap, but not enough to heat up the surrounding area.

One experimental device described in Ovshinsky and Hellmutt [1973], a 256-bit random access memory array, is converted to the conducting state by a 25 volt, 10 millisecond pulse, and is erased by a 120 milliamp, 5 microsecond pulse. The spot of material that is converted by these pulses has a diameter of about 1 micro-meter. Early devices broke down after a relatively small number of cycles, but this problem appears to have been solved, and lifetimes as long as 108 set-reset cycles have been reported. In any event, this figure is not really relevant to the network system envisioned here, since few of our connections will be switched more than once. According to Professor David Adler of M.I.T., an expert in the field, the technology has outgrown an initial period of uncertainty, and is now well on the way to being understood at a molecular and quantum-theoretic level [Adler, 1977].

The plan, then, is to lay down a pattern of north-south wires, spread the glass in a layer over these wires, and lay down the east-west wires on top of that. (Of course, many small sheets could be used instead of one large one.) To connect any link-wire to any node-terminal, we simply apply a 25v pulse between the two. The connection is then made, and we can use it indefinitely. If we ever want to break the connection, we apply an appropriate high-current pulse through it. The material used is relatively inexpensive, and it does not have to be laid down in a single, perfect crystal.

Of course, this is easier said than done. If the wires are spaced 10 micro-meters apart, this gives us a sheet that is 10 meters by 60 meters. If we cut this into 200 sheets and stack them with a centimeter of air-space between sheets, we get a box that is 2x2x1.5 meters, which is not altogether unreasonable. If we can reduce the inter-wire spacing and the inter-sheet gap by a factor of 10 each, we get a box smaller than a foot in each dimension. Of course, if we want more than a million elements, the required switching area (or volume) will go up as N^2: for a billion elements, we would need a million of these switching boxes. Once again, we have the packaging problem: how do you connect 1000 (or perhaps 10,000) IC packages to the seven million wires emerging from our connection box? I have no answer to this question, at present.

One possible ray of hope is the idea of neighborhooding: it seems probable that the elements form neighborhoods, with dense connectivity among the members of a given neighborhood, but with relatively few connections to outside nodes. It may be that the system could be divided into clusters of, say, 1000 densely-connected elements, and that only one-tenth of these would have any wires coming into them from outside the cluster. It might also be the case that such a cluster would have outgoing wires to only 100 external nodes. One could then imagine placing such a network in a single package with about 300 leads: 100 CPU-bus wires, 100 outgoing wires, and 100 incoming wires. This is a rather unwieldy, but not altogether unmanageable, number. The thousand-element packages could then be connected into a million-element system by a crossbar 600 times smaller in area than the crossbar discussed above. Note that we are not requiring that the neighborhood have only 100 outgoing or incoming *wires*, but rather that the total set of wires connects to only 100 *nodes*. Wires to a common destination can be tied together before they enter or leave the local package.

The only way to study the neighborhooding behavior of large real-world knowledge bases is to build a few, and this has not yet been done. My guess would be that the figures used above are about right, but this is only a guess. I also suspect that the assigment of elements to neighborhoods in the order in which they are created would probably be almost as effective as any more-complex allocation scheme. Further experience with the simulator on a variety of real-world domains should resolve this issue.

The one-stage crosspoint switch gives us a sort of upper limit on the number of potential connection points that must be considered. Given the low density of actual connections, there are a number of multi-stage connection strategies that would require fewer switches and that would grow more slowly than N^2. A number of variants of the sorting-network scheme described in the next section might be employed to achieve interconnection networks with connections on the order of $N(\log N)^2$ or possibly even $N(\log N)$. If such schemes are employed, a million-element system might be constructed with as few as 10^8 switching elements -- still a lot, but much better than 10^{12}. I am currently studying such schemes to determine how practical they might be.

In conclusion, I would say that implementation of a million-element parallel network system would not be inexpensive or easy -- at least, at first -- but neither does the idea belong entirely within the realm of science fiction. There was a time not long ago when the idea of threading three or four wires through each of a few million tiny ferrite doughnuts seemed equally improbable. If we want the parallel network badly enough, it will be built somehow. The simulator will tell us exactly what such a network can do for us, so we will have a very good idea of whether any given implementation scheme is worthwhile, before construction begins.

A.3 Implementation with a Micro-Processor Network

In the past few years, microprocessors have burst upon the scene, and their price drops lower every year. An obvious question, then, is whether some interconnected system of microprocessors, operating in parallel, could give us a significant speed advantage over a purely serial simulation.

At first glance, the idea seems attractive. Since we have replaced the complex, procedural, inherently serial component of knowledge-base search with a simple, brute-force search, and since this search proceeds by tracing out paths in parallel, we can simply assign a new micro-processor to the task whenever the path branches, until we either complete the search or we run out of micro-processors in the idle-pool. At that point each micro-processor completes its assigned task by itself, occasionally checking the idle-pool to see if help is available. When a processor's branch rejoins a portion of the tree that is already marked, the processor retires to the pool, ready to help its comrades. Of course, there is a certain overhead associated with finding and assigning free processors, and many processors would be idle much of the time. Still, the speedup should be significant. Depending on the exact shape of the network and the details of the strategy used, a thousand microprocessors might be expected to increase the system's speed by a factor between 10 and 100. Better still, the harder problems -- those with the greatest fan-out in the direction of the scan -- will be the ones that offer the best opportunities for such parallelism. It would appear, then, that a micro-processor network might occupy a large and important niche between serial simulation and the fully parallel hardware implementation described in the last two sections.

The problem with all of this is that the nodes and links of the system are not like roads that can be followed without getting in anyone else's way. The elements of the system would be represented as they are in the current implementation: as structures of pointers and flag-words in a standard random-access memory system. If a thousand micro-processors are to be used at once, there must be a thousand memory ports to serve them all. This would require a large amount of hardware to synchronize and arbitrate all of these requests, and contention would almost certainly wipe out any gains due to the parallelism.

The problem is not solved by allowing the micro-processors to copy the area of the tree that they are exploring into their own private memories. First, a path through the tree is likely to be spread all over the system's memory. Second, it takes as much time to copy a pointer as to follow it, and contention is almost as likely to occur during the copying accesses as during normal ones. Several adjacent pointers in memory might be copied as part of a single operation, but there is little likelihood that many of the extra pointers will be useful. Finally, serious problems are created by the existence of multiple copies of a single node. Some of these copies might be marked, others might be unmarked, and still others might be cancelled. Coordinating all of this would be very difficult.

The one multiple-processor scheme which looks promising would assign each processor permanently to a fixed chunk of the network, consisting of perhaps a thousand elements. For each of these elements, the processor (in its attached private memory) would store the element's marker-bit status and pointers indicating the element's link-wire and node-terminal connections. These local processors do not conduct searches on their own; rather, they simulate the combined effects of the thousand primitive elements which they represent. The propagation commands are generated by a central control computer and sent to the element-processors over a party-line bus, just as in the primitive-element system. Each element-processor handles all of the propagations that occur entirely within its own borders. When a marker must be propagated into an element owned by some other processor, a message-passing protocol is used.

If each processor represents a thousand primitive elements, a million-element system would require a thousand processors, each with perhaps 16K words of memory for data and programs. If the problems of message-passing contention are ignored for a moment, we might estimate that this system would run a thousand times more slowly than a true primitive-element system, since each processor would have to divide its attention among a thousand nodes. This does not sound very good, but by the same rough estimation a serial system would be a thousand times slower still. For most purposes, then, the parallel-processor system would probably be fast enough. If it is not, then we could use ten thousand processors, each with less memory and only a hundred elements to worry about.

Of course, we cannot ignore the message-passing problem. Such a system would generate a tremendous amount of message traffic, far more than could be handled by a common message bus. There is a possible way around this problem, however, using an scheme developed by Moravec [1976], a refinement of an earlier proposal by Batcher [1968]. This scheme would use Batcher sorting networks instead of a common bus-structure to handle the flow of messages between processors. Using the message-passing interface that Moravec describes, every processor can send one message to any other processor during each major cycle of the system. All of the messages are delivered at once, without interference, unless two messages are sent to the same destination. In that case, one of the messages is delivered, and the sender of the other message is notified that he must try again. Though I have not analyzed in detail the behavior of such a message-passing system for the present task, it seems probable that very little processor-time would be lost due to message contention. A processor with many popular high-level nodes might be assigned a few extra incoming ports to handle the message-load. It would appear, then, that we might be able to achieve a thousand-fold speed-up after all.

The message network requires a considerable amount of logic, but much less than would be required by a full crossbar interconnection. For the interconnection of N processors, the system would require an amount of logic proportional to $N(\log N)^2$. By Moravec's calculation, a network for a thousand processors would require about 4000 48-pin logic packages, a figure well within the reach of current technology. A million-processor network, which would be equivalent to a billion primitive elements, would require about 13 million logic packages, a very large but not altogether inconceivable number, especially when the possiblity of denser packaging is allowed for. Such a machine would be hard to outgrow.

Appendix B: Table of Node Types, Link Types, and Modifier Flags

Node Types:

*INDV   ·Represents the description of an individual entity in some
         universe or an individual role in some description.

         Parent wire: Creates a virtual *VC link to some special
                          superior *TYPE node.
         Existence wire: Indicates which universe, area, or *TYPE
                          description the *INDV exists in. Functions as
                          virtual *EXIN or *EXFOR link, depending on the
                          **EXIN flag. If **SPLIT is set, functions
                          as a virtual *SPLIT link as well.
         Modifiers: **EXIN, **SPLIT, **SPEC, **EXTERN, **RSPLIT.

*TYPE   Represents the description of the typical member of some set.
         The set is extensionally defined -- it contains whatever we
         say that it contains.

         Parent wire: Creates a virtual *VC link to some special
                          superior *TYPE node.
         Set wire: Connects the *TYPE node to the set that it
                          describes.
         Modifier: **PART

*MAP   The version of some individual role that appears in a given
         virtual copy or context area.

         Map wire: The individual role that is being mapped.
         Owner wire: The base-node of the description or area into
                          which the map is being made.

*TMAP   Like *MAP, but it is the map of a *TYPE node, and behaves
         like a *TYPE node in the copy.

         Map wire: The *TYPE role-node that is being mapped.
         Owner wire: The base-node of the description or area
                            into which the map is being made.
         Modifier: **PART

*IST   Represents an Individual STatement of some relation or
         predicate. Like an *INDV node in most respects.

         Parent wire: The type of statement that the *IST node
                            represents.
         Scope wire: The area within which the statement is
                            considered to be valid.
         Spec wire: If this relation is part of the spec of an
                            *EVERY-node, this wire points to the
                            *EVERY-node in question.
         Modifiers: **NOT, **UNK, **SPEC.

*EVERY   A *TYPE node modified to represent the definition of an
         intensionally-defined set. This node serves both as a
         specification for the set, and as a description of the
         typical member.

         Parent wire: As in the *TYPE node.
         Set wire: Connects the *EVERY-node to its set.
         Scope wire: The area within which the definition
                            operates. ("Every X in Y ...")
         Modifiers: **NOT, Digestion priority flags.

*OTHER   Represents an arbitrarily-chosen individual of the associated
          *TYPE, distinct from the one represented by the *TYPE-node
          itself. See section 3.7 for full explanation.

          Type wire: Tied to the *TYPE or *EVERY node with which
                              this node is associated. Can also be tied to
                              another *OTHER node to represent a third or
                              subsequent individual binding.

*INT   Like an *EVERY node whose set is the intersection-set of the
          two parents. If the same activation-mark appears on P1
          and P2, it is placed on the *INT-node as well.

          Parent wires: P1 and P2 connect to the two parent-nodes.
          Set wire: Connects the *INT-node to the set it defines.
          Modifiers: **NOT.

Links:

Each link has an integral node that represents the statement that the
link is making. These integral nodes behave as *IST nodes. The
following wires are therefore defined:

Parent wire: Used to indicate the type of the link. Usually this
                    will be totally redundant with the link's type-flags,
                    but sometimes it will indicate a sub-type of the basic
                    *TYPE-node for that link. Only the *TYPE-flags affect
                    marker propagations.

Scope wire: This indicates the area (spatial, temporal, subject,
                    or combination) within which the link is considered
                    to be active.

Spec wire: If the **SPEC flag is set, this link is part of the
                    specification of an *EVERY node. The spec-wire then
                    indicates which node is being specified.

A and B wires: These are the wires that do the actual linking. Their
                    meaning varies from one link-type to another.

Modifiers: **NOT, **UNK, **SPEC.

The following link-types are currently defined:

*VC   Virtual Copy link: A is a virtual copy of B.
          Special modifier: **LIKE.

*EQ   Equality link: A and B represent compatible views of
          the same entity.

*CANCEL   Cancellation link: In context or copy-layer A, relation B is
          cancelled. If B is an individual role-node, its existence is
          cancelled in copy A. To cancel a *VC or *EQ link creating an
          ancestor of A, use *CANVC on the ancestor instead.

*CANVC   Identity cancellation link: Node A is not a virtual copy of
          node B, despite any *VC or *EQ links to the contrary.

*SPLIT   Used in building exclusive type-splits and sets of distinct
          individuals. When a set of *SPLIT links share a common
          B-node, all of the A-nodes in this set represent distinct
          entities. Any attempt to *EQ them or to *VC a single
          individual under two of them should cause a clash.

*EXFOR   For every copy of B there exists a map of A.
          Special modifier: **RSPLIT.

*EXIN   A exists in area B. In every copy of B, there is a map
          of A. Special modifier: **RSPLIT.

*SCOPE   Statement A is valid within area B. Replaces scope-wire.

Modifier Flag Definitions:

**EXTERN   Flags *INDV nodes that are appropriate output symbols
                 for the knowledge-base system, and therefore
                 appropriate input symbols for the external programs
                 using the knowledge-base: LISP numbers or atom-names,
                 ASCII codes, muscle twitches, or whatever.

**SPEC   Marks those links, relations, and *INDV nodes that are
                 clauses in the specification of an *EVERY node.

**UNK   Unknown. Add this to a **SPEC statement, to indicate
                 that the case will be accepted if this condition
                 cannot be established. Kills statement during normal
                 accessing. If digestion finds this violated, case is
                 removed from the class specified by the **UNK.

**NOT   On a statement, negates it. Clashes with any attempt
                 to assert the same statement in non-negated form.
                 On an *EVERY-node, indicates that no item meeting the
                 specification exists within the given scope-area.

**LIKE   Weakens the sense of a *VC link to indicate that A
                 inherits the description of B, but is not strictly
                 speaking a member of B's class. Thus "A is like a B"
                 rather than "A is a B". Also used to create a copy
                 of an *INDV that is not *EQ to that *INDV.

**EXIN   Makes the existence-wire of an *INDV node carry the
sense of an *EXIN link rather than an *EXFOR.

**SPLIT   Makes the existence-wire of an *INDV node serve as a
virtual *SPLIT link. The *INDV cannot then be equated
with any other **SPLIT *INDV in the same area.

**RSPLIT   Used in *EXIN, *EXFOR links, *INDV nodes that define
roles. This role may not be played by the same *INDV
in a given context for two distinct owners. Each
owner-copy has its own player for this role.

**PART   Marks the PART *TYPE-role and all of its *TMAPS. Used
to make PART-OF hierarchy operations more efficient.

BIBLIOGRAPHY

Abelson, Robert P. (1975), "Concepts for Representing Mundane Reality in Plans", in *Representation and Understanding*, Bobrow and Collins (eds.), Academic Press.

Adler, David (1977), "Amorphous-Semiconductor Devices", *Scientific American*, May, 1977.

Anderson, John R. and Gordon H. Bower (1973), *Human Associative Memory*, V. H. Winston & Sons.

Asimov, Isaac (1950), *I, Robot*, Fawcett Crest (paperback).

Batcher, K. E. (1968), "Sorting Networks and their Applications", *1968 Spring Joint Computer Conference Proceedings*, IFIPS.

Bobrow, Daniel G., and Terry Winograd (1976), "An Overview of KRL, a Knowledge Representation Language", Xerox Palo Alto Research Center. (Also Stanford Artificial Intelligence Laboratory Memo AIM-239.)

Brachman, Ronald J. (1977), "A Structural Paradigm for Representing Knowledge", Ph.D. Thesis, Division of Engineering and Applied Physics, Harvard University.

Brown, Allen L. (1977), "Qualitative Knowledge, Causal Reasoning, and the Localization of Failures", AI-TR-362, MIT Artificial Intelligence Lab.

Bullwinkle, Candace L. (1975a), "Computer Performance of the Sentence Completion Task", M.S. Thesis, University of Pittsburgh.

Bullwinkle, Candace L. (1975b), "Picnics, Kittens, and Wigs: Using Scenarios for the Sentence Completion Task", IJCAI 4.

Carbonell, Jaime R., and Allan M. Collins (1973), "Natural Semantics in Artificial Intelligence", IJCAI 3. (Also in AJCL, 1974, Vol. 1, Mfc. 3.)

Cercone, Nick, and Len Schubert (1975), "Toward a State-Based Conceptual Representation", IJCAI 4.

Charniak, Eugene (1972), "Toward a Model of Children's Story Comprehension", AI TR-266, MIT Artificial Intelligence Lab.

Collins, Allan, Eleanor H. Warnock, Nelleke Aiello, and Mark L. Miller (1975), "Reasoning From Incomplete Knowledge", in *Representation and Understanding*, Bobrow and Collins (eds.), Academic Press.

Doyle, Jon (1977), "Truth Maintenance Systems for Problem Solving", AI TR-419, MIT Artificial Intelligence Lab.

Dreyfus, Hubert L. (1972), *What Computers Can't Do*, Harper & Row.

Dreyfus, Hubert L. (1976), Review of Minsky & Papert, Winston books in *Creative Computing*, March-April, 1976.

Evans, Thomas G. (1968), "A Program for the Solution of Geometric-Analogy Intelligence Test Questions", in *Semantic Information Processing*, Minsky (ed.), MIT Press.

Fahlman, Scott E. (1974a), "A Planning System for Robot Construction Tasks", *Artificial Intelligence* 5, pages 1-49.

Fahlman, Scott E. (1974b), "A Hypothesis-Frame System for Recognition Problems", Working Paper 57, MIT Artificial Intelligence Lab.

Fahlman, Scott E. (1975), "Thesis Progress Report", AI Memo 331, MIT Artificial Intelligence Lab.

Feldman, Jerome A., and Paul D. Rovner (1969), "An ALGOL-Based Associative Language", *Communications of the ACM*, August, 1969.

Fikes, Richard E., Peter E. Hart, and Nils J. Nilsson (1972), "Learning and Executing Generalized Robot Plans", *Artificial Intelligence 3*, 251-288.

Goldstein, Ira P., and R. Bruce Roberts (1977), "Nudge, A Knowledge-Based Scheduling Program", AI Memo 405, MIT Artificial Intelligence Lab. (To appear in IJCAI 5.)

Grossman, Richard W. (1976), "Some Data-Base Applications of Constraint Expressions", LCS TR-158, MIT Laboratory for Computer Science.

Hayes, Philip J. (1977), "On Semantic Nets, Frames, and Associations", Proc. IJCAI 5.

Hendrix, Gary G. (1975a), "Expanding the Utility of Semantic Networks Through Partitioning", Proc. IJCAI 4.

Hendrix, Gary G. (1975b), "Partitioned Networks for the Mathematical Modeling of Natural Language Semantics", Technical Report NL-28 (Ph.D. thesis), Dept. of Computer Sciences, The University or Texas at Austin.

Hendrix, Gary G. (1976), "The Representation of Semantic Knowledge", in Speech Understanding Research, Final Technical Report, Walker (ed.), Stanford Research Institiute.

Hewitt, Carl (1972), "Description and Theoretical Analysis (Using Schemata) of PLANNER", AI TR-258, MIT Artificial Intelligence Lab.

Katz, Jerrold J. and Jerry A. Fodor (1963), "The Structure of a Semantic Theory", in *The Structure of Language*, Fodor and Katz (eds.), Prentice-Hall.

Kuipers, Benjamin J. (1975), "A Frame for Frames: Representing Knowledge for Recognition", in *Representation and Understanding*, Bobrow and Collins (eds.), Academic Press.

Lasnik, Howard (1972), "Analyses of Negation in English", Ph.D. thesis, M.I.T. Dept. of Linguistics.

Marr, David, and Keith Nishihara (1977), "Representation and Recognition of the Spatial Organization of Three-Dimensional Shapes", AI Memo 416, MIT Artificial Intelligence Lab.

McCarthy, John, and Patrick J. Hayes (1969), "Some Philosophical Problems from the Standpoint of Artificial Intelligence", *Machine Intelligence 4*, Meltzer and Michie (eds.), Edinburgh University Press.

McDermott, Drew V. and Gerald J. Sussman (1972), "CONNIVER Reference Manual", AI MEMO-259, MIT Artificial Intelligence Lab.

McDermott, Drew V. (1975), "Very Large Planner-Type Data Bases", AI Memo 339, MIT Artificial Intelligence Lab.

McDermott, Drew V. (1976), "Artificial Intelligence meets Natural Stupidity", SIGART Newsletter, April, 1976.

McDermott, Drew V. (1977), "Flexibility and Efficiency in a Computer Program for Designing Circuits", AI-TR-402, MIT Artificial Intelligence Lab.

Meldman, Jeffrey A. (1975), "A Preliminary Study in Computer-Aided Legal Analysis", MAC TR-157, MIT Laboratory for Computer Science.

Minsky, Marvin L. (1975), "A Framework for Representing Knowledge", in *The Psychology of Computer Vision*, Winston (ed.), McGraw Hill.

Moore, Robert C. (1973), "D-SCRIPT: A Computational Theory of Descriptions", IJCAI 3.

Moravec, Hans (1976), "The Role of Raw Power in Intelligence", to appear as a Stanford AI Memo. Available from the author.

Mylopoulos, John, Alex Borgida, Philip Cohen, Nicholas Roussopoulos, John Tsotsos, & Harry Wong (1975), "TORUS -- A Natural Language Understanding System for Data Management", IJCAI 4.

Norman, Donald A., David E. Rumelhart, and the LNR Research Group (1975), *Explorations in Cognition*, W. H. Freeman.

Ovshinsky, Stanford R., and Hellmutt Fritzsche (1973), "Amorphous Semiconductors for Switching, Memory, and Imaging Applications", IEEE Transactions on Electron Devices, Vol. ED-20, No. 2, February, 1973.

Pople, Harry E., Jack D. Myers, and Randolph A. Miller (1975), "DIALOG: A model of Diagnostic Logic for Internal Medicine", IJCAI 4.

Quillian, M. Ross (1968), "Semantic Memory", in *Semantic Information Processing*, Minsky (ed.), MIT Press.

Quillian, M. Ross (1969), "The Teachable Language Comprehender: A Simulation Program and Theory of Language", Communications of the ACM, August, 1969.

Raphael, Bertram (1968), "SIR: Semantic Information Retrieval", in *Semantic Information Processing*, Minsky (ed.), MIT Press.

Rich, Charles, and Howard E. Shrobe (1976), "Initial Report on a LISP Programmer's Apprentice", AI-TR-354, MIT Artificial Intelligence Lab.

Rieger, Chuck (1975a), "Conceptual Overlays: a Mechanism for the Interpretation of Sentence Meaning in Context", IJCAI 4.

Rieger, Chuck (1975b), "One System for Two Tasks: A Commonsense Algorithm Memory that Solves Problems and Comprehends Language", Working Paper 114, MIT Artificial Intelligence Lab.

Rivest, Ronald L. (1974), "Analysis of Associative Retrieval Algorithms", Memo STAN-CS-74-415, Stanford University, Computer Science Department.

Roberts, R. Bruce, and Ira P. Goldstein (1977), "The FRL Manual", AI Memo 409, MIT Artificial Intelligence Lab.

Rosch, E. (1975), "Cognitive Representations of Semantic Categories", *Journal of Experimental Psychology: General 104*, 192-233.

Rosch, E. and C. Mervis (1975), "Family Resemblances: Studies in the Internal Structure of Categories", *Cognitive Psychology 7*, 573-605.

Rubin, Ann D. (1975), "Hypothesis Formation and Evaluation in Medical Diagnosis", AI TR-316, MIT Artificial Intelligence Lab.

Rumelhart, David E., Peter H. Lindsay, & Donald E. Norman (1972), "A Process model for Long-Term Memory", in *Organization of Memory*, Tulving and Donaldson (eds.), Academic Press.

Rumelhart, David E. (1975), "Notes on a Schema for Stories", in *Representation and Understanding*, Bobrow and Collins (eds.), Academic Press.

Sacerdoti, Earl D. (1975), "A Structure for Plans and Behavior", Stanford Research Institute Artificial Intelligence Center Technical Note 109.

Schank, Roger C. (1973), "Identifications of Conceptualization Underlying Natural Language", in *Computer Models of Thought and Language*, Schank and Colby (eds.), W. H. Freeman Press.

Schank, Roger C. (1975), "The Structure of Episodes in Memory", in *Representation and Understanding*, Bobrow and Collins (eds.), Academic Press.

Schank, Roger C., and Robert P. Abelson (1975), "Scripts, Plans, and Knowledge", IJCAI 4.

Schubert, Len K. (1975), "Extending the Expressive Power of Semantic Networks", IJCAI 4.

Scragg, Greg W. (1975a), "Frames, Planes, and Nets: A Synthesis", Working Paper 19, Instituto per gli Studi Semantici e Cognitivi, Castagnola, Switzerland.

Scragg, Greg W. (1975b), "A Structure for Actions", Working Paper 20, Instituto per gli Studi Semantici e Cognnitivi, Castagnola, Switzerland.

Scragg, Greg W. (1975c), "Answering Questions about Processes", in *Explorations in Cognition*, Norman & Rumelhart (eds.), W. H. Freeman & Co.

Shapiro, Stuart C. (1971), "A Net Structure for Semantic Information Storage, Deduction, and Retrieval", IJCAI 2.

Shortliffe, E. (1976), *MYCIN: Computer-Based Medical Consultations*, American Elsevier.

Simmons, Robert F. (1973), "Semantic Networks: Their Computation and Use for Understanding English Sentences", in *Computer Models of Thought and Language*, Schank and Colby (eds.), W. H. Freeman Press.

Strawson, P. F., (1971), "Identifying Reference and Truth-Values", in *Semantics: An Interdisciplinary Reader in Philosophy, Linguistics, and Psychology*, Steinberg & Jakobovits (eds.), Cambridge University Press.

Sussman, Gerald J., Terry Winograd, and Eugene Charniak (1971), "Micro-Planner Reference Manual", AI MEMO 203a, MIT Artificial Intelligence Lab.

Sussman, Gerald J. (1973), "A Computational Model of Skill Acquisition", AI-TR-297, MIT Artificial Intelligence Lab.

Sussman, Gerald J., and Allen L. Brown (1974), "Localization of Failures in Radio Circuits: A Study in Causal and Teleological Reasoning", AI MEMO-319, MIT Artificial Intelligence Lab.

Sussman, Gerald J. (1977), "SLICES, At the Boundary Between Analysis and Synthesis", MIT AI-MEMO 433, MIT Artificial Intelligence Lab.

Waltz, David (1975), "Understanding Line Drawings of Scenes with Shadows", in *The Psychology of Computer Vision*, Winston (ed.), McGraw Hill.

Wilensky, Robert (1976), "Using Plans to Understand Natural Language", in *Proceedings of the ACM, 1976.*

Winston, Patrick H. (1975), "Learning Structural Descriptions from Examples", in *The Psychology of Computer Vision*, Winston (ed.), McGraw Hill.

Winston, Patrick H. (1977), "Learning by Hypothesizing and Justifying Transfer Frames", AI Memo-414, MIT Artificial Intelligence Lab.

Winograd, Terry (1974), "Five Lectures on Artificial Intelligence", AIM-246, Stanford Artificial Intelligence Lab.

Winograd, Terry (1975), "Frame Representations and the Declarative-Procedural Controversy", in *Representation and Understanding*, Bobrow and Collins (eds.), Academic Press.

Woods, William A. (1975), "What's in a Link: Foundations for Semantic Networks", in *Representation and Understanding*, Bobrow and Collins (eds.), Academic Press.

INDEX